East Asian Strategic Review 2020

The National Institute for Defense Studies
Japan

This publication is an English translation
of the original Japanese edition published in April 2020.

Edited by:
The National Institute for Defense Studies
5-1 Ichigaya Honmura-cho, Shinjuku-ku, Tokyo 162-8808, Japan
URL: www.nids.mod.go.jp

Published by:
Interbooks Co., Ltd.
Kudan-Crest Bldg 6F, 5-10 Kudan-Kita 1-chome,
Chiyoda-ku, Tokyo 102-0073, Japan
Phone: +81-3-5212-4652
URL: https://www.interbooks.co.jp
books@interbooks.co.jp

ISBN 978-4-924914-65-0

The National Institute for Defense Studies
East Asian Strategic Review 2020

Printed in Japan

Cover photo
P-3C patrol aircraft (Japan Maritime Self-Defense Force)
First Japan-India 2+2 Foreign and Defence Ministerial Meeting
(Japan Ministry of Defense)
AAV7 amphibious assault vehicle (Japan Ground Self-Defense Force)

Preface

This edition of the *East Asian Strategic Review* (*EASR*) marks the twenty-fourth year of the flagship publication of the National Institute for Defense Studies (NIDS), Japan's sole national think-tank in the area of security affairs. Over those years, *EASR* has built up an established reputation as the only annual report in both Japanese and English that provides domestic and international audiences with insight into the Japanese perception of the increasingly challenging security situations of East Asia.

EASR comprises chapters examining strategic trends in regional countries that may affect Japan's security and covering timely topics in East Asian security. This edition deals with diverse themes such as Sino-American confrontation ranging from trade disputes to hegemonic competition, the Xi Jinping administration's response toward Hong Kong rocked by street protests, shaky situations of the Korean Peninsula over the "recurring crisis," and impacts that the termination of the INF Treaty would bring about. It also offers an explanation about the significance of the "Free and Open Indo-Pacific" vision for which Japanese government agencies have been working together.

EASR 2020 presents NIDS academics' analyses of major security developments that took place mainly during the period from January through December 2019, and is based on information compiled from public sources in Japan and overseas. The views contained herein do not necessarily represent the official position of the Government of Japan or the Ministry of Defense. The titles and ranks of people mentioned herein are, in principle, those that were current at the time of the events described.

As part of our editorial policy, this publication provides the names of the authors responsible for each chapter as well as chapter notes indicating information sources, so as to further strengthen its standing as a scholarly work founded on analyses personally made by the contributing researchers.

Japanese personal names throughout the text are presented according to Japanese custom (family name followed by given name) in reversal of standard Western order but in the same fashion as the Chinese and Koreans.

This edition was written by: Hashimoto Yasuaki (Introduction); Ichimasa Sukeyuki (Chapter 1); Momma Rira and Iwamoto Hiroshi (Chapter 2); Watanabe Takeshi and Koike Osamu (Chapter 3); Matsuura Yoshihide, Tomikawa Hideo and Manabe Yuko (Chapter 4); Hyodo Shinji, Hasegawa Takeyuki, Sakaguchi Yoshiaki and Sawada Hiroto (Chapter 5); Arakaki Hiromu and Kiridori Ryo (Chapter 6); and Satake Tomohiko (Chapter 7). It was edited by Kikuchi Shigeo, Sukegawa Yasushi, Fukushima Yasuhito, Hasegawa Takeyuki, Oshite Junichi, and Asami Asaki.

With East Asian security issues attracting the world's attention, it is our hope that *EASR* will help build interest in and understanding of the strategic environment in the region and will promote an intellectual discussion among the public with the aim to support Japanese security policymaking.

April 2020

Hashimoto Yasuaki
Editor-in-chief
Former Director, Policy Studies Department

Contents

List of Abbreviations

A2/AD	Anti-access/area denial
ACC	Air Combat Command
ACE	Aviation combat element
ACE	Agile combat employment
ACSA	Acquisition and cross-servicing agreement
ADMM	ASEAN Defense Ministers' Meeting
AIT	American Institute in Taiwan
ARF	ASEAN Regional Forum
ARMM	Autonomous Region in Muslim Mindanao
ASEAN	Association of Southeast Asian Nations
ASG	Abu Sayyaf Group
ATACMS	Army Tactical Missile System
BARMM	Bangsamoro Autonomous Region in Muslim Mindanao
BCT	Brigade Combat Team
BIAF	Bangsamoro Islamic Armed Forces
BIFF	Bangsamoro Islamic Freedom Fighters
BNPT	Badan Nasional Penanggulangan Terorisme
BOL	Bangsamoro Organic Law
BRN	Barisan Revolusi Nasional
BTA	Bangsamoro Transition Authority
C4ISR	Command, control, communications, computers, intelligence, surveillance and reconnaissance
CAB	Comprehensive Agreement on Bangsamoro
CCND	Creating the Conditions for Nuclear Disarmament
CD	Conference on Disarmament
CEND	Creating an Environment for Nuclear Disarmament
CEWG	Creating an Environment for Nuclear Disarmament Working Group
CIS	Commonwealth of Independent States
COC	Code of Conduct
CPGS	Conventional Prompt Global Strike
CSTO	Collective Security Treaty Organization
CTBT	Comprehensive Nuclear-Test-Ban Treaty
CUES	Code for Unplanned Encounters at Sea
D&SD	Diplomatic and Security Dialogue

Densus 88	Detasemen Khusus 88 Antiteror
DF	Dongfeng
DMO	Distributed maritime operations
DOM	Daerah Operasi Militer
EABO	Expeditionary advanced base operations
EAS	East Asia Summit
EEZ	Exclusive economic zone
ESSCom	Eastern Sabah Security Command
EU	European Union
EWG	Experts' Working Groups
FE	Foal Eagle
FFP	Future Forward party
FMCT	Fissile Material Cut-off Treaty
FOC	Full operational capability
FOIP	Free and Open Indo-Pacific
FSA	Force Structure Assessment
FYDP	Future Years Defense Program
GGK	Grup Gerak Khas
GLCM	Ground-launched cruise missile
GSOMIA	General Security of Military Information Agreement
HA/DR	Humanitarian assistance and disaster relief
HGV	Hypersonic glide vehicle
HIMARS	High Mobility Artillery Rocket System
HI-RAIN	HIMARS rapid infiltration
I2CEWS	Intelligence, information, cyber electronic warfare and space
IAEA	International Atomic Energy Agency
ICBM	Intercontinental ballistic missile
IFPC	Indirect Fire Protection Capability
INDOPACOM	Indo-Pacific Command
INF	Intermediate-range nuclear forces
IOC	Initial Operational Capability
IoT	Internet of Things
IPD19	Indo-Pacific Deployment 2019
IRBM	Intermediate-range ballistic missile
IRCM	Intermediate-range cruise missile
ISIL	Islamic State of Iraq and the Levant

JAD	Jamaah Ansharut Daulah
JASSM-ER	Joint Air-to-Surface Standoff Missile-Extended Range
JCPOA	Joint Comprehensive Plan of Action
KGB	Komitet Gosudarstvennoy Bezopasnosti
KOGABWILHAN	Komando Gabungan Wilayah Pertahanan
KOOPSUS	Komando Operasi Khusus
KOPASSUS	Komando Pasukan Khusus
KPK	Komisi Pemberantasan Korupsi
KR	Key Resolve
LCU	Landing craft utility
LPX-II	Landing Platform Experimental-II
LRASM	Long-range anti-ship missile
LRCM	Long-range cruise missile
LRPF	Long Range Precision Fires
LSC	Large surface combatant
LTAMDS	Lower tier air and missile defense sensor
MD	Missile defense
MDC2	Multi-domain command and control
MDO	Multi-domain operations
MDTF	Multi-Domain Task Force
MILF	Moro Islamic Liberation Front
MNLF	Moro National Liberation Front
MOU	Memorandum of understanding
MRBM	Medium-range ballistic missile
MRL	Multiple rocket launcher
M-SHORAD	Mobile Short-Range Air Defense
NAC	New Agenda Coalition
NATO	North Atlantic Treaty Organization
NDS	National Defense Strategy
NPT	Treaty on the Non-Proliferation of Nuclear Weapons
NSA	Negative security assurances
NSOF	National Special Operations Force
NSS	National Security Strategy
NTM	National technical means
ODA	Official development assistance
OEWG	Open-ended Working Group

OPM	Organisasi Papua Merdeka
PASKAL	Pasukan Khas Laut
PASKAU	Pasukan Khas TUDM
PCA	Permanent Court of Arbitration
PDD	Partnership for Democratic Development
PDI-P	Partai Demokrasi Indonesia Perjuangan
PHP	Philippine peso
PPRP	Palang Pracharath party
PSI	Proliferation Security Initiative
RAM	Rocket, artillery, mortar
RDT&E	Research, development, testing and evaluation
RIMPAC	Rim of the Pacific
SARA	Suku, Agama, Ras dan Antargolongan
SB-CTD	Special Branch Counter-Terrorism Division
SCM	Security Consultative Meeting
SCO	Shanghai Cooperation Organisation
SDGs	Sustainable Development Goals
SINKEX	Sinking exercise
SIPRI	Stockholm International Peace Research Institute
SLBM	Submarine-launched ballistic missile
SLCM	Sea-launched cruise missile
SMA	Special Measures Agreement
SRBM	Short-range ballistic missile
SRCM	Short-range cruise missile
SSC	Small surface combatant
START I	Strategic Arms Reduction Treaty I
THAAD	Terminal High Altitude Area Defense
TICAD	Tokyo International Conference on African Development
TPNPB	Tentara Pembebasan Nasional Papua Barat
TPNW	Treaty on the Prohibition of Nuclear Weapons
TRADOC	US Army Training and Doctrine Command
TTX	Tabletop exercise
UAS	Unmanned aircraft systems
UFG	Ulchi Freedom Guardian
ULMWP	United Liberation Movement for West Papua
UNICEF	United Nations Children's Fund

VLS	Vertical launching system
WFP	World Food Programme
WPNS	Western Pacific Naval Symposium
ZTE	Zhongxing Telecommunication Equipment Corporation
2MTW	Two major theater wars

Introduction

East Asia in 2019

HASHIMOTO Yasuaki

1. Termination of the INF Treaty and its Impacts

The Treaty between the United States of America and the Union of Soviet Socialist Republics on the Elimination of their Intermediate-Range and Shorter-Range Missiles (INF Treaty) was terminated on August 2, 2019. Furthermore, although the Treaty between the United States of America and the Russian Federation on Measures for the Further Reduction and Limitation of Strategic Offensive Arms (New START) is set to expire in 2021, negotiations to extend the treaty are not anticipated. The significance of these treaties lied in restraining a nuclear arms competition, bringing about transparency and predictability based on a strict verification regime. In reality, nuclear weapons and missile technologies proliferated, and the security environment transformed significantly. Debates have emerged that the arms control framework should be expanded to include countries other than the United States and Russia, and that negotiations should cover not only the issues around the definition of strategic/tactical nuclear weapons and caps on the number of nuclear weapons but also the treatment of new strategic arms and missile defenses. The international community places high expectations on US-Russia nuclear arms control for compliance with Article VI of the Treaty on the Non-Proliferation of Nuclear Weapons (NPT), which stipulates negotiations in good faith on nuclear disarmament. Negotiations on a successor treaty, which has been declared as being aimed at the "21st-century model of arms control," have attracted international attention.

Meanwhile, both the United States and Russia are officially developing intermediate-range missiles, especially after the INF Treaty expired, raising the possibility of a missile arms race in East Asia. Such an arms race could fundamentally alter international relations in Northeast Asia, including US-Russia, China-Russia, and Japan-Russia relations, and have major impacts on the East Asian strategic environment.

2. Hong Kong Rocked by Street Protests and the Xi Jinping Administration

China and the United States held ministerial trade negotiations intermittently and reached a Phase One agreement in December. In January 2020, both governments signed the Phase One agreement document and showed compromises on trade. Nevertheless, it is unforeseeable whether the Phase Two trade negotiations will lead to an agreement. The reason is that the two countries are not simply disputing conditions for remedying the trade imbalance; they are competing for overall national strength, including science and technological prowess. Pressed to make hard choices, President Xi Jinping of China is likely preparing for a long battle with the United States. Against this backdrop, President Xi has made ongoing efforts to enhance the military's loyalty toward him, strengthening his power base by appointing confidants to his circle and tightening his grip on the Communist Party of China (CPC).

For the Xi administration in 2019, chaos from the Hong Kong mass protests turned into an unexpectedly large issue. The Hong Kong police have taken stringent measures to suppress the people's protests aimed at repealing the Fugitive Offenders and Mutual Legal Assistance in Criminal Matters Legislation (Amendment) Bill, which was submitted to the Legislative Council in February 2019. As such, it has been difficult to bring the situation to normalcy. This effect had a considerable impact on the Taiwanese presidential election. Kuomintang (KMT) swept to victory in the local elections held in Taiwan in late November 2018, and it was believed that the presidential election would turn out in its favor. However, the Taiwanese masses saw the situation in Hong Kong and felt a sense of crisis toward Taiwan's future. This in turn resulted in the Democratic Progressive Party (DPP) turning the table. In the presidential election on January 11, 2020, President Tsai Ing-wen was reelected with the most ever votes in the history of the election. The DPP also kept its majority in the Legislative Yuan.

3. A Shaky Korean Peninsula over the "Recurring Crisis"

After the second summit meeting between the United States and the Democratic People's Republic of Korea (DPRK) ended without a joint statement, the DPRK resumed missile launches to make a point to the United States: it was capable of reintroducing a state of nuclear-missile crisis. Pyongyang also sought to establish bilateral alignment with China, hinting that Beijing would join the peace regime talks concerning the future US force presence. This was just over a year after the DPRK and the Republic of Korea (ROK) signed the Panmunjom Declaration that suggested the peace regime talks might be held without China. The DPRK takes actions fully cognizant of the strategic effects generated by nuclear weapon fears on the United States and the ROK and of China's threat perception of the US forces. In tandem with such actions, the DPRK has undertaken steps to avoid domestic emergence of a force that would substitute Kim Jong Un, Chairman of the State Affairs Commission of the DPRK (Chairman of the Workers' Party of Korea). Namely, it has reaffirmed the ideology that governmental institutions are constituents of the ruling power, denying them of political neutrality on the grounds of "bureaucratism," and that people belong to "Kim Il Sung's nation and Kim Jong Il's Korea."

The ROK's Moon Jae-in administration took the position that mutual trust and dialogue between the two Koreas are essential for establishing peace on the Korean Peninsula. In the wake of the second US-DPRK Summit that ended with no outcomes, the Moon Jae-in administration announced provision of humanitarian assistance to the DPRK through international organizations and offered to host President Trump's meeting with Chairman Kim Jong Un at Panmunjom. Despite these efforts, no progress was made in inter-Korean relations.

Japan-ROK relations deteriorated amidst the emergence of issues, including the incident of an ROK naval vessel directing its fire-control radar at a Maritime Self-Defense Force (MSDF) patrol aircraft and the ROK government's negative action related to the hoisting of the MSDF flag at an international fleet review. Regarding the Japan-ROK General Security of Military Information Agreement (GSOMIA), the ROK government notified its termination to the government of Japan in August 2019 but announced in November that the ROK government would suspend the expiry of the agreement.

4. Japan's Pursuit of a "Free and Open Indo-Pacific"

In recent years, Japan has undertaken whole-of-government initiatives toward maintaining and bolstering an open maritime order based on the rule of law and freedom of navigation under the "Free and Open Indo-Pacific" (FOIP) concept.

The Ministry of Defense (MOD)/the Self-Defense Forces (SDF) have also been promoting various initiatives toward realizing FOIP as shown by the National Defense Program Guidelines for FY 2019 and beyond (2019 NDPG). The 2019 NDPG stressed: "in line with the vision of free and open Indo-Pacific, Japan will strategically promote multifaceted and multilayered security cooperation, taking into account characteristics and situation specific to each region and country."

Maintaining and strengthening the international order based on principles such as the rule of law and freedom of navigation are the main objectives of FOIP. FOIP is certainly not a new concept, but rather a goal that Japan has consistently pursued since the Cold War era. At the same time, under the influence of India's rapid economic growth and China's maritime advances beginning in the latter half of the 2000s, FOIP has been characterized by unprecedented focus on maritime security and strengthening cooperation with democratic countries with ocean borders.

Based on the above perspective, in recent years the MOD/SDF, notably the MSDF, have been expanding their presence and partnerships in the Indo-Pacific region. In addition, the MOD/SDF are strengthening initiatives to provide capacity building assistance to other countries in the region as well as multilateral security cooperation. Nevertheless, amidst the ongoing severe financial situation and personnel shortages, the feasibility of further project expansion poses as an issue.

With increasingly tight budget and personnel constraints going forward, it is becoming more important to develop a whole-of-department approach as well as to strengthen cooperation with other ministries and agencies in order to promote defense exchanges and cooperation. Additionally, to review each project and set an order of priority for these projects, it is essential to have a long-term strategy for defense exchanges and cooperation in the Indo-Pacific. Considering the placement of the ROK and China in FOIP is also an important pending issue.

Chapter 1

Nuclear Arms Control

Modernizing Nuclear Forces and Creating a Positive Environment for Nuclear Disarmament

ICHIMASA Sukeyuki

The nuclear arms control architecture since the Cold War has undergone considerable changes in recent years. In today's era called the "second nuclear age," it is not an overstatement to say that the post-Cold War wave of arms control has receded, and that the world has entered a new cycle of nuclear expansion driven by modernization of nuclear weapons. The Treaty between the United States of America and the Union of Soviet Socialist Republics on the Elimination of their Intermediate-Range and Shorter-Range Missiles (INF Treaty) was terminated in August 2019. Furthermore, there is no prospect for negotiations to extend the Treaty between the United States of America and the Russian Federation on Measures for the Further Reduction and Limitation of Strategic Offensive Arms (New START), which is set to expire in 2021. These treaties have been meaningful, for example, in restraining a nuclear arms competition, bringing about transparency and predictability based on a strict verification regime. However, the security environment has transformed significantly amidst the proliferation of nuclear weapons and missile technologies. There are debates that the arms control framework should be expanded to include countries other than the United States and Russia, and that negotiations should cover not only the issues around the definition of strategic/tactical nuclear weapons and numerical caps on nuclear weapons but also the treatment of new strategic arms and missile defenses. Meanwhile, the international community places high expectations on US-Russia nuclear arms control for compliance with Article VI of the Treaty on the Non-Proliferation of Nuclear Weapons (NPT), which stipulates negotiations in good faith on nuclear disarmament. Negotiations on a successor treaty, which has been declared as being aimed at the "21st-century model of arms control," have attracted international attention.

These circumstances have had reverberations on multilateral nuclear disarmament and non-proliferation efforts. The NPT failed to adopt the draft Final Document at the 2015 Review Conference, and expectations are building for a successful 2020 Review Conference on the milestone 25th anniversary of the indefinite extension of the NPT. On the other hand, new developments in nuclear disarmament have emerged, including the Treaty on the Prohibition of Nuclear Weapons (TPNW), which focuses on the humanitarian impact of nuclear weapons and seeks their total elimination. In the face of opposition from nuclear-weapon states and nuclear umbrella states, negotiations on the TPNW were held with the involvement of the civil society, and the treaty was adopted by the United

Nations (UN) General Assembly in July 2017. Amid concerns about a divided international community on nuclear disarmament approaches, nuclear-weapon states that have benefited from the indefinite extension of the NPT have also been required to engage in nuclear disarmament. In view of the multifarious security environment of various countries, the current situation calls into question how to constructively pursue discourse concerning new initiatives on nuclear disarmament, taking into account nuclear deterrence needs, the international community's concerns over delays in nuclear disarmament negotiations, nuclear risk reduction, and the humanitarian impact of nuclear weapons.

1. US-Russia Nuclear Arms Control: Developments and Challenges

(1) Implications of Terminating the INF Treaty

The INF Treaty was a breakthrough agreement that was signed toward the end of the Cold War. In order to eliminate ground-launched ballistic and cruise missiles with ranges of 500 to 5,500 km and their launchers and verify compliance with the agreement, the treaty introduced verification measures with a high level of intrusiveness under the slogan, "trust but verify." As time passed, however, US and Russian postures gradually diverged. In the mid-2000s when horizontal proliferation of intermediate-range missile technologies increased, Russia began to hint at withdrawing from the treaty, citing China's intermediate-range missiles and the United States' deployment of missile defense systems in Europe.[1]

In May 2013, the United States first conveyed concerns to Russia regarding its treaty violation, and Russia denied it.[2] In July 2014, the US Department of State (DOS) published a report stating that Russia's development of a ground-launched cruise missile (GLCM) is in violation of the INF Treaty.[3] In an April 2018 report, the DOS

Russia's GLCM, 9M729 (SSC-8) (Reuters/Kyodo News)

disclosed for the first time its analysis finding that this GLCM is 9M729 (SSC-8).[4] However, Russia refuted that it is not a violation of the treaty.[5] In December 2018, Mike Pompeo, US Secretary of State, issued a statement that the United States will inevitably have to withdraw from the INF Treaty unless Russia remedies its violation.[6] Conversely, Sergei Ryabkov, Deputy Minister of Foreign Affairs of the Russian Federation, condemned that the United States' SM-3 and Aegis Ashore were in breach of the treaty,[7] noting if the United States deploys ground-launched missiles, Russia will have to take retaliatory measures of all sorts, which could plunge them into a missile crisis that no one desires.[8] In addition, Vladimir Putin, President of the Russian Federation, raised alarm bells, stating that the United States' withdrawal from the INF Treaty may ruin the entire architecture of arms control and non-proliferation of weapons of mass destruction.[9] The situation could not be defused even after the United States suspended its obligations under the INF Treaty in February 2019. The treaty's termination became probable when Russia similarly suspended its obligations, too. In April, Donald Trump, President of the United States, instructed his administration staff to begin considering a new US-Russia-China "21st-century model of arms control," according to reports.[10] On August 2, the INF Treaty was terminated.

Such developments took place against the background of differences in the security environment between now and the time that the INF Treaty was concluded owing to missile technology proliferation, as well as a decline in the post-Cold War momentum to nuclear disarmament dubbed the "end of the arms control era," and an increasing dependence on nuclear deterrent.

In the post-Cold War era, horizontal proliferation of missile technology occurred across the globe as symbolized by the rise of China, which has become one of the world's largest missile holders. In particular, since the mid-1990s, China has built up its missile forces, including those that match INF definitions. Its DF-17 hypersonic glide vehicle (HGV), which is seen as a new means for delivery of nuclear weapons, was showcased for the first time in October 2019 at a military parade celebrating the 70th anniversary of China's founding.[11]

The momentum to nuclear disarmament, namely, discourse on a "world without nuclear weapons," subsided in many nuclear-weapon states. To the contrary, a wave of worldwide nuclear modernization, which had been underway behind the scenes, appears to be re-emerging. The TPNW negotiations discussed

Figure 1.1. Status of development and possession of noteworthy missiles with INF ranges by nuclear-weapon states, de facto nuclear-weapon states, and nuclear threshold states

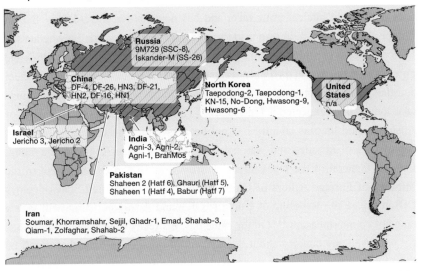

Source: Compiled by the author based on the CSIS Missile Defense Project website "Missiles of the World."

later have revealed that around one-fourth of the entire world depends on nuclear deterrent. Moreover, there is logic that the changes in the security environment have made Cold War-style arms control unfit for the status quo, and therefore, the termination of the INF Treaty was unavoidable. While President Trump's proposal of a "21st-century model of arms control" involving China[12] may offer a new step toward a "world without nuclear weapons," i.e., if and when China's participation is realized in the future, the country itself has refused the proposition.

In connection with the INF Treaty's termination, in July 2019, Vladimir Dzhabarov, First Deputy Chair of the Federation Council Committee on Foreign Affairs of the Russian Federation, indicated that if the United States deploys intermediate- and short-range missiles in Europe, Russia will follow suit.[13] On August 2, Mark Esper, US Secretary of Defense, stated that the United States has no plans to develop INF, and that for some time to come, it expects to enhance defense capabilities needed in the European and the US Indo-Pacific Command

(INDOPACOM) theaters.[14] On the other hand, Jens Stoltenberg, NATO Secretary General, affirmed on the same day that while NATO's nuclear deterrence must remain safe and effective, NATO need not take the same actions as Russia, does not want a nuclear arms race, and has no intention to re-deploy INF in Europe.[15] On August 3, in response to a question from the media on whether the United States is considering deployment of ground-launched intermediate-range missiles in Asia, Secretary Esper responded that he would like to deploy them and that while he personally would prefer within several months, these things take longer than expected.[16] On August 5, Scott Morrison, Prime Minister of Australia, said that his country had not been asked by the United States about deployment of missiles and was not considering it.[17] On August 6, Fu Cong, Director General of the Department of Arms Control and Disarmament of the Ministry of Foreign Affairs of China, stated that if the United States deploys INF in Japan, the Republic of Korea (ROK), and Australia, China will take a range of countermeasures.[18] On the same day, Secretary Esper noted that he has not yet asked any country about deployment of missiles in Asia, that it will be quite a long ways away, and that it will require a few years to actually be able to deploy some type of initial operational-capable missiles, whether they are ballistic or cruise missiles.[19] On August 7, at his press conference regarding a Japan-US defense ministerial meeting, Iwaya Takeshi, Minister of Defense, stated that there was no talk of deployment in Japan, saying Secretary Esper explained to him that the United States had not reached the stage of considering where to deploy missiles and that it was reviewing how it should respond to the situation. According to reports on August 18, Sergei Shoigu, Defense Minister of the Russian Federation, remarked that he thinks Russia will not take any actions as long as the United States does not deploy new missiles in Europe.[20] On August 22, Defense Minister Iwaya noted as follows: "Countries other than the United States and Russia, which had a treaty, are beginning to develop intermediate-range missiles and deploy operational missiles; a key challenge will be increasing transparency of military capabilities in East Asia," adding, "A new framework must be explored to prevent an excessive race in missile development."[21]

On August 18, the United States conducted a ground flight test of a GLCM, a variant of the Tomahawk with a range of more than 500 km, using the Mk41 Vertical Launching System (VLS).[22] As a response from Russia, which has already deployed the operational 9M729,[23] Deputy Foreign Minister Ryabkov criticized the US flight test, and at the same time, announced that Russia does not wish an arms race and will not deploy new missiles as long as the United States does not deploy them first.[24] Geng Shuang, Deputy Director of the Foreign Ministry Information Department of the People's Republic of China, which has deployed the most missiles with INF ranges of any country, criticized the US action for triggering a new round of arms race.[25]

On September 25, it was reported that President Putin of Russia sent a proposal to the government of Germany for a moratorium on deploying INF in the European region, and that the President also asked several countries, including European member states of NATO, to freeze INF deployment in Europe and other regions.[26] Meanwhile, on October 3, Suga Yoshihide, Chief Cabinet Secretary, stated at his press conference, "The United States explained to us that there will be no immediate deployment and it is not considering specific deployment locations, and that the United States has not asked any ally about new missile acceptance or deployment."[27] On October 22, it was reported that Japan and the United States commenced consultations on possible deployment of intermediate-range missiles in Asia.[28] On November 28, Emmanuel Macron, President of France, who held a meeting with NATO Secretary General Stoltenberg, said France cannot accept the proposal for a moratorium on deploying missiles, while on the other hand advocated that European countries should discuss a new treaty with the United States and Russia.[29] On December 6, Sergey Lavrov, Minister of Foreign Affairs of the Russian Federation, remarked that if the United States deploys missiles, Russia will respond with a mirror reaction.[30] On December 12, the United States announced that it conducted a flight test of a ground-launched ballistic missile, the first since the termination of the INF Treaty, and that it was successful.[31] In regard to the US announcement, Dmitry Peskov, Deputy Chief of Staff of the Presidential Executive Office, Presidential Press Secretary of the Russian Federation, said the test made clear the INF Treaty was terminated because of US policy.[32]

No conclusive information has come to light about the high-profile deployment of intermediate-range missiles. There were notable moves by China and Russia to restrain deployment. For example, at a China-ROK foreign ministers' meeting on December 4, Wang Yi, State Councilor and Minister of Foreign Affairs of China, allegedly warned Kang Kyung-wha, Minister of Foreign Affairs of the ROK, not to have US intermediate-range missiles deployed in the ROK.[33] At a bilateral foreign ministers' meeting on December 19, Foreign Minister Lavrov of Russia, too, raised concerns with Motegi Toshimitsu, Minister for Foreign Affairs, that deployment of intermediate-range missiles in Japan and elsewhere may enable the missiles to reach the Ural region in central Russia, according to reports.[34]

Intermediate-range missiles proliferated worldwide while the United States and Russia were restrained by the INF Treaty. From a strategic viewpoint, it is understandable that some observers believe measures are necessary to address this issue. Against the backdrop of the proliferation of intermediate-range missiles, there is also the view that regional deterrent will newly increase if the United States and Russia, which had been bound by the INF Treaty, re-deploy nuclear forces or intermediate-range missiles with conventional warheads. The INF Treaty for verifiable elimination, while its violation was not remedied, is now obsolete, and verification and inspection information accumulated over 30 years has been reset. Going forward, it is anticipated that both the United States and Russia will further rely on their own intelligence in place of verification, inspection and national technical means (NTM). A drop in transparency is inevitable, and a rise in uncertainties related to the size and deployment status of nuclear forces will cause security concerns about a decline in strategic stability.

China is seen as unlikely to participate in the "21st-century model of arms control" for some time.[35] But if the model is pursued, the creation of a more effective agreement will rest on the question of how to maintain or make appropriate revisions to elements such as: classification of weapons according to ranges and verifications with high intrusiveness; and balance with the reduction margin and inventory caps. While China may modernize and enhance its nuclear forces, its inventory is no more than about one-twentieth that of the United States and Russia. Meanwhile, only China and Russia possess the HGV, which has gained attention as a delivery vehicle for nuclear weapons. A challenge will be how to put this on the arms control agenda. The exterior appearance of missiles may not reveal whether nuclear warheads are mounted on missiles with certain payloads deployed by nuclear-weapon states. For this reason, the United States' Conventional Prompt Global Strike (CPGS) concept involving non-nuclear weapons may be contested during the negotiations. Furthermore, if China participates in the negotiations, it may seek revisions to the definition of strategic arms (strategic nuclear weapons, non-strategic nuclear weapons, or tactical nuclear weapons), which was set forth based on the geographical separation between the United States and Russia. This matter also concerns the negotiations on a successor treaty of New START. Moreover, the inclusion of more nuclear-weapon states in a nuclear arms control agreement itself will reduce nuclear risk and contribute to strengthening strategic stability and should be welcomed. It is expected that the agreement will be succeeded and not overlook the important lessons and know-how regarding arms control that the United States and Russia have accumulated over many years, including mutual verifications between the two countries.

(2) The Outlook for New START

New START was signed between the US and Russian leaders in April 2010 and entered into force in February 2011. It has a duration of ten years and is set to expire in 2021 if the United States and Russia do not agree to extend it. The treaty: (1) reduces the number of deployed warheads to 1,550 or less, (2) reduces the total number of deployed intercontinental ballistic missiles (ICBMs), submarine-launched ballistic missiles (SLBMs), and heavy bombers to 700 or less, and (3) reduces the total number of deployed and non-deployed ICBM and SLBM launchers as well as deployed and non-deployed heavy bombers to 800 or less in seven years, respectively. The treaty's verification regime is worthy of mention. It stipulates not only use of NTM but also biannual notifications concerning declared databases, ten annual Type One inspections of deployed and non-deployed strategic systems, and eight annual Type Two inspections of non-deployed strategic systems and their elimination and conversion. This stands in contrast to the Treaty between the United States of America and the Russian Federation on Strategic Offensive Reductions (Moscow Treaty, entered into force 2003), which contained no detailed verification provisions and relied on the verification provisions of the Treaty between the United States of America and the Union of Soviet Socialist Republics on Strategic Offensive Reductions (START I).

In terms of treaty compliance, the United States announced in September 2017 that it had achieved the levels required under the treaty, namely, 660 deployed ICBMs, SLBMs, and heavy bombers; 1,393 warheads on deployed ICBMs, SLBMs, and heavy bombers; and 800 deployed and non-deployed launchers of ballistic missiles, SLBM launchers, and heavy bombers.[36] Likewise,

Russia announced in February 2018 that it had achieved the required levels, namely, 527 deployed ICBMs, SLBMs, and heavy bombers; 1,444 warheads on deployed ICBMs, SLBMs, and heavy bombers; and 779 deployed and non-deployed launchers of ballistic missiles, SLBM launchers, and heavy bombers.[37]

As the expiration date for New START approaches, the fate of negotiations on a successor treaty or on the extension of New START has drawn attention in recent years. As of October 2018, Foreign Minister Lavrov of Russia stated that his country was ready for consultations on extending the treaty and would wait for a reply from the United States.[38] In May 2019, Tim Morrison, senior director on the US National Security Council, stated that President Trump will determine whether or not to extend the treaty at some point in 2020.[39] In August, Andrea Thompson, Under Secretary for Arms Control and International Security, US DOS, stated that discussions are ongoing between the relevant US and Russian agencies on what new weapons they have developed or are developing would fall under the New START parameters.[40] In the same month, Presidential Press Secretary Peskov of Russia noted that while President Putin has raised the issue of extension with President Trump, the United States has not responded, and that global strategic stability would be undermined if they lose the only agreement that substantially regulates the area of nuclear weapons.[41] The prospects remain uncertain for successor treaty negotiations and the treaty's extension in the immediate term. Since the ratification of the treaty, the United States had issues with its exclusion of Russia's tactical nuclear weapons, which outnumber those of the United States, and stockpile of nuclear warheads.[42] Barack Obama, former President of the United States, showed motivation for negotiating a successor treaty that covers these arsenals. On the other hand, Russia has expressed concerns over US missile defenses and non-nuclear strategic arms, such as the CPGS concept.[43] Indeed, in 2011, Deputy Foreign Minister Ryabkov made reference to concluding a legally binding missile defense-related treaty.[44] In 2013, then President Obama proposed in his Berlin speech to further reduce US deployed strategic nuclear weapons by up to one-third, and subsequently mentioned removing US tactical nuclear weapons deployed in Europe. Nevertheless, the response from Russia was cold. Yury Ushakov, Aide to the President, noted the need for discussions engaging other countries possessing nuclear weapons and opposed moves that would distort the balance in the system of strategic deterrence and undermine the efficacy of Russian nuclear forces.[45]

On the future outlook for New START, in August 2019, Defense Secretary Esper stated that, in light of Russia's development of new strategic arms after New START was concluded, the United States should consider if the treaty will continue to serve US interests while keeping strategic stability in mind. In doing so, the Defense Secretary said the United States should take into account the possibility of multi-lateralizing the treaty for avoiding a future arms race, as well as the pros and cons of including non-strategic nuclear weapons in the treaty.[46] In the following month, John Bolton, National Security Advisor, was dismissed[47] and left the administration. He previously criticized it would be inappropriate to extend New START as it cannot effectively address new strategic arms like HGV possessed by China and Russia,[48] and had expressed his intention to involve China and focus on negotiations for reaching a more comprehensive agreement that covers new weapons not regulated by the treaty. While it depends on what category of nuclear weapons and their delivery vehicles are envisioned for the "21st-century model of arms control" pursued by the United States, the dismissal of National Security Advisor Bolton may have some impacts on White House policy. Meanwhile, at the Eastern Economic Forum in September, President Putin of Russia referred to the "21st-century model of arms control" advocated by the United States. On this occasion, President Putin criticized the United States for still not ratifying the Comprehensive Nuclear-Test-Ban Treaty (CTBT), while showing understanding toward China's contention that its nuclear forces are smaller in scale than those of the United States and Russia, and therefore, China's arsenal of nuclear weapons and their delivery vehicles is too small for reduction. President Putin also quoted himself as asking President Trump how new hypersonic weapons will be included in an arms control agreement when the two met on the margins of the G20 Osaka Summit, and said that Russia has not received a clear answer from the United States.[49] Under these circumstances, on November 27, Deputy Foreign Minister Ryabkov underscored that Russia is open to extending the treaty for less than

Meeting between President Trump and President Putin at the Osaka G20 Summit
(UPI/Newscom/Kyodo News Images)

five years.[50] On December 22, Foreign Minister Lavrov stated that if New START will be extended, Russia is ready to include the RS-28 Sarmat and the Avangard HGV under the treaty's regulations.[51] On the other hand, on December 24, President Putin stated that Russia will continue to strengthen its nuclear forces as long as US-Russia consultations do not make progress. Defense Minister Shoigu also referred to deploying Avangard by the end of the week.[52] On December 25, Deputy Foreign Minister Ryabkov revealed that the two sides were coordinating toward holding discussions on bilateral strategic stability in a third country in a few weeks' time.[53]

The significance of New START is as was presented by the US DOS in February 2018. In short, New START is significant because compliance with the treaty enhances the security of the United States and its allies and makes strategic relations between the United States and Russia more stable, transparent, and predictable. This will be critically important when trust in the relationship deteriorates or the threat of miscalculation and misperception rises.[54] However, some note that, even if the United States and Russia agree to extend New START and it is extended until 2026, this alone will not directly resolve the issues that led to setbacks in the successor treaty negotiations, such as treatment of missile defense, the CPGS concept, and tactical nuclear weapons, and that the extension will not necessarily produce a constructive outcome for the negotiations involving China.[55]

(3) The Second Nuclear Age: Modernization of Nuclear Forces and New Strategic Arms

The second nuclear age has long been discussed in the context of the international nuclear security environment. Paul Bracken calls the "second nuclear age" a post-Cold War situation in which independent nuclear decisions are made in key regions and globally, led by the world major powers, in contrast to the first nuclear age epitomized by Cold War US-Soviet nuclear confrontations.[56] Rod Lyon notes that there are three variants of the second nuclear age discourse: (1) the second nuclear age discussion that flourished from 1995 to around 1998 warning of nuclear proliferation to rogue status, and by extension, the potential failure of the nuclear deterrence doctrine; (2) the second nuclear age discussion in around 2004 contending that nuclear proliferation chains will undermine nuclear non-proliferation norms; and (3) the second nuclear age discussion from around 2015 to the present reflecting the modernization of nuclear forces and their increasing strategic importance.[57] All of these discussions are closely linked to nuclear deterrence and concern issues related to horizontal and vertical nuclear proliferations—precisely challenges of nuclear non-proliferation under the NPT regime and of nuclear arms control agreements among nuclear-weapon states.

In actuality, the recent situation of nuclear weapon modernization backs up the second nuclear age discussion elaborated above. Russia develops arsenals, such as the new sea-launched cruise missile (SLCM) Kalibr, the short-range ballistic missile (SRBM) system Iskander-M (SS-26), and the 9M729 (SSC-8) that was alleged to be in violation of the INF Treaty. In the March 2018 State of the Union address, President Putin announced development of new weapons, such as the RS-28 Sarmat ICBM, the Avangard HGV, the Burevestnik nuclear-powered cruise missile, and the Poseidon nuclear-powered unmanned underwater vehicle carrying thermonuclear warheads. China, too, develops and possesses arsenals, such as the DF-21 and DF-15 ground-launched medium-range ballistic missiles (MRBMs) and the DF-16 SRBM, the DF-26 intermediate-range ballistic missile (IRBM), short-range cruise missile (SRCM), and the HN1, HN2, HN3, and DF-17 intermediate-range cruise missiles (IRCMs). In the Nuclear Posture Review (NPR) of February 2018, the United States expresses that it will maintain its policy of modernizing nuclear weapons, that as a short-term plan it will develop a lower-yield nuclear warhead for the SLBM, and that as a long-term plan it will develop SLCM.[58] In January 2019, it was reported that the United States produced a new model of low-yield nuclear warhead.[59] In August, the United States referred to developing a low-flying long-range cruise missile (LRCM) and a ballistic missile.[60]

Nuclear tests have also drawn attention. In May 2019, in his address at the Hudson Institute in the United States, Robert Ashley, Director of the Defense Intelligence Agency, cast doubt on Russia's adherence to the nuclear testing moratorium based on the zero-yield standard, which prohibits explosions that produce self-sustaining, supercritical chain reaction.[61] Russia immediately objected, saying the remark was a groundless defamation, and emphasized it is in compliance with the ratified CTBT.[62] The Comprehensive Nuclear-Test-Ban Treaty Organization (CTBTO) Preparatory Commission issued a statement that it had not detected signs of nuclear testing.[63] Meanwhile, radiation leakage from a small explosion in August in northern Russia that resulted in fatalities[64] gained attention as a possible indication of new nuclear weapon development in the country.

It is a fine line between modernization of aging nuclear forces and a new nuclear arms race. If removal from a nuclear arms control treaty leads to loss of transparency and ability to prevent nuclear expansion, this may pave the way for a more unstable and unpredictable international security environment. From the perspective of reducing nuclear risk, it is time to once again review the balance between deterrence and security on the one hand and nuclear arms control and nuclear disarmament on the other hand.

(4) US and Russia Nuclear Arms Control Obligations under NPT Article VI

The INF Treaty and New START are arms control treaties between the United States and Russia, along with being treaties that have come under the spotlight in the global context. The conclusion of the INF Treaty eliminated certain delivery vehicles in a verifiable manner. It also generated the trend for the subsequent START I and Presidential Nuclear Initiatives, including reduction, abolition, and strengthened control of tactical nuclear weapons, and heightened the post-Cold War international momentum to nuclear disarmament. On the other hand, New START curbed the nuclear arms race by introducing numerical caps on nuclear weapons and their delivery vehicles and contributed to improving the security environment by creating transparency and predictability under a verification regime. As with US-Russia nuclear arms control and nuclear disarmament treaties, both refer to the obligations under Article VI of the NPT in their preamble, i.e., negotiations in good faith on nuclear disarmament.

The NPT, which forms the core of today's international nuclear order, has a backbone consisting of a political transaction known as a "grand bargain": in exchange for non-nuclear weapon states' acceptance of nuclear non-proliferation obligations, nuclear-weapon states engage in nuclear disarmament and promote peaceful uses of nuclear power.[65] In the second half of the 1960s when the NPT was negotiated, the Non-Aligned Movement sought Negative Security Assurances (NSA) from nuclear-weapon states and their clear engagement in nuclear disarmament. At the time, NSA took the form of non-legally binding pledges made through the UN Security Council. As for nuclear disarmament, negotiations in good faith on nuclear disarmament were stipulated under Article

VI of the NPT. In addition, such engagement of nuclear-weapon states has been confirmed in Nuclear-Weapon-Free Zones (NWFZ). In 1995, 25 years after the NPT's entry into force in 1970, nuclear-weapon states promoted the indefinite extension of the treaty under the provision of Article X, Paragraph 2 of the NPT. Against the backdrop of the CTBT negotiations at the Conference on Disarmament (CD), the 1995 Review and Extension Conference made three decisions (1. extension of the NPT, 2. strengthening the review process for the treaty, and 3. principles and objectives for nuclear non-proliferation and disarmament) and adopted a resolution on the Middle East, and the indefinite extension of the NPT was agreed. This not only fixed the definition of nuclear-weapon state stipulated in Article IX, Paragraph 3 of the NPT into the future, but also made the negotiations in good faith on nuclear disarmament under Article VI an indefinite requirement.

2. Multilateral Nuclear Disarmament, Nuclear Non-Proliferation Efforts, and Discourse concerning New Initiatives on Nuclear Disarmament

(1) Challenges for the 2020 NPT Review Conference

The "grand bargain" has become a focal point of the NPT Review Conference, which continues to be held every five years since the NPT's indefinite extension. Ahead of the 2020 NPT Review Conference, what attracted attention at the 2019 session of the Preparatory Committee for the NPT Review Conference were Cluster 1 (nuclear disarmament) discussions regarding nuclear disarmament obligations and the points at issue pertaining to the legal prohibition of nuclear weapons.[66] At the session, a number of states parties noted the slow pace of progress on NPT Article VI obligations related to the signing and ratification of the CTBT, commencement of negotiations on the Fissile Material Cut-off Treaty (FMCT), as well as the uncertain outlook of the termination of the INF Treaty and New START.[67] In response, the United States noted the deterioration of the international security environment in recent years, and stated that, while Washington cannot offer a universal NSA, it would not threaten to use nuclear weapons against non-nuclear weapon states that comply with their nuclear non-proliferation obligations. Regarding the criteria for the use of nuclear weapons, the United States said that it would consider their use only in extreme circumstances to defend the vital interests of the United States or those of its allies and partners, and that it would maintain effective deterrence against non-nuclear attacks that could constitute extreme circumstances. In order to pursue a world without nuclear weapons as a long-term goal, it stressed the need to find a remedy for the current security environment that makes nuclear deterrence necessary.[68] Meanwhile, the United States did not articulate about the extension of New START, prospects for a successor treaty, or arms control issues related to intermediate-range missiles following the termination of the INF Treaty. Russia, on the other hand, distributed a working paper regarding future practical nuclear disarmament measures and creating prerequisites for their implementation. In this context, Russia vowed that it did not want New START to have the same fate as the INF Treaty, and supported the extension of New START upon solving the problem related to the considerable amount of strategic arms unilaterally excluded from accountability under the treaty. Furthermore, taking into account the role that nuclear weapons play in the security of many countries, Russia criticized the United States' missile defenses, CPGS concept, deployment of weapons in outer space, and nuclear sharing policy with NATO countries.[69]

Concerning the legal prohibition of nuclear weapons, Austria and Brazil as well as other Asian, African, and Latin American countries and regional groups expressed support for the TPNW, adopted in 2017, in response to nuclear-weapon states' concerns that the TPNW would weaken the NPT regime and their calls for developing a nuclear disarmament environment centered around improving the security environment. Based on these discussions, the Preparatory Committee for the NPT Review Conference's recommendations drafted by the chair included the need for a legally-binding norm to prohibit nuclear weapons[70] but were not adopted by consensus.[71]

In 2020, on this milestone year of 25 years since the NPT's indefinite extension, there are a number of difficult challenges, including North Korean nuclear issues, issues related to the United States' withdrawal from the Joint Comprehensive Plan of Action (JCPOA) on Iran, as well as non-nuclear disarmament challenges such as the establishment of the Middle East Zone Free of Nuclear Weapons and Other Weapons of Mass Destruction. The 2019 session of the Preparatory Committee for the NPT Review Conference achieved agreement on procedural matters, while on the other hand discussions on nuclear disarmament have seen a deepening rift between nuclear-weapon/nuclear umbrella states and non-nuclear weapon states. Some observers have sternly noted that discussions outside of the NPT framework and diplomatic efforts are necessary.[72]

(2) Prospects for the TPNW's Entry into Force and Apprehension of a Divided International Community

The adoption of the Final Document at the 2010 NPT Review Conference, which expressed "its deep concern at the catastrophic humanitarian consequences of any use of nuclear weapons," led to the holding of the sessions of the Preparatory Committee for the NPT Review Conference in 2012 and beyond and to the holding of the International Conference on the Humanitarian Impact of Nuclear Weapons since 2013 in Oslo, Nayarit, and Vienna. In particular, the Vienna conference in 2014 was attended by the United States and the United Kingdom and discussed the impact of nuclear weapons explosions and of nuclear testing, risk drivers for nuclear weapons use, scenarios and capabilities regarding nuclear weapons use, and international norms and the humanitarian impact of nuclear weapons.[73] Additionally, the conference issued a "humanitarian pledge"[74] supported by 127 states. Subsequently, pursuant to the 2015 UN General Assembly resolution (A/RES/70/33), the Open-ended Working Group (OEWG) taking forward multilateral nuclear disarmament negotiations held discussions on the legal prohibition of nuclear weapons in the absence of nuclear-weapon states. The 2015 NPT Review Conference discussed the inhumane nature of nuclear weapons and released a joint statement on the humanitarian consequences of nuclear weapons with the support of 159 states, including Japan. In 2016, TPNW negotiations were conducted following the adoption of the resolution by the General Assembly on taking forward multilateral nuclear disarmament negotiations (A/RES/71/258). On July 7, 2017, the TPNW was adopted at the UN General Assembly by a vote of 122 states in favor and was opened for signature. This means approximately two-thirds of all countries in the world supported the multilateral TPNW, which prohibits development and possession of nuclear weapons as well as using and threatening to use nuclear weapons. However, as of December 2019, the TPNW has been signed by 80 states and ratified by 34 states and has not yet reached the 50 states required for entry into force.

As was already stated, all nuclear-weapon states and nuclear umbrella states disapproved the TPNW since the negotiations. For example, in July 2017, five nuclear-weapon states noted in a statement that accession to the TPNW is incompatible with the policy of nuclear deterrence, which has been essential to keeping the peace in Europe and Northeast Asia for more than 70 years.[75] In September, NATO criticized that a treaty that will not engage nuclear-weapon states will not be effective, will not contribute to reducing nuclear arsenals, and will not only not contribute to a country's security and to international peace and stability but will also risk creating divisions in the international community, notwithstanding the fact that a unified approach is required as nuclear proliferation and security threats increase more than ever.[76] Japan has also presented a path forward based on a practical approach toward the elimination of nuclear weapons. Japan expressed the view that, with the engagement of nuclear-weapon states and upon building confidence and trust among states, agreeing on measures to reduce nuclear weapons, and creating an enabling security environment, an effective and meaningful treaty should be made for the elimination of nuclear weapons as the final building block after reaching a "minimization point" at which the number of nuclear weapons is sufficiently low. While showing understanding that the TPNW negotiations are an outcome of the frustration toward the slow pace of nuclear disarmament and a sincere desire to urgently achieve progress, Japan expressed that it cannot participate in the negotiations, which will not involve nuclear-weapon states, may divide the international community, and which will likely not lead to a resolution of real security issues.[77]

There are deep-rooted divisions between these discussions on the humanitarian impact of nuclear weapons and the discourse on security realities. Both discuss security; however, humans (humanity) are the subject of the former, whereas states (nuclear-weapon states, allies, and partners) are the subject of the latter. The debates have not stopped even after the TPNW negotiations have ended. At the annual International Atomic Energy Agency (IAEA) General Conference in September 2019, five nuclear-weapon states jointly noted the TPNW's harmful impact on the non-proliferation regime and reaffirmed that they will neither sign nor be bound by the treaty.[78] In order to avoid a further deepening of this divide in nuclear disarmament discourse, interested countries have recently raised issues in the lead-up to the 2020 NPT Review Conference. Below, the proposals for the following are described: Creating an Environment for Nuclear Disarmament (CEND) initiative, Stockholm Initiative on Nuclear Disarmament, and Group of Eminent Persons for Substantive Advancement of Nuclear Disarmament (EPG).

CEND was proposed by the United States in 2018 at CD under the name of "Creating the Conditions for Nuclear Disarmament (CCND)"[79] and was unveiled by its current name at the 3rd Preparatory Committee for the 2020 NPT Review Conference in the following year, 2019. At the CEND Working Group (CEWG) kickoff meeting in July 2019 also attended by NPT non-member states, Christopher A. Ford, Assistant Secretary of State for International Security and Nonproliferation, US DOS, sought a realistic and new disarmament discourse under the current security environment, along with diplomatic dialogue for exploring solutions to making progress on nuclear disarmament. Namely, he asked participants to discuss three topics: (1) reducing perceived incentives for states to retain, acquire, or increase their holdings of nuclear weapons; (2) multilateral and other types of institutions and processes to bolster non-proliferation efforts and build confidence in, and further advance, nuclear disarmament; and (3) interim measures to address risks associated with nuclear weapons and to reduce the likelihood of war among nuclear-armed states.[80]

The Stockholm Initiative was launched in June 2019 at the Stockholm Ministerial Meeting on Nuclear Disarmament and the Non-Proliferation Treaty, which adopted a joint declaration of 16 states including Japan. The declaration advocates an ambitious and realistic "steppingstones approach" for compliance with NPT Article VI, based on the engagement of states that attended the 1995, 2000, and 2010 NPT Review Conferences. Specifically, it notes transparent and responsible declaratory policies, measures to reduce the role of nuclear weapons in doctrines and policies, ways of enhancing transparency and of reducing risks of any uses of nuclear weapons, strengthened NSA, work on nuclear disarmament verification, and the importance of FMCT. In particular, the declaration notes that the extension of New START could be a key contribution to preserving strategic stability.[81]

In April 2019, the EPG, comprised of Japanese and foreign experts, submitted the Kyoto Appeal to Kono Taro, Minister for Foreign Affairs, and made it public. In October, Professor Shiraishi Takashi, EPG Chair, submitted the Chair's Report of the Group of Eminent Persons for the Substantive Advancement of Nuclear Disarmament to Wakamiya Kenji, State Minister for Foreign Affairs. The Kyoto Appeal urges, among other items: (1) sustaining bilateral and multilateral nuclear arms control treaties, including monitoring and verification; (2) compliance with obligations under nuclear arms control and disarmament treaties; (3) restoring civility and respect as well as practices of cooperation on nuclear arms control and threat reduction; and (4) respecting the contribution of civil society in cultivating innovative ideas and in nurturing mutual understanding and cooperation. In addition, the Kyoto Appeal proposes 11 items for the 2020 NPT Review Conference, including that nuclear-weapon states explain and share information regarding their nuclear doctrines, deterrence policies, risk reduction measures, and security assurances to non-nuclear weapon states through the P-5 (five nuclear-weapon states) process.[82] The Chair's Report lists actions that can be started before the 2020 NPT Review Conference, including resuming Russia-US engagement for nuclear forces reduction, as well as nuclear risk reduction measures and information sharing by nuclear-weapon states and explaining the consistency between their nuclear posture/policy and international humanitarian law. The report also presents actions that can be taken between 2020 and 2025, including US-Russia-China discussions on mitigating security dilemmas and assessing the impact that emerging technologies, such as artificial intelligence, can have on strategic stability and arms control.[83]

(3) The Humanitarian Impact of the Use of Nuclear Weapons and the Perspective of Nuclear Deterrent-Based Security

Since around 2015, there have been increasing opportunities for discussing the humanitarian impact of nuclear weapons, including at the Preparatory Committee for the NPT Review Conference, the New Agenda Coalition (NAC), and international meetings led by humanitarian initiative countries. Such discussions have provided an impetus for the civil society and brought about major changes in international politics, resulting in the adoption of the TPNW. Nevertheless, nuclear weapons still have a significant presence in today's international security environment that has long been called the second nuclear age. In recent years, along with the modernization of nuclear weapons, countries are beginning to enter a new cycle of the race to develop nuclear weapons, according to some observers.[84] Nuclear weapons, which have both political and military dimensions, are deemed necessary in countries that benefit from their deterrent effect with respect to security. On the other hand, it cannot be denied that use of nuclear weapons, including by mistake or accident, could have direct and indirect impact on surrounding countries beyond the countries concerned. Therefore, reviews have been undertaken in the past as to how such threats should be eliminated.[85]

Cross-regional discussions are ongoing regarding practical efforts to achieve a world of decreased nuclear risks from a mid- to long-term perspective.[86]

On the other hand, according to nuclear deterrence logic, the presence of nuclear weapons offers a source of power for dissuading the opponent's actions. Increasing the survivability of nuclear weapons and strengthening second-strike capability will further enhance the nuclear deterrent. Additionally, in the sense of readying for an uncertain future, the notion that there is still high political demand for nuclear deterrent applies not only to NATO, which emphasizes the Nuclear Alliance, but also to security in Northeast Asia where the Cold War structure remains and where nuclear issues still shake up the region.

However, after the INF Treaty's termination was decided in August 2019, European member states of NATO that wavered about INF deployment in the 1980s have made their stance clear: they do not want INF re-deployed in their territories like during the Cold War. By no means is it desirable for the world to be split on the 50-year NPT regime, creating an upheaval since the Cold War era. At the same time, given the current situation referred to as the second nuclear age, countries which have enjoyed the benefits of the indefinitely extended NPT must take another look at the "grand bargain" and confirm the obligation to pursue negotiations in good faith on nuclear disarmament. The future direction of the counter discourse on security and nuclear disarmament is drawing attention. In this context, a multifaceted consideration must be given to the humanitarian impact of the use of nuclear weapons, nuclear deterrence, disarmament, nuclear risk reduction, and the humanitarian dimension, bearing in mind the destructive impact of nuclear weapons on the global environment and scientific studies. Accordingly, a new discourse is sought for nuclear disarmament that takes into account many standpoints.

Two Ways of Looking at Reduction of Nuclear Weapons

Nuclear weapons play no small part in international politics. Under such circumstances, the inventory of nuclear weapons in the world numbering over 70,000 during the Cold War has decreased considerably. For example, the total number of nuclear weapons including estimates was 13,865, according to "World Nuclear Forces" in *SIPRI Yearbook 2019* published by the Stockholm International Peace Research Institute whose *Yearbook* attracts much attention every year.[87] The number alone suggests that, as a result of the reduction, overkill due to use of nuclear weapons has become less of a concern, and that the world has moved further away from a nuclear arms race, which has placed an economic burden on nuclear-weapon states.

On the other hand, such efforts to reduce nuclear weapons are still at a halfway point to eliminating nuclear weapons. The Bulletin of the Atomic Scientists' Doomsday Clock was set at two minutes to midnight in 2018.[88] This record worst setting is the same as when the United States and the Soviet Union successfully conducted thermonuclear tests in 1953. The Bulletin gives reasons, including North Korea's nuclear development, the termination and an uncertain future of nuclear arms control agreements, and the modernization of nuclear weapons. In addition, a study presents that even with the current reduced number of nuclear weapons in the world, an all-out nuclear war between nuclear powers can cause a nuclear winter to occur globally.[89] At present, US and Russian nuclear forces, which have come under the spotlight with the termination of the INF Treaty and the uncertain future of New START, still make up approximately 93% of the world's nuclear arsenals.[90] In this way, how one views the reduction in nuclear weapons varies depending on whether one is pursuing elimination of nuclear weapons, or initially seeking the creation and maintenance of a stable strategic environment through practical nuclear deterrence.

NOTES

1) Daryl Kimball and Kingston Reif, "The Intermediate-Range Nuclear Forces (INF) Treaty at a Glance," Arms Control Association, August 2019.

2) US Department of State, "Fact Sheet: Timeline of Highlighted US Diplomacy regarding the INF Treaty Since 2013," July 30, 2019.

3) US Department of State, "Adherence to and Compliance with Arms Control, Nonproliferation, and Disarmament Agreements and Commitments," July 31, 2014, p. 8.

4) US Department of State, "2018 Report on Adherence to and Compliance with Arms Control, Nonproliferation, and Disarmament Agreements and Commitments," 2018, p. 12.

5) US Department of State, "INF Myth Busters: Pushing Back on Russian Propaganda regarding the INF Treaty," July 30, 2019.

6) CNBC, December 5, 2018.

7) TASS, November 26, 2018.

8) TASS, December 19, 2018.

9) TASS, December 18, 2018.

10) *Washington Post*, April 25, 2019.

11) AP News, October 1, 2019.

12) Bloomberg, June 28, 2019.

13) Sputnik Japan, July 6, 2019.

14) US Department of Defense, "Secretary of Defense Esper Media Engagement en Route to Sydney, Australia," August 2, 2019.

15)　NATO, "Secretary General: NATO Response to INF Treaty Demise Will Be Measured and Responsible," August 2, 2019.

16)　Reuters (Japanese edition), August 5, 2019.

17)　AFP-JIJI, August 5, 2019.

18)　Reuters, August 6, 2019.

19)　Bloomberg (Japanese edition), August 7, 2019.

20)　Reuters, August 18, 2019.

21)　Japanese Ministry of Defense, "Boei Daijin Kisha Kaiken" [Press Conference by the Defense Minister], August 22, 2019.

22)　US Department of Defense, "DOD Conducts Ground Launch Cruise Missile Test," August 19, 2019; "Update: US Tests Ground-Launched Missile Concept Previously Banned under INF," *Jane's Defence Weekly*, August 22, 2019.

23)　NATO, "NATO and the INF Treaty," August 2, 2019.

24)　Reuters, August 20, 2019.

25)　Ibid.

26)　TASS, September 25, 2019.

27)　Jiji Press (online edition), October 3, 2019.

28)　*Asahi Shimbun* (online edition), October 22, 2019.

29)　Reuters, November 28, 2019.

30)　Reuters, December 6, 2019.

31)　US Department of Defense, "DOD Tests Prototype Conventionally-Configured Ground-Launched Ballistic Missile," December 12, 2019.

32)　*Newsweek*, December 13, 2019.

33)　*Yomiuri Shimbun*, December 6, 2019.

34)　NHK News Web, December 24, 2019.

35)　*Washington Post*, October 23, 2018.

36)　US Embassy & Consulates in Russia, "Fact Sheet: Key Facts about New START Treaty Implementation," February 5, 2018.

37)　TASS, February 5, 2018.

38)　TASS, October 22, 2018.

39)　*Asahi Shimbun* (online edition), May 30, 2019.

40)　US Embassy & Consulates in Russia, "Telephonic Press Briefing with Andrea L. Thompson, Under Secretary of State for Arms Control and International Security Affairs," August 13, 2019.

41)　Sputnik International, October 26, 2019.

42)　*Washington Free Beacon*, June 18, 2019; "Keynote: Thomas Donilon 2011 Carnegie International Nuclear Policy Conference," Carnegie Endowment for International Peace, March 29, 2011.

43)　Jonathan Pearl, "After New START: Challenges and Opportunities for 21st Century Arms Control," *Bulletin of the Atomic Scientists*, February 18, 2011.

44)　Tom Z. Collina, "Russia Makes New Proposal on Missile Defense," *Arms Control Today*, April 2011.

45) *Washington Post*, June 19, 2013.

46) US Department of Defense, "Secretary of Defense Esper Media Engagement en Route to Sydney, Australia."

47) Kingston Reif and Shannon Bugos, "US-Russian Nuclear Arms Control Watch," Arms Control Association, September 13, 2019.

48) *Washington Free Beacon*, June 18, 2019.

49) President of Russia, "Plenary Session of the Eastern Economic Forum," September 5, 2019.

50) Kingston Reif and Shannon Bugos, "Moscow Sends Warning on New START," *Arms Control Today*, December 2019.

51) *Sankei Shimbun*, December 23, 2019.

52) *Nikkei Shimbun*, December 25, 2019.

53) *Nikkei Shimbun*, December 26, 2019.

54) US Department of State, "Press Statement: New START Treaty Central Limits Take Effect," February 5, 2018.

55) Iain King, "The New Start Arms Control Treaty: Extend it, Go for More, or Let it Lapse?" Center for Strategic & International Studies, July 19, 2019.

56) Paul Bracken, *The Second Nuclear Age: Strategy, Danger, and the New Power Politics*, Times Books, 2012, pp. 1-2.

57) Rod Lyon, "Re-envisioning the Second Nuclear Age," Australian Strategic Policy Institute, February 19, 2015.

58) US Department of Defense, *Nuclear Posture Review*, February 2018, p. XII.

59) *Guardian*, January 28, 2019.

60) US Department of Defense, "Secretary of Defense Esper Media Engagement en Route to Sydney, Australia."

61) Rebeccah L. Heinrichs, "Transcript: The Arms Control Landscape ft. DIA Lt. Gen. Robert P. Ashley, Jr." Hudson Institute, May 31, 2019.

62) Reuters, May 30, 2019.

63) 47NEWS, May 30, 2019.

64) *New York Times*, August 12, 2019.

65) Akiyama Nobumasa, "Kakuheiki Fukakusan Joyaku (NPT) no Naritachi" [The Origin of the Treaty on the Non-Proliferation of Nuclear Weapons (NPT)], Akiyama Nobumasa, ed., *NPT Kaku no Gurobaru Gabanansu* [NPT: Nuclear Global Governance], Iwanami Shoten, 2015, p. 22.

66) Alicia Sanders-Zakre, "Reporting on the 2019 NPT PrepCom," Arms Control Association, May 10, 2019; "NPT PrepCom 2019: Live CNS Updates," Middlebury Institute of International Studies at Monterey James Martin Center for Nonproliferation Studies (CNS), April 29, 2019.

67) Ibid.

68) NPT Prepcom, "Statement by the United States in Cluster 1: Nuclear Disarmament Third Session of the Preparatory Committee for the 2020 Review Conference of the Parties to the Treaty on the Non-Proliferation of Nuclear Weapons, Ambassador Robert Wood, US Permanent Representative to the Conference on Disarmament," New York, May 2, 2019.

69)   NPT Prepcom, "Statement by the Delegation of the Russian Federation at the Third Session of the Preparatory Committee for the 2020 Review Conference of the Parties to the Treaty on the Non-Proliferation of Nuclear Weapons (General Debate)," New York, April 29, 2019.

70)   Chugoku Shimbun Hiroshima Peace Media Center, "Kakugunshuku meguri Umaranu Mizo: NPT Jikkosei Iji e Kadai" [Unbridgeable Nuclear Arms Control Divide: Challenges for Maintaining the NPT's Effectiveness], May 13, 2019.

71)   *Asahi Shimbun* (online edition), May 11, 2019.

72)   Nagasaki University Research Center for Nuclear Weapons Abolition, "RECNA NPT Blog 2019 Dai 10 Go (Sokatsu) (2) 2020 nen ni Mukete: Kienai Fuan" [RECNA NPT Blog 2019 No. 10 (Summary) (2) Toward 2020: An Unending Anxiety], May 12, 2019.

73)   Japanese Ministry of Foreign Affairs, "Dai 3 Kai Kakuheiki no Jindoteki Eikyo ni kansuru Kaigi" [Third Conference on the Humanitarian Impact of Nuclear Weapons], December 25, 2014.

74)   Federal Ministry Republic of Austria, "Vienna Conference on the Humanitarian Impact of Nuclear Weapons," December 8–9, 2014; Federal Ministry Republic of Austria, "Formal Endorsements and/or Expressions of Support for the Humanitarian Pledge," April 7, 2016.

75)   United States Mission to the United Nations, "Joint Press Statement from the Permanent Representatives to the United Nations of the United States, United Kingdom, and France following the Adoption," July 7, 2017.

76)   NATO, "North Atlantic Council Statement on the Treaty on the Prohibition of Nuclear Weapons," September 20, 2017.

77)   Japanese Ministry of Foreign Affairs, "Statement by H.E. Mr. Nobushige Takamizawa, Ambassador Extraordinary and Plenipotentiary, Permanent Representative of Japan to the Conference on Disarmament at the High-level Segment of the United Nations Conference to Negotiate a Legally Binding Instrument to Prohibit Nuclear Weapons, Leading towards their Total Elimination," March 27, 2017.

78)   Kyodo News (online edition), September 20, 2019.

79)   NPT Prepcom, "Creating the Conditions for Nuclear Disarmament: Working Paper Submitted by the United States of America (NPT/CONF.2020/PC.II/WP.30)," April 18, 2018.

80)   US Department of State, "Inaugurating a New and More Realistic Global Disarmament Dialogue, Remarks Dr. Christopher Ashley Ford, Assistant Secretary Bureau of International Security and Nonproliferation, 1st Plenary Meeting of the Creating the Environment for Nuclear Disarmament Working Group," July 2, 2019.

81)   Japanese Ministry of Foreign Affairs, "Stockholm Ministerial Meeting on Nuclear Disarmament and the Non-Proliferation Treaty (NPT)," June 11, 2019; Government Offices of Sweden, "The Stockholm Ministerial Meeting on Nuclear Disarmament and the Non-Proliferation Treaty: Ministerial Declaration, Stockholm," June 11, 2019.

82)   Group of Eminent Persons for Substantive Advancement of Nuclear Disarmament, "Kyoto Appeal: Appeals for the 2020 Review Process for the Treaty on the Non-Proliferation of Nuclear Weapons (NPT)," Ministry of Foreign Affairs Japan, April 2019.

83)   Japanese Ministry of Foreign Affairs, "'Kakugunshuku no Jisshitsuteki na Shinten no tame no

Kenjinkaigi' Gicho Repoto no Teishutsu" [Submission of the Chair's Report of the Group of Eminent Persons for Substantive Advancement of Nuclear Disarmament], October 21, 2019.

84)   Alexey Arbatov, "Mad Momentum Redux? The Rise and Fall of Nuclear Arms Control," *Survival*, Vol. 61, No. 3, June-July 2019, p. 9.

85)   Gareth Evans and Kawaguchi Yoriko, "Eliminating Nuclear Threats: A Practical Agenda for Global Policymakers," Report of the International Commission on Nuclear Non-proliferation and Disarmament, November 2009, pp. 230-231; Group of Eminent Persons for Substantive Advancement of Nuclear Disarmament, "Kyoto Appeal."

86)   Japanese Ministry of Foreign Affairs, "Foreign Minister Taro Kono Exchanged Views with the Heads of States of the Non-Proliferation and Disarmament Initiative," April 24, 2018.

87)   Shannon N. Kile and Hans M. Kristensen, "SIPRI Yearbook 2019: 6. World Nuclear Forces," Stockholm International Peace Research Institute, June 2019.

88)   Gayle Spinazze, "It is Still 2 Minutes to Midnight," *Bulletin of the Atomic Scientists*, January 24, 2019.

89)   Joshua Coupe, Charles G. Bardeen, Alan Robock and Owen B. Toon, "Nuclear Winter Responses to Nuclear War between the United States and Russia in the Whole Atmosphere Community Climate Model Version 4 and the Goddard Institute for Space Studies ModelE," *JGR Atmospheres*, July 23, 2019, pp. 8522-8543.

90)   Hans M. Kristensen and Matt Korda, "Status of World Nuclear Forces," Federation of American Scientists, May 2019.

Chapter 2
China

China-US Relations' Transformation into a Hegemonic Struggle

MOMMA Rira (Lead author, Sections 1 and 2)
IWAMOTO Hiroshi (Sections 1 and 3, Column)

China and the United States held ministerial trade negotiations intermittently, and amidst a continuation of progress and setbacks, reached a Phase One agreement in December. In January 2020, both governments signed the Phase One agreement document and showed compromises on trade. Nevertheless, it remains to be seen whether the Phase Two talks will lead to an agreement. The underlying reason: the two countries are not simply disputing conditions for remedying the trade imbalance; they are competing for overall national strength, including science and technological prowess. This is salient in US moves to drive out five major Chinese companies that lead the world in the 5G next-generation communications technology, and in the United States urging its allies to do the same. Not following suit of the United States are the European Union (EU) and the member states of the Association of Southeast Asian Nations (ASEAN), which generally have a favorable view toward China as an inexpensive provider of advanced technological capabilities. Pressed to make hard choices, President Xi Jinping is prepared for a long battle with the United States, as media reports suggest. President Xi is set on strengthening his power base by appointing confidants to his circle and on tightening his grip on the party, including visiting the site where the Communist Party of China (CPC) and the Red Army started the Long March. Furthermore, President Xi sets his sights on maintaining the nature of the People's Liberation Army (PLA) as the armed forces of the CPC, seizing opportunities such as China's 70th anniversary parade. However, even if its diplomacy, security, and military are strengthened, China has an inherent social structural vulnerability that cannot be avoided, namely, the rapid onset of an aging society. This situation will quickly tighten its financial circumstances. China is in effect entering a period toward slow growth.

Strained relations with the United States have also had implications for China's diplomacy with other countries. This is evident in China's multilateral frameworks, notably the Belt and Road Forum for International Cooperation, and in bilateral efforts, including improvement of China-Japan relations. Moreover, proactive diplomacy with Pacific Island countries is seen as China's groundwork for not limiting itself to the Belt and Road Initiative (BRI) and gaining freedom of action in all areas of the Western Pacific.

The people's protests in Hong Kong, triggered by the Fugitive Offenders and Mutual Legal Assistance in Criminal Matters Legislation (Amendment) Bill, are intensifying alongside the efforts of the Hong Kong police to suppress the protests, and there is no clear end in sight. This situation had a large impact on the Taiwanese presidential election. Kuomintang (KMT) swept to victory in the local elections held in Taiwan in late November 2018, and it was believed that the presidential election would turn out in its favor. However, the Democratic Progressive Party (DPP) turned the table, winning the hearts of the Taiwanese masses who saw the situation in Hong Kong and felt a renewed sense of crisis toward Taiwan's future. In the presidential election on January 11, 2020, President Tsai Ing-wen was reelected with the most ever votes in the history of the presidential election. The DPP also kept its majority in the Legislative Yuan. With the Tsai government now in a strong position to stand up to China, the situation in the Taiwan Strait is expected to become severer.

As regards the PLA, moves have been made to strengthen President Xi's authority, as well as to maintain and enhance the PLA's status as the CPC's armed forces. At the same time, the PLA is engaged in partnership with Russia and modernization of its equipment. In 2019, there was a noticeable strengthening of Taiwan-US relations, especially in the military domain. Underpinning the favorable Taiwan-US relationship has been the deepening discord between China and the United States.

Faced with not only China-US confrontation, but also issues including the reelection of President Tsai in Taiwan, the situation in Hong Kong that fails to find compromise, and the spread of COVID-19, improving Sino-Japanese relations is increasing in importance for the Xi Jinping government.

1. Xi Jinping's Statecraft Tested by China-US Confrontation

(1) China-US Confrontation: Radicalization of Trade Friction into Hegemonic Struggle

As anyone will acknowledge, China and the United States are closely interdependent economically. The United States imports a considerable amount of cost-effective products from China, such as home appliances, furniture, household goods, personal computers, smartphones, network servers, and solar panels. China depends on the United States for advanced electronic devices, cutting-edge production equipment, robots, artificial intelligence-related technologies, pharmaceuticals, agricultural products, feedstuffs, and more.[1] However, China-US relations, which have worsened since the end of 2017, showed no clear path toward improvement in 2019. Even amidst this lack of direction, the two countries conducted ministerial trade negotiations frequently. In June, a China-US Summit was convened on the margins of the G20 Summit held in Osaka but did not give rise to any prospect of resolving the trade negotiations. Under such circumstances, both countries imposed the fourth round of sanctions and retaliatory tariffs in September, following on from September 2018.

China and the United States are locked in a tit-for-tat struggle not simply over conditions for remedying the trade imbalance. The two countries are competing for overall national strength, including state-of-the-art technologies such as 5G. The United States is moving to drive out Huawei and ZTE Corporation that lead the world in the 5G next-generation communications technology, and is urging its allies to do the same. Five countries, namely, the United States, the United Kingdom, Canada, Australia, and New Zealand (known as the "Five Eyes"), which are parties to a multilateral agreement on joint use of facilities that intercept communications and radio waves to collect information, have created

Figure 2.1. Flow of Section 889 of the National Defense Authorization Act (NDAA) for Fiscal Year 2019

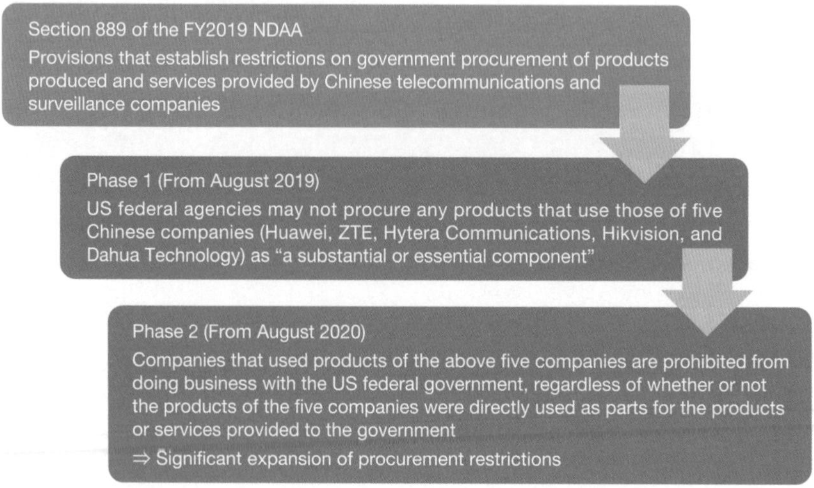

Section 889 of the FY2019 NDAA
Provisions that establish restrictions on government procurement of products produced and services provided by Chinese telecommunications and surveillance companies

Phase 1 (From August 2019)
US federal agencies may not procure any products that use those of five Chinese companies (Huawei, ZTE, Hytera Communications, Hikvision, and Dahua Technology) as "a substantial or essential component"

Phase 2 (From August 2020)
Companies that used products of the above five companies are prohibited from doing business with the US federal government, regardless of whether or not the products of the five companies were directly used as parts for the products or services provided to the government
⇒ Significant expansion of procurement restrictions

Source: Compiled by the authors based on the National Defense Authorization Act for Fiscal Year 2019.

a new framework for sharing information on cyber attacks in collaboration with Japan, Germany, and France.[2] In addition, US Secretary of State Mike Pompeo visited the Eastern European countries of Hungary, Slovakia, and Poland to warn them against the use of Huawei communications equipment in their countries. Furthermore, Section 889 of the National Defense Authorization Act for Fiscal Year 2019, which was passed in the United States in 2018, has been brought to attention for establishing significant restrictions on government procurement of products produced and services provided by Chinese telecommunications and video surveillance companies. For the first phase of the restrictive measures, Section 889 states that US federal agencies may not procure any products that use those of five Chinese companies (Huawei, ZTE, Hytera Communications, Hikvision, and Dahua Technology) as "a substantial or essential component" from August 2019. It specifies that, in the second phase from August 2020, the United States intends to take more comprehensive and extremely stringent measures and to exclude Chinese companies from the list of government suppliers.

That is not to say that all countries are on the same page. On March 26, the European Commission issued a recommendation on cybersecurity of 5G networks. The recommendation did not seek a uniform ban of Huawei and other Chinese companies' products and entrusted member states to make their own decision. Germany has reportedly indicated that it will not prohibit Huawei products from its 5G networks.[3] On April 9, Premier Li Keqiang, who was visiting Brussels, held a meeting with EU leaders. They issued a joint statement expressing that there should not be "forced transfer of technology."[4] Given the United States' distrust of China's assurance on eliminating "forced transfer of technology," the joint statement may reflect China's plan to create a US-EU divide, foreseeing the disagreements over their policies on China.

ASEAN member states, too, are largely keen on strengthening their relations with China. Prime Minister Mahathir bin Mohamad of Malaysia attaches importance to its relationship with Chinese IT companies, and committed to cooperating with Huawei on 5G trials. At a Business Summit held in Bangkok in June, Prime Minister Mahathir showed a friendly stance toward China, stating, "We should not take sides." At the Shangri-La Dialogue held in June, Prime Minister Lee Hsien Loong of Singapore also warned against the United States for over-emphasizing the threat of Huawei. Many countries welcome Chinese companies whose selling point is advanced technological capabilities at low prices. For this reason, the China-US battle for hegemony is not necessarily unfolding to China's disadvantage.

In May, President Xi Jinping visited Ganzhou, Jiangxi Province, a chief producer of rare earth, and noted, "Rare earth is an important strategic resource."[5] The National Development and Reform Commission later issued a press release, stating that experts recommended strengthening export controls for rare earth and establishing a full-process traceability and review system for exports.[6] This development recalls China's use of rare earth to apply pressure on Japan in 2010. It is deemed that China again seeks to use rare earth as a trump card in its trade negotiations with the United States.

On June 2, the State Council Information Office published a white paper titled, "China's Position on the China-US Economic and Trade Consultations," in which China justified its position. In the white paper, China notes as follows: (1) its science and technological innovations are based on self-reliance; condemning China of intellectual property theft and forced technology transfer is unfounded, (2) the additional tariff measures that the United States imposed undermine its own and others' interests, (3) the trade war cannot "make America great again," and (4) US hegemonic behavior harms the world. Furthermore, the white paper underscores that China and the United States should hold dialogues and consultations to avoid disagreement and friction in the economic and trade area.[7]

Subsequently, the United States and China worked toward compromise, and on December 13, announced the Phase One agreement, respectively. The two countries unveiled the details of the agreement independently. China's announcement was as follows: (1) the United States will fulfill its consent to phase out its additional tariffs on Chinese products, (2) the United States will achieve a switch from hiking to cutting additional tariffs, and (3) an agreement document will be prepared that includes intellectual property rights, technology transfer, food products, agricultural products, financial services, exchange rate and transparency, trade expansion, and bilateral assessment and dispute settlement.[8] On the other hand, the Office of the US Trade Representative announced that the agreement includes China's commitment to make substantial additional purchases of US goods and services in the coming years.[9]

Under the Phase One agreement, China has significantly increased purchases of US products, including agricultural products such as soybeans and energy resources. Meanwhile, the United States has lowered tariffs on $120 billion of

Table 2.1. US-China trade and commerce negotiations (2019–2020)

Date	Place	Issue and Outcome
2019　January 30 and 31	Washington, DC	Consultations on intellectual property rights protection, suspension of forced technology transfer, etc. China expressed intent to purchase US soybeans (5 million t).
February 14 and 15	Beijing	Work began for creating a memorandum on bilateral issues.
February 21–24	Washington, DC	
March 28 and 29	Beijing	Details unknown
April 3–5	Washington, DC	No agreement reached on vital matters.
April 30–May 1	Beijing	
May 9 and 10	Washington, DC	No de facto achievements
May 10		The United States increased the tariff rate on Chinese goods (equivalent to $200 billion) for the third round of sanctions and retaliatory tariffs. China announced countermeasures (equivalent to $60 billion).
July 30 and 31	Shanghai	No de facto achievements
September 1		The United States and China simultaneously imposed some of the fourth round of sanctions and retaliatory tariffs.
October 10 and 11	Washington, DC	First negotiations since July. Provisional agreement reached on agricultural products, currency, etc.
October 25	Telephone meeting	The US Trade Representative announced the holding of a ministerial-level telephone meeting and progress toward a Phase One agreement.
December 13		The two countries announced the Phase One agreement, respectively. The United States scrapped tariffs on China scheduled for December 15. China also retracted retaliatory tariffs.
December 20	Telephone meeting	US and Chinese leaders held a telephone meeting on the trade negotiations.
2020　January 13–15	Washington, DC	Phase One agreement document signed.

Source: Compiled by the authors based on media reports.

Chinese imports it imposed in September 2019, from 15% to 7.5%. While this is the first time that the United States relaxed sanctions since imposing import restrictions on steel and aluminum in March 2018, it maintains 25% tariffs on

$250 billion of Chinese imports. China, too, has maintained most of its retaliatory tariffs. It is thought that the two countries moved toward compromise due to President Trump's desire to stress his achievements for the US presidential election scheduled in autumn 2020, and due to the China-US trade friction putting a damper on China's growth rate. Despite such motives, the path to a Phase Two agreement is expected to be mired in difficulties—the reason being that the consultations on outstanding matters pertain to issues related to China's structural reforms, such as excessive industrial subsidies and tax breaks for state-owned enterprises, along with issues concerning Huawei, which the United States perceives as having security implications.

(2) Xi Jinping's Pursuit of Long-term Rule While Tightening Grip on Party and Armed Forces

It is well known that President Xi Jinping brings acquaintances into the central government and appoints them to his circle. They include people he has known from his local government years, such as: Li Zhanshu, Chairman of the National People's Congress (NPC) of the People's Republic of China (PRC); Liu He, Vice-Premier of the State Council; Chen Miner, Secretary of the Chongqing Municipal Committee of the CPC; and Cai Qi, Secretary of the Beijing Municipal Committee of the CPC. These individuals occupy Central Politburo member or higher posts, which are reserved for only 25 of the more than 90 million CPC members throughout China. Wang Qishan, who retired from his Central Politburo Standing Committee member post and became a mere party member at the 19th Party Congress in 2017, was elected Vice President of the PRC in March 2018 and has been given the important role of overseeing diplomacy. In media reports about the PLA military parade on October 1, Vice President Wang Qishan's

Giant portrait of Xi Jinping shown at the parade
(Xinhua/Kyodo News Images)

name was listed after the seven members of the CPC Politburo Standing Committee and before former Presidents Jiang Zemin and Hu Jintao.[10] As a special envoy of President Xi, Vice President Wang Qishan attended the Ceremonies of the Accession to the Throne in Japan and the inauguration ceremony for the Indonesian President.[11] They demonstrate President Xi's continued deep confidence in Vice President Wang Qishan, as well as President Xi's intention to assemble confidants to his circle for strengthening his power base.

An increasing display of loyalty toward President Xi Jinping has been observed on various occasions. At the largest ever military parade held in Beijing on October 1, 2019 to coincide with the country's 70th anniversary, a group comprised of generals, field officers, and company officers was formed for the first time in the history of the military parade since China's founding and took part in the procession. All 25 members who led this formation are reportedly generals. At the review, they all gave a unified salute to President Xi at the podium.[12] The *PLA Daily* reported that it was a demonstration of "all service members' wholehearted commitment and absolute loyalty toward President Xi" and of "the new structure following the rebuilding of the military's leadership management and operational command system."[13] After the military parade, a parade by the people was held, featuring giant portraits of China's past and incumbent party leaders: Mao Zedong, Deng Xiaoping, Jiang Zemin, Hu Jintao, and Xi Jinping. The portraits are thought to represent the people's loyalty to the party's leaders.

During Deng Xiaoping's rule, it became routine for the leader to deliver an address at military parades held on milestone years since the PRC's founding. Furthermore, it was customary for the address to mention past leaders. Nevertheless, Xi's latest address mentioned only Mao Zedong. By drawing a direct link between Mao Zedong and himself, it is believed that Xi intended to portray himself as the "core of the party" to consolidate his authority and power.

In China, recent years have seen moves for maintaining and strengthening the PLA's nature as the armed forces of the party. In the *PLA Daily,* it was reaffirmed that, "The military is the people's armed forces under the absolute leadership of the party; its purpose is always the party's purpose, and its original aspirations are the party's original aspirations."[14] At the military parade held on China's 70th anniversary, President Xi noted on the party's position as follows: the PLA "must adhere to the leadership of the CPC." At the parade, helicopters and guards of honor raised the party flag, the state flag, and the army flag in this order, highlighting the superiority of the party.

The CPC theory's strong influence on military affairs was also observed at the Military Olympics (Military World Games) held for the first time in China on

October 18. The lighting ceremony for its torch relay was held on August 1 at a memorial hall in Nanchang, Jiangxi Province, which is connected to the armed uprising led by the CPC in this area on August 1, 1927. At the ceremony, the flame was reportedly lit by the great-granddaughter of Fang Zhimin, a proletarian revolutionist from Jiangxi Province.[15] In this way, even before the events began, China's first Military Olympics was largely used to make people aware that the PLA is the armed forces of the party.

President Xi Jinping is set on tightening his grip on the party. In May, he visited Yudu County, Jiangxi Province, which was the starting point of the Long March. It began in October 1934 as the Communists were no longer able to resist the encirclement campaign of the KMT army led by Chiang Kai-shek, and were forced to abandon the Chinese Soviet Republic. During the visit, President Xi noted that the CPC's original aspirations and mission, along with the revolution's ideals and purpose, should never be forgotten.[16] He may have intended to emphasize that the negotiations and battle with the United States will be a long arduous journey similar to the Long March. "不忘初心、牢記使命 (Staying true to our founding mission)"[17] was the theme of the 19th Party Congress held in October 2017 and has since been reiterated on various occasions. Wang Huning, Politburo Standing Committee member and the fifth-ranking member of the party, and General Zhang Youxia, Vice Chairman of the Central Military Commission, were appointed to head the Education Leading Group on the theme of "staying true to our founding mission," which was established under the CPC Central Committee and the Central Military Commission, respectively. President Xi has stated that the "original aspirations" and "mission" of CPC members refer to seeking happiness for the Chinese people and rejuvenation for the Chinese nation.[18]

On September 3, President Xi delivered an important address at the Party School of the Central Committee that educates CPC senior officials. In this address, President Xi remarked, "The world today is undergoing dramatic change not seen in the past 100 years." "The great rejuvenation of the Chinese nation will not be achieved easily by mere drum-beating and gong-clanging, and realizing the great dream requires a great struggle." Xi added that the struggle would continue at least until 2049, the 100th anniversary of China.[19] The phrase "unprecedented changes unseen in the past 100 years" refers not only to the international situation in which China finds itself. Having a population that is

Figure 2.2. Changes in China's population by age (in millions)

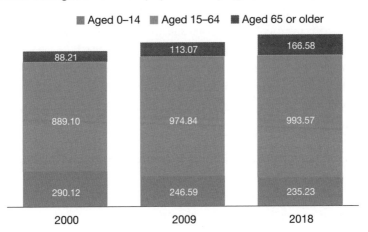

■ Aged 0–14　■ Aged 15–64　■ Aged 65 or older

	2000	2009	2018
Aged 65 or older	88.21	113.07	166.58
Aged 15–64	889.10	974.84	993.57
Aged 0–14	290.12	246.59	235.23

Source: Compiled by the authors based on the Chinese National Bureau of Statistics website.

more than quadruple that of the United States, China has drawn the interests of various countries attracted to its massive market. Therein also lies the reason the United States continued to uphold its policy of engagement with China. That very China faces a rapid onset of population aging and decline, as has been pointed out from before, and this is now becoming a reality. According to information released by the National Bureau of Statistics, the Chinese population as of the end of 2018 was 1.395 billion; the proportion of the working-age population (age 15 or older and under age 65) and the population of young people under age 15 decreased, whereas conversely, the elderly population that is age 65 or older increased. This trend will rapidly tighten Beijing's financial situation. The Report on the Work of the Government presented at the March NPC set the GDP target growth rate at 6 to 6.5%.[20] While this is slightly lower than the previous year's growth rate of around 6.5%, the numerical target appears to be sufficiently high. Nevertheless, it represents the end of China's high economic growth in the 10% range, considered one of the grounds that gave legitimacy to the CPC's rule, and China's entry into a period of slow growth.

Such changes in Chinese society are putting pressure on its economic situation. On top of this, the country faces intensifying confrontation with the United States, the Hong Kong issue, and a worsening economy. President Xi seeks to fully fulfill his role as a helmsman of the party, the government, and the PLA by enhancing party solidarity and unifying its thinking, while the party shares a sense of crisis over foreign and domestic affairs. However, concentrating power in himself also means no one else can be held accountable. If President Xi were to mismanage Sino-US relations or fail to adapt to a rapidly changing aging society, he could become a target of criticism from both inside and outside the party and be forced to retire, even if he abolished the term limit system and wished to stay in power for the long term.

(3) The Xi Government's Efforts to Improve Foreign Relations as a Hedge

With China-US relations under duress, Beijing is taking pains to strengthen or stabilize its relations with neighboring countries. In particular, China and Russia identify each other as a comprehensive strategic partner. On June 5, 2019, President Xi Jinping visited Russia for the eighth time since assuming the presidency in 2013 and held a meeting with President Putin. At the meeting, the Chinese and Russian leaders discussed such matters as the issue of the Korean Peninsula and Iran's nuclear issue, and affirmed that China and Russia, as core members of the United Nations (UN), will protect the international system founded on international law and maintain the multilateral trading system.[21] It is believed that President Xi and President Putin sought to define themselves as a counterbalance to the Trump administration, which gives top priority to US interests. On July 23, Chinese and Russian bombers conducted a joint flight over the East China Sea and the Sea of Japan.[22] Some note that this joint flight reveals the continuously deepening China-Russia relationship, and that it was strategically intended to counter the United States with which confrontation is increasing.[23] The spokesperson for the Chinese Ministry of National Defense stated that China and Russia "conducted their first-ever joint strategic air patrol," and that it deepened their strategic coordination, including the level of joint actions and operation capabilities.[24] Furthermore, a scholar has pointed to the possibility of China and Russia continuing to announce new joint military trainings.[25]

Criticized as a "debt trap," China's BRI has come under the stern eye of the international community, and China has made a series of efforts to dispel this negative image. From April 25 to 27, the Second Belt and Road Forum for

International Cooperation was held in the suburbs of Beijing. The First Forum in 2017 was attended by approximately 1,500 people from over 130 countries, including leaders of 29 countries, and over 70 international organizations. In contrast, the Second Forum was attended by 6,000 people from over 150 countries, including leaders of 38 countries, and 92 international organizations. As is demonstrated, the BRI's marked increases in participating nations and international organizations have risen China's influence on the international community.[26] In his keynote speech, President Xi stated that the BRI will introduce widely accepted rules and standards on all fronts and respect the laws of participating countries, showing that considerations would be given to criticisms and concerns expressed by beneficiary countries.[27]

Sino-Japanese relations are also improving. On April 24, Nikai Toshihiro, Secretary-General of the Liberal Democratic Party, visited China as a special envoy of Prime Minister Abe Shinzo and held a meeting with President Xi. President Xi himself attended the G20 Summit held in Osaka in June. Vice President Wang Qishan attended the Ceremonies of the Accession to the Throne held in October.

Nonetheless, it is clear that improvements in China-Japan foreign relations have not necessarily worked to the favor of security affairs. On July 24, China published a national defense white paper entitled, "China's National Defense in the New Era."[28] For the first time in approximately four years since May 2015, a national defense white paper was published. Among the clear differences with previous national defense white papers is the hardline rhetoric used with regard to the Senkaku Islands. The latest white paper uses wording not seen in previous white papers, namely, that navigation of Chinese government vessels in the waters of the Senkaku Islands constitutes China's exercise of national sovereignty under the law. Indeed, China Coast Guard (CCG) vessels have stepped up their activities in these waters. From April to June, CCG vessels entered the contiguous zone around the Senkaku Islands on 64 consecutive days, the longest on record. Although this record ended on June 15, the consecutive entries resumed the following day on June 16 and continued for 32 days. Since September 2012, there have only been five confirmed cases in which Chinese government vessels conducted activities in these waters for more than 30 days, excluding the aforementioned entries. Moreover, it was unprecedented for entries to resume after a mere one-day interval. On an annual basis, both the number of days and the number of total CCG vessels that entered the contiguous zone were record highs in 2019.

From September to November 2019, a Hokkaido University professor was detained by Chinese authorities. In November that year, an employee of a Japanese company was sentenced to three years in prison. Since 2015, 15 Japanese nationals have been detained in China, 9 of whom have been sentenced to prison, according to reports. China has established laws, such as the Counter-Espionage Law (2014), the National Security Law (2015), the National Intelligence Law (2017), and the Law on the Administration of Activities of Overseas Non-Governmental Organizations within the Territory of China (2017), and has used the laws to reinforce its domestic surveillance system. It appears China has actively applied such laws to foreign nationals as well. While there have been remarkable improvements in China-Japan foreign relations, the above events reveal that Sino-Japanese relations by no means have seen an overall easing of tensions.

China conducts proactive diplomacy with Pacific Island countries. In September, China established diplomatic relations with the Solomon Islands and the Republic of Kiribati, both of which had diplomatic relations with Taiwan. As a result, the number of countries that have maintained diplomatic relations with Taiwan has decreased from 22 to 15 since the initial inauguration of the Tsai Ing-wen government (May 2016). China's moves should be considered not only as efforts to raise its national prestige ahead of its 70th anniversary and as a blow to Taiwan, but also as part of China's Pacific strategy based on the BRI.

Beijing provides large-scale economic assistance to Pacific Island countries, including Papua New Guinea and Fiji. This region is expected to assume greater importance in the area of space business, a field into which Beijing has focused its efforts. In Kiribati, with which China had diplomatic relations from 1997 to 2003, it operated an observation station for satellite tracking, position measurement, and control. A ground-based observation station is cheaper than dispatching tracking ships each time, and for such reasons, China may resume the station.[29] In addition, Kiribati is located along the equator, the most advantageous position for launching satellites into the geostationary orbit. China engages in the business of launching high-demand satellites, such as communication and broadcasting satellites and meteorological satellites, and may build a satellite launching facility in Kiribati.

Pacific Island countries are anticipated to gain important geopolitical standing from a military strategic perspective. At this point in time, China does not have the ability to exercise sea control in these vast waters. However, Beijing already has the ability to pass through the "first island chain" and carry out frequent trainings in this area. At the same time, China is thought to be steadily deploying anti-ship ballistic missiles, such as DF-21D and DF-26, that deny US naval access. Important sea lanes for transporting crude oil to East Asia include the route from the Indian Ocean to the Strait of Malacca and the South China Sea. The route from the Indian Ocean, transiting the Lombok Strait, the Makassar Strait, and the Celebes Sea, is also a vital route. Palau, which lies at the exit of the route, along with Papua New Guinea, is located at the southern tip of the "second island chain." Palau currently maintains firm diplomatic relations with Taiwan. However, if China were to establish diplomatic relations with Palau that will enable deployment of military capabilities from the country, China will acquire a bridgehead for securing freedom of action in all areas of the Western Pacific. Furthermore, China can now access areas where its fleet could not make port calls previously because of their diplomatic relations with Taiwan, such as Kiribati and the Solomon Islands. China has been pursuing a gradual strategy of passing through the "first island chain" and aiming for forays into the "second island chain." Depending on its relations with Pacific Island countries, China's future strategy will include the option of targeting Guam from behind. Many of the Pacific Island countries scattered between Hawaii, Guam, and Australia are under the strong influence of the United States. Nevertheless, there is plenty of room for China to leverage economic assistance to strengthen its relations with these countries.

2. Taiwan's Increasingly Fluid Situation Linked with the Hong Kong Protests

(1) The Fugitive Offenders Amendment Bill Deepens Anxiety over Chinese Rule

Hong Kong was probably under the most spotlight in 2019 since its return to China in 1997. The circumstance giving rise to this was the large-scale protests that unfolded virtually every week against the Fugitive Offenders and Mutual

Legal Assistance in Criminal Matters Legislation (Amendment) Bill, which would have enabled the extradition of Hong Kong nationals to police in mainland China, and there is still no end in sight to the protests. The Bill was proposed after a Hong Kong man murdered his girlfriend in Taiwan in February 2018. Afterwards, the man fled back to Hong Kong. The government of Hong Kong has no extradition arrangement with Taiwan, making it difficult for Taiwan to institute criminal prosecution. To resolve this situation, the government of Hong Kong introduced the Bill in the Legislative Council. The extradition countries and regions included not only Taiwan but also mainland China and Macao. For Chinese authorities, it was natural for Hong Kong, a special administrative region of China, to conclude a criminal justice agreement on extradition with mainland China, and the authorities endorsed the Bill. However, the people of Hong Kong strongly opposed it, fearing that those who criticize the CPC government will be extradited to China on unfounded charges. Staff of Causeway Bay Books, which sold books critical of the CPC, disappeared in 2015, and their detainment by Chinese authorities later came to light. It is no surprise that the people of Hong Kong who know this incident felt an increasing sense of danger.

On April 28, approximately 130,000 people (source: protest organizer) took to the streets in the largest protest since the Umbrella Movement in 2014. The protests drew unprecedented numbers: 1.03 million people (source: organizer) participated on June 9 and 2 million people (source: organizer) on June 16. The enormity of the participants can be understood if Hong Kong's population of 7.52 million people (2019) is considered. The protests initially took place mostly on Hong Kong Island but later expanded to the opposite shore, the Kowloon Peninsula, which is connected to mainland China by land. Amidst severe criticisms,

June 16, 2019; People filling the streets of Hong Kong (UPI/Newscom/Kyodo News Images)

the Fugitive Offenders Amendment Bill was de facto withdrawn (June 18, Chief Executive Carrie Lam) and then formally withdrawn (September 4, Chief Executive Carrie Lam). Nonetheless, the situation has not been resolved and has even worsened. The following months have seen escalating protests, including the burning of

Chinese flags by demonstrators, a break-in and temporary occupation of the Legislative Council (July 1), spray-painting on the Hong Kong Liaison Office of the Hong Kong and Macao Affairs Office of the State Council, one of China's branch offices (July 21), a sit-in at Hong Kong International Airport (August 9), damages to a Bank of China branch (October 4), provocations (shining of laser lights) against the PLA's Hong Kong garrison (thousands of personnel) stationed in the New Territories, vandalism of subway stations, and an attack on Xinhua News Agency's Hong Kong branch (November 2). Meanwhile, the Hong Kong police have intensified activities to suppress the protests, resulting in some casualties, and the clashes show no sign of abatement. The PLA is unlikely to come into to bring the situation under control. On the other hand, videos have been released showing the People's Armed Police assembling in Shenzhen, adjacent to Hong Kong, and conducting suppression drills.[30] On August 14, the spokesperson for the Hong Kong and Macao Affairs Office stated, "We condemn in the strongest terms this almost terrorist act,"[31] perhaps to create a basis for suppressing the situation. On November 14, President Xi Jinping commented on and expressed a sense of crisis over the situation in Hong Kong, stating, "The most urgent task for Hong Kong at present is to...restore order."[32]

(2) From the KMT's Ascendancy to the DPP Government's Catch-up

The situation in Hong Kong is having a large impact on the Taiwanese political situation. The DPP suffered a major defeat in the local elections held in November 2018, and the reelection of President Tsai Ing-wen in the 2020 presidential election was considered hopeless. This situation changed dramatically with the outbreak of the largest protests in Hong Kong's history related to the aforementioned Fugitive Offenders Amendment Bill. Han Kuo-yu, Mayor of Kaohsiung (KMT), and Ko Wen-je, Mayor of Taipei (independent, later established the Taiwan People's Party), who were thought to be President Tsai's rivals in the presidential election, adopted the stance of not criticizing China. In contrast, President Tsai expressly vowed support for the people of Hong Kong and opposition to "one country, two systems." The Taiwanese people's approval rating for President Tsai increased gradually. She won against former Premier Lai Ching-te in the DPP primary election and was formally appointed the party's official presidential candidate on June 13. The DPP Central Executive Committee, which endorsed President Tsai, postponed the party's primary election from the original mid-April date and succeeded in weakening former Premier Lai Ching-te's momentum. The DPP Central Executive Committee has authority over how the party's primary is conducted. Making full use of that was a winning strategy for the Tsai camp.

As for the KMT, its primary election was fought between mainly Mayor of Kaohsiung Han Kuo-yu and Terry Gou, who is famous for founding Foxconn, the world's largest company in the electronics contract manufacturing service. Mayor Han Kuo-yu won the primary on July 15. This win was backed by the KMT's victory wave created in the previous year's local elections and by Han himself recapturing the mayoral seat of Kaohsiung, a DPP stronghold, for the first time in 20 years. Terry Gou left the party on September 12. Although he indicated he would run in the presidential election as an independent, he ultimately did not declare his candidacy. The final candidates for the presidential election were three political party-nominated individuals: President Tsai Ing-wen (DPP), Mayor of Kaohsiung Han Kuo-yu (KMT), and Chairman James Soong (People First Party). There were no independent candidates.

According to an opinion poll by a Taiwanese media outlet, the approval rating of President Tsai surpassed that of Mayor Han in around mid-August. As can be seen, the effects of the large-scale Hong Kong protests started to appear in approval rating polls for Taiwan's presidential candidates after one to two months. From then on, President Tsai successfully captured the hearts and minds of the Taiwanese people who began to harbor fears about Taiwan's future, and dominated the election campaign. Additionally, as Taiwan became ever more important for the United States as a result of deteriorating US-China relations, the United States' explicit support for President Tsai became an element that gave reassurance to the Taiwanese people. Mayor Han, on the other hand, advocated to the Taiwanese people that he would restore the Taiwanese economy by improving relations with China, as revealed by his Facebook slogan, "Safety for Taiwan, money for the people." Economic recovery is certainly a critical issue in a national election. In a presidential election in which the policy on China took on great significance, however, the slogan of economic recovery slightly lacked in impact. In the final stage of the election campaign, Mayor Han attacked the DPP for being a political party steeped in corruption, and even lodged intense criticism of Taiwanese mainstream media outlets with which he had poor relations. It is believed that Mayor Han's criticism of the media adversely affected his election campaign. Voting for the presidential election took place on January 11,

Figure 2.3. Approval rating of the presidential election candidates (2019)

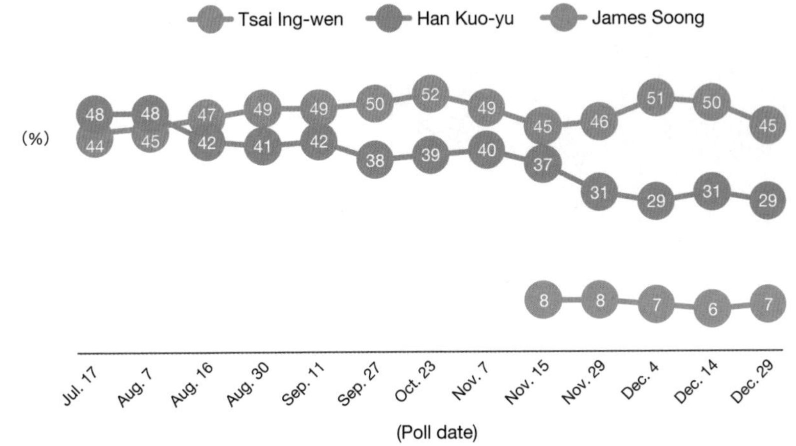

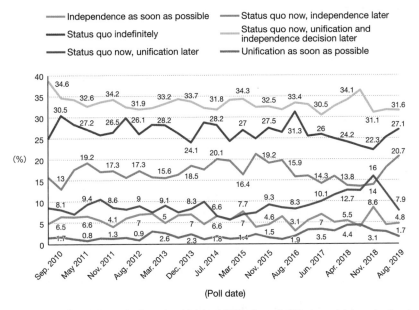

Tsai Ing-wen   Han Kuo-yu   James Soong

Source: Compiled by the author based on TVBS, December 30, 2019.

Figure 2.4. Taiwan's public opinion on unification and independence

Source: Compiled by the author based on Mainland Affairs Council, "Minzhong dui dangqian liang'an guanxi zhi kanfa" [Public Opinion on Cross-Strait Relations], July 25–29, 2019.

President Tsai Ing-wen following her reelection (left: Vice President-elect Lai Ching-te) (Kyodo News)

2020. Tsai Ing-wen and Lai Ching-te won 8.17 million votes (57.1% of total votes), the most in the election's history, and secured an overwhelming victory by a margin of about 2.65 million votes over Han Kuo-yu and Chang San-cheng. James Soong and Sandra Yu won just under 610,000 votes. President Tsai acknowledged that the situation in Hong Kong contributed to her reelection by a large margin. In addition, President Tsai called on China to abandon its hopes for China-Taiwan unification under "one country, two systems."

As Figure 2.4 shows, the proportion of Taiwanese people who want status quo indefinitely and people who want status quo now and independence later bottomed out in October 2018 and has risen significantly since January 2019. On the other hand, the proportion of people who want status quo now and unification later has decreased sharply. It is believed that this trend also had a direct impact on the approval ratings of potential candidates in the presidential election.

(3) Taiwan's Strengthened Partnership with the United States

The year 2019 saw a marked strengthening of the Taiwan-US partnership. In July, on the occasion of her trip to Latin American and Caribbean countries, President Tsai attended a welcome reception in New York during her transit. The reception was held by UN ambassadors and others from countries that have diplomatic relations with Taiwan. This was the first time that a President of Taiwan met with UN ambassadors and others from its diplomatic allies in New York, the home of the UN headquarters.[33] In cases where a Taiwanese dignitary transits the United States to visit a country with which Taiwan has diplomatic relations, the two countries must coordinate carefully regarding what level of activities would be conducted in the transit city and to what extent they would be disclosed. In the recent transit, the United States conveyed its intent to offer a warm welcome to Taiwan, and likely had it leak this information with the intention of reining in China.

It has also come to light that senior Taiwanese and US officials held a meeting. According to reports, David Lee, Secretary-General of the National Security

Council, who was visiting the United States from May 13 to 21, held a meeting with John Bolton, Assistant to the President for National Security Affairs. This was the first time that the Secretary-General of the National Security Council of Taiwan met with the National Security Advisor of the United States since the breaking of Taiwan-US relations in 1979. Advisor Bolton is known for his hardline approach to China and for his pro-Taiwan stance, and he drew attention for being one of the people China is cautious of.[34] While Advisor Bolton resigned in September, US-China confrontation remains intransient. The US White House, Congress, and the public have consistently maintained a severe stance toward China to a great extent. The exit of a single senior official with a harsh view on China from the White House alone is not expected to change this trend significantly.

On June 1, the US Department of Defense (DOD) released the Indo-Pacific Strategy Report, in which it states that Singapore, New Zealand, Mongolia, and Taiwan are reliable, capable, and natural partners of the United States as democracies in the Indo-Pacific region.[35] The report puts Taiwan on an equal footing with other nations, and notes that the United States is pursuing a strong cooperative relationship with Taiwan and will faithfully implement the Taiwan Relations Act, as part of a broader commitment to the security and stability of the Indo-Pacific region.[36]

In regard to arms sales, the United States has provided unprecedented preferential treatment to Taiwan. On July 8, the US DOD notified Congress that it intends to sell M1A2 tanks and other equipment worth a total of $2.2 billion to Taiwan. Primary weapons upgrades for the Taiwanese Army have been postponed vis-a-vis those of the Navy and Air Force. The M1A2 tank to be purchased is a weapon used by the US Army on active duty. The Taiwanese Navy and Air Force have been provided with weapons from a generation ago. If you compare them with the Army, the US preferential treatment to Taiwan is evident, and this in and of itself has significance. Furthermore, on August 15, the US DOD notified Congress of its intention to sell 66 F-16C/D Block 70 fighters to Taiwan. Past US administrations have remained cautious about selling fighters to Taiwan. The latest decision to sell fighters is the first since 150 F-16A/B fighters were last sold 27 years ago. This marks the fifth time that the Trump administration will sell arms to Taiwan. The sales total has already reached $12.417 billion. The Trump administration's provision of preferential treatment to Taiwan is all the more apparent when one looks at the Obama administration, which sold arms to Taiwan three times during its eight years, amounting to $13.962 billion in total, and which sold no primary weapons.[37] Moreover, on August 20, William Christensen, Director of the American Institute in Taiwan's (AIT) Taipei office, visited Kaohsiung where he toured a naval base, boarded a Keelung-class destroyer, and observed AAV7 Assault Amphibious Vehicles.[38] It is apparently not unusual for Americans affiliated with supplying weapons in Taiwan to visit its armed forces. However, the AIT disclosing the visit at its initiative has a different meaning from the media reporting on the visit. It can be inferred that the AIT disclosed the visit to show that the United States supports the Tsai government.

US naval vessels transit the Taiwan Strait frequently. The total number of US naval vessels that transited the Taiwan Strait from 2007 to May 2019 was 92, according to a Hong Kong newspaper report.[39] The media has also reported that US naval vessels sailed through the Taiwan Strait eight times from January to September 2019.[40] The vessels that have sailed through included not only naval vessels, such as Aegis warships and dock landing ships, but also Coast Guard ships. In addition, 2019 saw US aircraft operations, including flight of the US Navy's P-8 patrol aircraft over the Taiwan Strait keeping in line with US vessels and southward flight of the US Air Force's MC-130J special operations aircraft over the Taiwan Strait. On March 31, it was confirmed that Chinese Air Force fighters flew across the median line in the Taiwan Strait for the first time since 2011. Such flights by US military aircraft may be intended to keep Chinese flights in check.

With regard to the sailing of US warships in the Taiwan Strait, of note is whether or not they will include US aircraft carriers. When the first direct presidential election was held in 1996 and the Chinese forces conducted a missile drill, the United States urgently deployed two aircraft carriers to waters surrounding Taiwan—the USS *Independence* and the USS *Nimitz*. In November 2007, the aircraft carrier USS *Kitty Hawk* was refused from making a port call in Hong Kong and transited the Taiwan Strait. Excluding these two cases, US Navy aircraft carriers have not sailed through the Taiwan Strait for more than ten years since then. Nevertheless, Chief of US Naval Operations John M. Richardson has affirmed that the United States considers the Taiwan Strait as part of the high seas, and that there is no limitation on any type of vessel navigating these waters.[41]

The favorable US-Taiwan relations are underpinned by the United States' increasingly confrontational posture toward China. The Trump administration sees past US policy on engagement with China as a failure,[42] and this has led to strengthening engagement with Taiwan. The Trump administration is comprised of individuals known to be pro-Taiwan, including Matt Pottinger, National Security Council Senior Director for Asian Affairs, and Randall Schriver, Assistant Secretary of Defense (who was later replaced). Congress has also taken a stern stance toward China, and pro-Taiwan Congress members are on the rise in both the Republican and Democratic parties. The result is evident in laws, such as the Taiwan Travel Act (February 2018) and the Asia Reassurance Initiative Act (enacted December 2018). The latter reaffirms US commitment to Taiwanese security and contains provisions supporting closer US-Taiwan relations.

As is known, the Taiwan Relations Act (enacted 1979) provides the legal basis for such US engagement with Taiwan. But it is China that the United States sees as a negotiation partner and a rival. Taiwan is viewed as a lever that will help steer the negotiations with China to the United States' favor. As China's national strength continues to grow, Taiwan's geopolitical value has proportionally risen to unprecedented levels, and in turn, the US commitment to Taiwan has strengthened. Therein also lies the reason that US support of Taiwan during peacetime has become increasingly clear. As there will likely be no easy end to the US-China rivalry, this phenomenon is expected to last for a relatively long time. The United States' very clear support of Taiwan appears to be inconsistent with its traditional policy of strategic ambiguity, i.e., remaining vague about whether it will intervene in contingencies in the Taiwan Strait and preventing a flare-up between China and Taiwan. But actually, the United States has consistently maintained the "one China policy" and neither supports Taiwan's independence nor is considering establishing diplomatic relations with Taiwan. In this regard, US support of Taiwan is limited.

3. The PLA's Rapid Modernization of Training and Equipment

(1) Military Training for Becoming a "World-class Military"
Since the end of 2015, bold military reforms have been implemented under President Xi Jinping. It appears that work is also under way to develop a system

for conducting trainings compatible with the military reforms. In two consecutive years, the New Year mobilization order for the training of the armed forces stated that military training was considered strategically important.[43] The year 2018 was the first in the PLA's history in which the head of the PLA himself promulgated the New Year training mobilization order.[44] In January 2019, it was reported that the new Outline of Military Training was almost complete,[45] and in March, the Trial Regulation on the Supervision of Military Training entered into force.[46] President Xi is thought to give priority to military trainings, and steps are being taken to develop the training system. The PLA is working to introduce trainings in new fields. Alongside these efforts, it appears the PLA gives particular priority to training commander-level officers, the strengthening of which was also sought in the Military Training Regulations (entered into force in 2018).[47] In 2018, the "QIBING (Unconventional Troops)" competition was held in five provinces and cities simultaneously. Troops competed with each other on combat capabilities and other skills in five areas: intelligence, surveillance, reconnaissance (ISR); special operations; communications security; electronic countermeasures; and aerial assaults.[48] A photo showing a row of commanders (colonels) immersed in a BeiDou terminal operation test was published in the *People's Daily*,[49] likely to make this training situation widely known. It is said that, "The training of troops must begin with training of senior officers; the training of a strong army must begin with training of strong commanders." In June 2018, the first-ever test of group army heads was conducted.[50] This trend continued into 2019. According to reports, under the banner of "General commanders taking the lead, everyone participating," 52 general-class commanders from the army gathered together for the first time and were screened in accordance with the Military Training Regulations and the Outline of Military Training. Commanding abilities and stamina were covered in the screening.[51] The QIBING competition was also made into a series, and it appears that it was held in more fields and locations in 2019.[52] In recent years, it is reported that exercise forces are often defeated by the opponent's forces, suggesting that drills have become more realistic and practical. PLA trainings are implemented more rigorously than before, from commanders down to the troops at the bottom. China is focused on improving capabilities in new domains for becoming a first-class military,[53] and it is expected that trainings and institutional development to this end will be strengthened and expanded.

China's partnership with Russia appears to be deepening also in the area of military exercises. China participated in Tsentr 2019 held in Orenburg, Russia from September 16 to 21 (from China, 1,600 personnel, 300 weapons and equipment, and 30 aircraft participated).[54] This was China's second time participating in a large drill in Russia, following on from its first-ever participation in the Vostok 2018 exercise held in the Far East and Siberia in September 2018 (from China, 3,200 personnel, approximately 1,000 equipment and vehicles, and 30 aircraft participated).[55] A press release issued by China's Ministry of National Defense (MND) following participation in the Vostok 2018 exercise noted its achievements as including strengthening friendship and trust and enhancing various capabilities. In comparison, the MND's press release following participation in Tsentr 2019 stated: (1) the exercise improved capabilities related to long-distance deployment and command as well as capacities in joint operation and comprehensive logistics, and demonstrated outcomes from progress in military force reform, and (2) the exercise has further developed the China-Russia strategic partnership relationship and improved strategic coordination between the two militaries.[56] The MND's use of more explicit wording compared to the previous year suggests a deepening in exercise content. Meanwhile, as the above figures show, China's participation in 2019 was smaller in scale than the previous year. It has been reported that PLA forces used rail and air travel for both exercises. However, a clear difference exists between the two exercises. In Vostok 2018 held in the Far East and Siberia, personnel and equipment were transported across a relatively short distance from China. On the other hand, Tsentr 2019 was conducted in Orenburg at the southern tip of the Ural Mountains. Difficulties were likely entailed in crossing Siberia on Russian railroad to arrive at the exercise location.

Previous Vostok exercises were thought to have taken into account warfare with Japan and the United States and warfare with China.[57] In this respect, the participation of the PLA in these exercises, albeit partially, was symbolic from the viewpoint of China-Russia partnership. Attention must continue to be paid to the PLA's participation in Russian exercises, including size, equipment, and exercise content.

(2) Steady Modernization of Equipment and Related Technologies

When the Rocket Force was established in December 2015, President Xi Jinping emphasized improvements in medium- and long-range precision strike capability and strategic deterrence capability.[58] And in fact, China's missile attack

Various equipment related to information communications and electronic warfare were showcased at the 2019 parade (Xinhua/Kyodo News Images)

capabilities appear to have made considerable improvements. At the military parade for China's 70th anniversary, the missiles showcased by the PLA included: the DF-41, which has the longest range in the world and can reportedly carry up to ten nuclear warheads;[59] the DF-17, which can reach a speed beyond Mach 5 and change orbit in midair, and therefore, is difficult for the existing missile defense network to accommodate;[60] and the CJ-100 (DF-100), which is an improvement on the CJ-10 with better speed and precision and is considered a cruise missile mainly targeting US carrier strike groups.[61] While China exhibited the JL-2 submarine-launched ballistic missile (SLBM) at the parade, it conducted a JL-3 launch test in June, according to reports. Whereas the JL-2 has a range of approximately 8,000 km, the JL-3 reportedly has a range of approximately 12,000 km[62] and can cover nearly all areas of the United States even from China's coastal waters. Such missile force may be intended to show China's strength to other countries, including the United States. The parade was also unique in that it displayed many types of equipment related to information communications and electronic warfare. The status of the equipment displayed in the parade was entirely different from a decade ago. It seems China is steadily developing equipment related to the electromagnetic domain to adapt to the strategic environment.

In addition, China places priority on building and operating aircraft carriers. In November, its first indigenous aircraft carrier following on from the *Liaoning* aircraft carrier, a refurbished *Varyag*, transited the Taiwan Strait.[63] A commissioning ceremony for this aircraft carrier named "*Shandong*" was held in Sanya on the island of Hainan in December, attended by President Xi.[64] Zhu Yingfu, chief designer of the *Liaoning*, expressed the view that possessing three to five aircraft carriers was appropriate for China, and emphasized the need for possessing a nuclear-powered aircraft carrier.[65]

China refers to the Internet of Things (IoT) as "*wu lian wang*" and is taking steps to incorporate it into the military. The *PLA Daily* notes the importance of doing so.[66] In September 2019, a PLA website published an article on *wu lian wang* that makes use of satellites.[67] It is expected that such networks will be developed in an array of forms in China and will be used in the military. The use of *wu lian wang* for the military's management of supplies has been reported from before.[68] One of the ways of tracking the state of the goods and their data is two-dimensional (2D) code.[69] The use of 2D codes for managing supplies has also been reported.[70] At the 70th anniversary parade, troops were seen wearing a 2D code next to their rank badge on camouflage clothing. Perhaps the code is also used for managing personal data.

China is making steady progress in modernizing its space technology, which is closely interlinked with the military. In January 2019, the Chang'e 4 unmanned explorer landed on the far side of the moon. It was a first in the world. It also represents China's entry into space—one of the United States' areas of specialty. Direct communication cannot be made from the Earth to the far side of the moon. The relay satellite Queqiao was launched in May 2018.[71] In the recent mission, Queqiao fulfilled its expected function. China's advanced technological capabilities are noteworthy. This latest project was already stated in China's space white paper published in December 2016. The white paper discusses the peaceful use of space, and states that the purpose of developing China's space program is to meet its national security needs, maintain national interests, and strengthen comprehensive national strength. Attention will be on whether or not China uses its space program for military purposes. Another development to follow is whether a Mars probe will be successfully launched in 2020, as stated in the space white paper.

China has steadily modernized its equipment and related technologies, and attention must continue to be paid to new developments.

As discussed above, as China and the United States repeat the cycle of confrontation and rapprochement, President Xi Jinping seeks long-term rule by seizing power while tightening his grip on the party and the military. However, the several issues facing his government are becoming ever more challenging. They include China-US confrontation, the reelection of President Tsai Ing-wen of Taiwan, a growing anti-China posture among the people of Hong Kong, response to the COVID-19 outbreak, a deteriorating international image of China in connection with COVID-19, and an unprecedented display of public dissatisfaction. In this international situation, improving Sino-Japanese relations is increasing in importance for the Xi Jinping government. For Japan, it means gaining leverage over China. Under these circumstances, the question is how Japan will be able to turn relations with China to its advantage.

What Can We Make Out of the Closer Ties between China and Russia?

China and Russia share a long border. Armed conflicts have arisen between China and the Union of Soviet Socialist Republics over the Damansky Island in 1969. China and Russia are not surrounded by any nations that could immediately pose a substantial and direct military threat, aside from themselves. Both perceive the other as a potential threat. Accordingly, Russia's major drills are thought to take China's presence into account. Likewise, China's Northern Theater Command is thought to have scenarios dealing with the Russian forces.

Nevertheless, since its founding and even after the period of Sino-Soviet clashes, China has needed Soviet and Russian technologies, especially for modernizing its military. For Russia of recent years, China has a growing presence day by day, economically and trade-wise. It is certain that some adjustments have been made to the exercise scenarios of the Russian forces.

At the Conference on Interaction and Confidence Building Measures in Asia held in Shanghai, China in May 2014, President Xi Jinping stated in his address, "It is for the people of Asia to...uphold the security of Asia," and proposed the "New Asian Security Concept" for establishing a security architecture that eliminates US influence. Furthermore, under the BRI, China has enhanced its presence in and outside of the region.

The United States has responded by changing its posture toward China. This trend has become conspicuous particularly since the establishment of the Trump administration. On November 7, 2017, on the 100th anniversary of the Bolshevik Revolution, the White House issued a statement announcing that the US government has designated this day as the National Day for the Victims of Communism. In the same statement, the White House noted that communism is "a political philosophy incompatible with liberty, prosperity, and the dignity of human life," and expressed sympathy with "all who continue to suffer under communism." Furthermore, whereas the United States during the Obama administration had "[welcomed] the rise of a China that is peaceful, stable, prosperous," the National Security Strategy released in December that year puts China in the same category as Russia. The National Security Strategy made it clear that the United States adopts a confrontational posture toward China, identifying it as a "revisionist power" that seeks to shape a world antithetical to US values and interests. Russia has been subject to economic sanctions of various countries since the Ukraine issue emerged. Meanwhile, the confrontation between China and the United States has begun to shift from negotiations over remedying the trade imbalance to a hegemonic struggle. In light of such circumstances, it is natural that China and Russia develop closer ties.

In June 2019, President Xi and President Putin held a meeting on the 70th anniversary of the establishment of diplomatic relations between China and Russia. The joint statement released at this time states that the two countries will raise their military relations to a new level through a range of measures, including cooperating on military technologies and conducting joint military exercises. While China and Russia have concluded the Treaty of Good-Neighborliness and Friendly Cooperation in July 2001, which is effective for 20 years (automatically extended every five years), changes in the recent strategic situation suggest that they could conclude a new treaty. However, as was already mentioned, the two countries represent potential threats, and the aforementioned joint statement sets forth that they will not conclude an alliance. In addition, President Putin commented on relations with China in his year-end press conference in December 2019, saying that Russia "[does] not plan to create [a military alliance with China]." Structural changes are unlikely to emerge if such factors are taken into consideration. Several Central Asian countries have acceded to the China-led Shanghai Cooperation Organization. Nevertheless, Russia has significant influence on the military technologies and know-how of former Soviet countries, and the situation does not call for China to take military initiative. That said, China and Russia could very well develop strong relations by treating the United States as a common enemy, just as in the 1970s when the United States and China grew closer by treating the Soviet Union as a common adversary. One of the indicators to find this out is China-Russia joint military drills and trainings. China and Russia have previously conducted the Peace Mission joint counter-terrorism drill series and the Maritime Cooperation naval drill series. In July 2019, the two countries conducted a joint bomber flight over the East China Sea and the Sea of Japan. In 2021, China may participate in the Zapad drills. The activities of the two military forces in around Japan, Taiwan, and other regions require continued attention.

NOTES

1)   Goto Yasuhiro, "Beichu 'Shinreisen'ka de Kiki ni tatsu Gurobaru Keizai" [Global Economy in Crisis in the Face of the US-China 'New Cold War'], *Toa* [East Asia], No. 621, March 2019, p. 14.

2)   *Mainichi Shimbun*, February 4, 2019.

3)   Hamamoto Ryoichi, "Chugoku no 'Ittai Ichiro' Senryaku de Bundan sareru Oshu" [A Divided Europe over China's Belt and Road Strategy], *Toa*, No. 623, May 2019, p. 46.

4)   *People's Daily*, April 10, 2019.

5)   *People's Daily*, May 23, 2019.

6)   Chinese National Development and Reform Commission, "Guojia fazhan gaigewei zhaokai xitu hangye zhuanjia zuotanhui yanjiu tuidong xitu chanye gaozhiliang fazhan" [Rare Earth Industry Experts Meeting Held by the National Development and Reform Commission: Reviews and Promotes Quality Development of Rare Earth Industry].

7)   Chinese State Council Information Office, "Guanyu Zhong-Mei jingmao cuoshang de Zhongfang lichang" [China's Position on the China-US Economic and Trade Consultations], June 2019.

8) *People's Daily*, December 14, 2019.

9) Office of the United States Trade Representative, "United States and China Reach Phase One Trade Agreement," December 13, 2019.

10) *People's Daily*, October 2, 2019.

11) *People's Daily*, October 15, 2019.

12) *PLA Daily*, October 2, 2019.

13) Ibid.

14) *PLA Daily*, August 27, 2019.

15) *PLA Daily*, August 2, 2019.

16) *People's Daily*, May 23, 2019.

17) *People's Daily*, October 28, 2017.

18) *People's Daily*, June 1, 2019.

19) *People's Daily*, September 4, 2019.

20) *People's Daily*, March 17, 2019.

21) *People's Daily*, June 6, 2019.

22) Joint Staff, "Chugokuki oyobi Roshiaki no Higashishinakai oyobi Nihonkai ni okeru Hiko ni tsuite" [Flights by Chinese and Russian Aircraft over the East China Sea and the Sea of Japan], July 23, 2019.

23) Chinese Ministry of National Defense, "Zhong-E shouci lianhe zhanlüe xunhang tisheng liangjun zhanlüe xiezuo shuiping" [China and Russia's First Joint Strategic Cruise Improves Strategic Coordination between the Two Militaries], August 29, 2019.

24) Ibid.

25) Yamazoe Hiroshi, "Roshia Gunki Chugoku Gunki no Takeshima Shuhen Hiko" [Flights around Takeshima by Russian and Chinese Military Aircraft], *NIDS Commentary*, August 13, 2019.

26) JETRO, "Dai 2 kai 'Ittai Ichiro' Hai Reberu Foramu, Shushi wa Jizokukanosei no Kakuho wo Kyocho" [Second Belt and Road High-Level Forum: Xi Stresses Ensuring Sustainability], *Bijinesu Tanshin* [Business Short Report], May 22, 2019.

27) *People's Daily*, April 27, 2019.

28) *PLA Daily*, July 25, 2019.

29) *South China Morning Post*, September 21, 2019.

30) Kyodo News, August 16, 2019.

31) Hong Kong and Macao Affairs Office of the State Council, press release, August 14, 2019.

32) *People's Daily*, November 15, 2019.

33) *Taiwan Weekly Review* (online edition), July 12, 2019.

34) *Nikkei Shimbun* (online edition), May 25, 2019.

35) US Department of Defense, *Indo-Pacific Strategy Report: Preparedness, Partnerships, and Promoting a Networked Region*, June 1, 2019, p. 30.

36) Ibid., p. 31.

37) Momma Rira, "Deta kara Yomitoku Bei Tai no Kinmitsudo" [US-Taiwan Closeness as Seen from Data], *Gaiko* [Diplomacy], Vol. 57, September 2019, p. 29.

38) *Liberty Times* (online edition), August 20, 2019.

39) *Liberty Times* (online edition), May 3, 2019.

40) *Liberty Times* (online edition), September 21, 2019.

41) *Navy Times*, January 18, 2019.

42) The White House, *National Security Strategy of the United States of America*, December 2017, p. 25.

43) *PLA Daily*, January 4, 2018 and January 5, 2019.

44) *PLA Daily*, January 4, 2019.

45) Ibid.

46) Central People's Government of the People's Republic of China, "Zhongyang junwei zhuxi Xi Jinping qianshu mingling fabu 《Zhongguo renmin jiefangjun junshi xunlian jiancha tiaoli (shixing)》" [Chairman Xi Jinping of the Central Military Commission Signs "Trial Regulation on the Supervision of PLA Military Training" Proclamation Order], February 11, 2019.

47) *PLA Daily*, December 31, 2017.

48) *China Military Net*, August 20, 2018.

49) *People's Daily*, July 11, 2018.

50) *Xinhua Net*, June 19, 2018.

51) *PLA Daily*, March 22, 2019.

52) KK NEWS, June 5, 2019.

53) *Qiushi Journal Online*, September 5, 2018.

54) *PLA Daily*, September 8, 2019.

55) *PLA Daily*, September 12, 2018.

56) Chinese Ministry of National Defense, "'Zhongbu-2019' yanxi tisheng Zhong-E liangjun zhanlüe xiezuo shuiping" [Tsentr 2019 Exercise Improves Strategic Coordination between Chinese and Russian Militaries], September 26, 2019.

57) Koizumi Yu, "'Vosutoku 2018' 29 man 7,000 nin Doin" [Vostok 2018 Mobilizes 297,000 Personnel], *Gunji Kenkyu* [Japan Military Review], No. 634, January 2019, p. 83.

58) *PLA Daily*, January 2, 2016.

59) *Newsweek Japan*, October 2, 2019.

60) Japanese Ministry of Defense, *Defense of Japan*, 2019, p. 63.

61) *Central News Agency*, October 2, 2019.

62) *Global Times Online*, June 28, 2019.

63) CCTV, November 19, 2019.

64) *PLA Daily*, December 18, 2019.

65) *Sichuan Daily*, April 7, 2017.

66) *PLA Daily*, March 2, 2018.

67) *China Military Net*, September 11, 2019.

68) *PLA Daily*, November 25, 2010.

69) Wu Zhanghong, "Jiyu wulianwang jishu de jungong tixi xinfazhan" [New Military Developments Based on Internet of Things Technology], *Shidai Jinrong* [Times Finance], September 2019, p. 213.

70) *PLA Daily*, September 18, 2012.

71) *China Military Net*, January 7, 2019.

Chapter 3
The Korean Peninsula

Diplomacy and Politics of Reintroducing a State of Nuclear-Missile Crisis

WATANABE Takeshi (Lead author, Section 1)
KOIKE Osamu (Section 2)

After the second summit meeting between the United States and the Democratic People's Republic of Korea (DPRK, or North Korea) ended without a joint statement, North Korea resumed missile launches to make a point to the United States: North Korea was capable of reintroducing a state of nuclear-missile crisis. Alongside this, Pyongyang has sought to entrap China into a bilateral alignment, hinting that Beijing would join the peace regime talks that have implications for the future of the US force presence. This was just over a year after the DPRK and the Republic of Korea (ROK, or South Korea) signed the Panmunjom Declaration that suggested the peace regime talks might be held without China. North Korea takes actions fully cognizant of the strategic effects generated by nuclear weapon fears on the United States and the ROK and of China's threat perception of the US forces. Against these backdrops, North Korea has undertaken steps to prevent the internal emergence of a force that would substitute Kim Jong Un, Chairman of the State Affairs Commission of the DPRK (Chairman of the Workers' Party of Korea [WPK]). Namely, it has reaffirmed the ideology that governmental institutions are constituents of the ruling power, denying them of political neutrality on the grounds of "bureaucratism," and that people belong to "Kim Il Sung's nation and Kim Jong Il's Korea."

The ROK's Moon Jae-in administration takes the position that mutual trust and dialogue between the two Koreas are essential for establishing peace on the Korean Peninsula, and has aimed to lift sanctions and implement other measures in return for progress in North Korea's denuclearization. In the wake of the second US-North Korea Summit, the Moon Jae-in administration announced provision of humanitarian assistance to North Korea through international organizations and offered to host President Trump's meeting with Chairman Kim Jong Un at Panmunjom. Despite these efforts, no progress was made in inter-Korean relations.

Japan-ROK relations deteriorated amidst the incident of an ROK naval vessel directing its fire-control radar at a Maritime Self-Defense Force (MSDF) patrol aircraft and the ROK government's negative action related to the hoisting of the MSDF flag at an international fleet review. In August 2019, the ROK government notified the government of Japan that it was terminating the Japan-ROK General Security of Military Information Agreement (GSOMIA), but in November, announced it would suspend the expiry of the agreement. As for the US-ROK alliance, US-ROK joint military exercises have been scaled down and/

or renamed to facilitate negotiations with North Korea.

The 2018 Defense White Paper, the first defense white paper published after Moon Jae-in came to office, deleted reference to North Korea as "an enemy" and stressed readiness for "other potential threats," thought to refer to neighboring countries other than North Korea. The ROK's national defense budget was established with priority given to self-defense capabilities, including building a system against nuclear and missile threats.

1. North Korea: A Strategy Reliant on the Nuclear Crisis Option

(1) Maintaining and Enhancing the Diplomatic Capabilities of Military Force

Pre-nuclear weapon military force is generally thought to pose a threat to people only after it has destroyed the military force of the adversary. In contrast, nuclear weapons provide the option of directly attacking the population at large without inter-troop clashes, and based on this power to hurt, are considered effective as a coercive means for ensuring enemy leaders' compliance.[1] North Korea does not have the readiness to wage a nuclear war against the United States, but by developing nuclear weapons, has raised alarm among people in the countries concerned. This nuclear crisis option forms the crux of Pyongyang's foreign relations strategy.

The DPRK has taken actions that help maintain this foreign relations strategy. The first is establishment of a "denuclearization" ideology that enables North Korea to keep its nuclear stockpile. In the previous year, 2018, North Korea committed to "denuclearization" in the Panmunjom Declaration and other agreements. North Korea's definition of "denuclearization" is likely different from non-proliferation in the Treaty on the Non-Proliferation of Nuclear Weapons (NPT). North Korea defines its phased denuclearization as aiming for "worldwide nuclear disarmament," along the lines of the "general and complete disarmament" target in Article VI of the NPT accepted by states which are permitted to possess nuclear weapons.[2] If this is construed to mean North Korea will not completely abandon nuclear development until there is "worldwide nuclear disarmament," Chairman Kim Jong Un's "we would neither make and test nuclear weapons any longer nor use and proliferate them" remark in his January 2019 New Year Address would mean not Pyongyang's abandonment of nuclear development but continued retention of the nuclear option. Indeed, this New Year Address threatened resumption of nuclear development: "if the United States does not keep the promise" and it "persists in imposing sanctions and pressure against our Republic," "we may be compelled to find a new way for defending the sovereignty of the country."[3] On April 12, a little over a month after the second US-North Korea Summit in Hanoi in late February ended without a joint statement, Chairman Kim Jong Un gave a specific deadline for retaining this option, noting he "will wait for a bold decision from the US with patience till the end of this year."[4]

Secondly, North Korea has continued to supplement its deterrence against US preventive attacks. The diplomatic strategy of not concealing but revealing nuclear development cannot be sustained without retaliatory capabilities that can deter an adversary even without relying on nuclear weapons. The reason is: once a country finds out about an opposing country's nuclear weapons development, a reasonable action would be to launch a preventive attack that destroys the nuclear weapons before they are completed.[5] North Korea embarked on nuclear diplomacy for the first time in 1993, after it had deployed several multiple rocket launchers (MRL) and long-range artillery in range of the Seoul metropolitan area in the vicinity of the demilitarized zone, giving US and ROK forces a strong motive to avoid military action.[6] If North Korea did not have retaliatory capabilities to turn Seoul into a "sea of fire," notably MRL and long-range artillery, it would have been considerably easier for the US forces to launch a preventive attack on North Korea.[7] The DPRK cites the US forces' attacks on Iraq and Libya to justify nuclear armament;[8] unlike these two countries, however, North Korea has developed nuclear weapons upon securing deterrence against preventive attacks. Following the US-North Korea meeting in Hanoi that ended without a joint statement, North Korea fired short-range ballistic missiles (SRBM) and MRL to display its ability to reintroduce a nuclear-missile crisis. These launches were conducted also for the purpose of developing weapons that have adapted to the missile defenses and the base realignment of the United States Forces Korea (USFK) and supplementing North Korea's retaliatory capabilities against ROK territory.

On April 17, 2019, not long after the remark on holding off a return to nuclear crisis until the "end of this year," a North Korean media outlet reported that Kim Jong Un, Chairman of the State Affairs Commission of the DPRK, instructed the launch of a "new-type tactical guided weapon," which is thought to have "the peculiar mode of guiding flight and the load of a powerful warhead," and presented "strategic goals for keeping munitions production going on and putting national defense

Missile, noted to have similarity to Russia's Iskander, launched by North Korea on the Sea of Japan side; reported by KCNA on May 5, 2019 (UPI/Newscom/Kyodo News Images)

science and technology on cutting edge level."[9] "Peculiar mode of guiding" suggests an ability to evade ambush by missile defenses. Analysts have noted similarities between the SRBM that North Korea actually launched on May 4 (flight distance approx. 250 km[10]) and the Russian forces' 9K720 Iskander-M (range approx. 500 km; or the 9M723 export model with a range of approx. 280 km).[11] The 9K720 is said to be capable of maneuvering at a trajectory that makes ambush difficult by existing US missile defenses[12] (the SRBM subsequently launched on May 9 had a flight distance reaching approx. 400 km[13]).

Furthermore, two types of MRL were launched in tandem with the SRBM, the 240 mm and 300 mm systems, and reportedly had a flight distance of over 70 km.[14] The 300 mm MRL is said to have similarities with China's WS-1B[15] and is thought to have a range (approx. 170 km) that reaches Pyeongtaek (US Army Garrison Humphreys), where the USFK has concentrated its facilities under recent years' base realignment.[16] Pyeongtaek had been outside the range of North Korea's conventional MRL models and long-range artillery. North Korea later announced at the end of July that it test launched a new MRL model with a "large-caliber multiple launch guided rocket system"[17] (however, this was an SRBM launch according to the ROK Joint Chiefs of Staff's analysis[18]). In August, North Korea said it test fired a "super-large" MRL.[19] (This, too, is thought to be an SRBM[20] like the systems North Korea launched in September, October, and November under the same designation.[21])

Pyongyang's intention to weaken the US-ROK allied force posture as examined above is consistent with North Korea urging the United States to make a decision by the "end of this year." Prior to the stalemate at the US-North Korea Summit in Hanoi, Chairman Kim Jong Un stated in his New Year Address: it is North Korea's steadfast will to eradicate military hostility between the North and South and "make the Korean Peninsula a durable and lasting peace zone," and given that the ROK agreed in the previous year to advance along "the road of peace and prosperity," "the joint military exercises with foreign forces, which constitute the source of aggravating the situation on the Korean Peninsula, should no longer be permitted and the introduction of war equipment including strategic assets from outside should completely be suspended." North Korea's intent may have been to make progress on the nuclear issue at the ensuing US-North Korea Summit in order to begin peace regime consultations, and in the consultation process, weaken the readiness and deterrence posture of the US-ROK allied forces. In the New Year Address, Kim Jong Un went on to state, "It is also needed to actively promote multi-party negotiations for replacing the current ceasefire on the Korean Peninsula with a peace mechanism in close contact with the signatories to the armistice agreement so as to lay a lasting and substantial peace-keeping foundation."[22]

The SRBM and MRL launches that followed the second US-North Korea Summit were designed to remind the United States of the demands North Korea made in the New Year Address on account of the United States' reneging on its previous year's commitment. In the wake of the May launch, the North Korean Foreign Ministry noted that the United States had not taken measures corresponding with the actions Pyongyang had taken for "peace and stability" and that the implementation of the previous year's Joint Statement of the first US-North Korea Summit had fallen into a stalemate, and condemned the US-ROK joint military exercise "Dong Maeng (Alliance) 19-1" as "provocative military drills."[23] On July 16, the North Korean Foreign Ministry noted on the United States and the ROK's attempt to conduct the joint military exercise "Alliance 19-2" and condemned the exercise as a "breach of the main spirit" of the Joint Statement. In this press statement, North Korea expressed dissatisfaction with the Proliferation Security Initiative (PSI) exercise held in early July with the participation of Japan, the United States, and the ROK, and once again confirmed its option of reintroducing a nuclear-missile crisis, stating, "With the US unilaterally reneging on its commitments, we are gradually losing our justifications to follow through on the commitments we made with the US as well."[24]

Shortly after this Foreign Ministry statement, North Korea began to publicly reaffirm its intention to further develop submarine-launched ballistic missiles (SLBM). On July 23, the WPK official newspaper *Rodong Sinmun* reported that Chairman Kim Jong Un, during an inspection of a "newly built submarine," unveiled "the Party's strategic plan for the use of submarine and underwater operation" and assigned this duty to the field of national defense science. It stated that this submarine would be turned into a war asset in the near future for operation on the side of the Sea of Japan.[25] Satellite images showed a submarine at the facility likely visited by Kim Jong Un. The submarine appeared to be based on the Romeo-class submarine and was larger than the Gorae-class submarine supposedly used in the test firing of the two-stage "Pukguksong" SLBM. Based on the shape of the submarine, it is assumed to have a larger SLBM carrying capacity than the Gorae-class submarine.[26]

Following the submarine inspection, North Korea continued to launch missiles as a threat to avert US-ROK joint military exercises and to prevent strategic assets of the US forces from being brought into the ROK. On July 25, a new type of SRBM (flight distance approx. 600 km[27]) was launched, which Chairman Kim Jong Un described as "part of the power demonstration to send a solemn warning to the South Korean military warmongers" that seek to "introduce the ultramodern offensive weapons into South Korea and hold military exercises." At this time, North Korea cited Chairman Kim Jong Un's remark that the SRBM operates on a "low-altitude gliding and leaping flight orbit," using more concrete language to assert Pyongyang's capability to launch attacks by evading US-ROK missile defenses. He stressed, "It is a work of top priority and a must activity for the security of the country to steadily develop powerful physical means and conduct the tests for their deployment for neutralizing those weapons posing undeniable threats to the security of the country immediately and turning them to scrap iron at an early stage when it is considered necessary."[28] On August 6, North Korea again launched the same SRBM system as a "demonstration fire." On observing the launch, Chairman Kim Jong Un stated that it will "send an adequate warning to the joint military drill now underway by the US and South Korean authorities."[29]

Missiles that were subsequently launched show similarities with the United States' Army Tactical Missile System (ATACMS), according to analysts.[30] After repeated SRBM launches, North Korea announced on October 1 that an agreement was reached with the United States to hold working-level consultations. On the following day, North Korea fired an SLBM, the launch of which it had previously hinted at. The "Pukguksong-3" launched by North Korea on October 2 reached a maximum altitude of 900 km and flew 450 km before falling into Japan's exclusive economic zone (EEZ).[31] In connection with the SLBM launch, the North Korean Foreign Ministry released a statement on October 10, noting that "the DPRK can give tit for tat, but exercises restraint" in response to the United States' testing of an intercontinental ballistic missile (ICBM), and "there is a limit to the patience of the DPRK."[32]

The WPK convened a plenary meeting of its Central Committee from December 28 to 31, ahead of the "end of this year" deadline for North Korea's aforementioned demands that were made under threat. At the meeting, Chairman Kim Jong Un condemned that, despite the measures North Korea had taken, including halting ICBM launches, the United States had not accepted its demands, e.g., repeatedly conducting "big and small joint military drills," the termination of which was promised by the President, and shipping "ultra-modern warfare equipment" into the ROK. Kim Jong Un vowed that North Korea will "steadily develop necessary and prerequisite strategic weapons" until a "peace regime" is established.[33] While this declaration suggests North Korea's intention to suspend development of strategic weapons once a peace regime is established, it stops short of promising to agree to a renunciation of strategic weapons conditioned on a peace regime. Chairman Kim Jong Un reaffirmed that a strategy reliant on the nuclear crisis option would be maintained, even if the negotiations on the peace regime make progress. "Denuclearization" was already off the negotiating table with the United States, according to a statement released earlier on December 7 by North Korea's United Nations Ambassador.[34]

(2) China and North Korea Strengthen Bilateral Alignment via Shared Concept of "Denuclearization"

Chairman Kim Jong Un, who had begun to stress his ability to reintroduce a state of nuclear-missile crisis by launching SRBM and MRL, revealed that he received a letter with "satisfaction" from President Donald Trump of the United States (June 23, 2019) soon after Chinese President Xi Jinping returned from his first visit to North Korea. It is highly likely that Pyongyang interlinked President Xi's first visit to North Korea with its US relations. During his visit, President

Xi "spoke highly of" "the DPRK side's" "efforts" to "promote the denuclearization of the Peninsula."[35] Comparing it with Xi's "China sticks to the goal of denuclearization of the Peninsula"[36] comment, which was made over a year earlier during Chairman Kim Jong Un's first visit to China (March 2018) that kicked off the China-North Korea summit meetings, it can be inferred that China has leaned toward affirming North Korea's position on "denuclearization."

President Xi Jinping of China shaking hands with Kim Jong Un, Chairman of the Workers' Party of Korea (right), before returning to China; June 21, 2019, Pyongyang International Airport (KCNA/Kyodo)

China's stance a year earlier to "[stick] to the goal of denuclearization" was nothing more than an expression of neutral support for achieving non-proliferation as defined in existing international law, the NPT. Affirming a predetermined rule does not entail arbitrary decisions and choices, and therefore, represents a neutral position. Over a year later, during his visit to North Korea, President Xi Jinping "spoke highly of" "the DPRK side"—a country that was far from making non-proliferation "efforts" in conformity with the existing NPT rule. By speaking highly of "the DPRK side," which advocates a new "denuclearization" rule that permits possession of nuclear weapons until there is "worldwide nuclear disarmament," China was effectively siding with the political position of North Korea that is not complying with non-proliferation.

It was not without hesitation that China spoke highly of North Korea's efforts for "denuclearization" that is not equivalent to non-proliferation. This is evident from Beijing's incremental display of its stance at successive summit meetings with North Korea. China's position to speak highly of such efforts grew firmer in the course of North Korea's announcements that China would not be left out of the peace regime consultations that have possible future implications for the USFK.

Chairman Kim Jong Un attended the Inter-Korean Summit not long after President Xi Jinping expressed his neutral stance at the first China-North Korea Summit. In the Panmunjom Declaration (April 2018) released at the Inter-Korean Summit, the Chairman officially indicated the possibility of holding

"North-South-US tripartite" talks without China "for the building of durable and lasting peace mechanism." A month after China's exclusion was indicated (May 2018), President Xi stated to Chairman Kim Jong Un during his second visit to China that "China supports the DPRK's adherence to the denuclearization of the Peninsula."[37] Compared to its previous neutral stance, China appears to have gone a step further. However, "denuclearization of the Peninsula" was not necessarily in line with North Korea's definition. Based on the wording, it can be interpreted that China was requesting the "DPRK side" to "stick" to non-proliferation under the NPT. The fact that a China-North Korea Summit was held even as the two sides remained in disagreement is implied by the foreign ministers' meeting that immediately preceded it. According to the Chinese side's announcement, North Korea stated at this meeting that it would maintain close communication with China toward denuclearization and creation of a "peace regime."[38] This statement, however, was not included in the report of the North Korean state-run Korean Central News Agency.[39]

During Chairman Kim Jong Un's third visit to China in June 2018, President Xi Jinping stated, "Comrade Chairman has made positive efforts for realizing denuclearization," a remark leaning closer to the North Korean position. In addition, Chairman Kim Jong Un noted, "the DPRK side hopes to work with China and other concerned parties to promote the establishment of a lasting and solid peace mechanism on the Korean Peninsula."[40] At this summit meeting, the Chairman indicated in his own words that North Korea would not exclude China from the peace regime consultations. However, this too was disclosed only by the Chinese side's announcement and was not reported by North Korea's official media.[41] In fact, President Xi praised the achievements of the first US-North Korea Summit before commenting on Chairman Kim Jong Un's "positive efforts." Thus, the Chinese President could have still been neutrally affirming North Korean "efforts" limited to those that can be agreed upon with the United States.

Following these meetings, in January 2019, when Chairman Kim Jong Un paid his fourth visit to China, President Xi at last expressed a position that was nearly identical to viewing "highly" the "efforts" to "promote the denuclearization of the Peninsula"—the remark President Xi made during his first visit to North Korea in June 2019. The difference was that the President affirmed not "efforts" but "measures." As of January, China "spoke highly of the positive measures taken by the DPRK side [for promoting] the realization of denuclearization on the Peninsula."[42] This is to say, when Chairman Kim Jong Un visited China ahead of his Hanoi meeting with US President Trump, the Chairman had already received China's word which was closer to North Korea's view. In his January 1 New Year Address released just prior to visiting China, Chairman Kim Jong Un, while avoiding direct reference to Beijing, stated he will "actively promote multi-party negotiations for replacing the current ceasefire on the Korean Peninsula with a peace mechanism" "so as to lay a lasting and substantial peace-keeping foundation," "in close contact with" "the signatories to the armistice agreement," including China. North Korea's stance on excluding China was waning.

Though this China-North Korea meeting brought the two countries closer together, it did not lead to official media reports in North Korea that Chairman Kim Jong Un acknowledged the prospect of China's participation in the peace regime consultations. This may have been because President Xi affirmed North Korean "measures" rather than the "efforts" he later affirmed during his first visit to North Korea in June, and "measures" may have been inadequate for North Korea. It can be logically deduced that the concrete "measures" North Korea had already taken, including nuclear test site measures, do not necessarily include the "denuclearization" ideology that does not comply with the NPT. Chairman Kim Jong Un's interpretation may have been: only if China affirms "efforts" not limited to concrete "measures" will it mean China supports North Korea's wish to "denuclearize" based on its unique ideology.

Indeed, it was only in June, after the Chinese President spoke "positively" of the "DPRK's efforts" rather than "measures" that Chairman Kim Jong Un allowed media reports related to the summit meeting to directly inform the people of North Korea that China seeks peace regime consultations in tandem with North Korea. When President Xi first visited North Korea that same month, the President was able to express his view in North Korea's *Rodong Sinmun* namely, his hope to work with the "Korean side and the related parties" via diplomatic talks and negotiations regarding "Korean issues."[43]

For many countries, it is not easy to express clear agreement with "the DPRK side's" "denuclearization"—an ideology which is not based on the neutral criterion of non-proliferation under international law and which has significant room for contention. If North Korea deemed it would be effective to use its ability to approve or disapprove China's participation in the peace regime consultations to entrap Beijing to its side, Pyongyang may have had this foresight since the early phase of the nuclear and missile tests from 2016. From that year, China has pursued the "dual track approach" of simultaneously holding talks on the peace regime and the nuclear issue before its resolution; in other words, China elevated the order of priority of the peace regime.

China was motivated to change its stance presumably to thwart the deterrence guarantee of the US-ROK allied forces provided by missile defenses. At the time, then Vice Foreign Minister Liu Zhenmin of China, one of the first people to advocate denuclearization and peace regime parallel talks, spoke critically of the USFK's deployment of the Terminal High Altitude Area Defense System (THAAD). According to Vice Minister Liu, the deployment of THAAD by the US-ROK alliance was a case in point of "the relevant bilateral military alliances are a product of a bygone era."[44] China allegedly imposed de facto economic sanctions on the ROK over the deployment of THAAD. More than a year later, at the end of October 2017 when the start of the meetings between North Korea and the ROK drew closer, China expressed concerns to the ROK, which was seeking improvement in relations. The concerns were related to: (1) missile defense, (2) THAAD deployment, and (3) US-Japan-ROK military cooperation. In response, the ROK reportedly explained its "public position with respect to the issues."[45] In regard to the points noted, the ROK unveiled the "three no-policies" for maintaining or strengthening its "existing" position (the ROK would not join the US missile defense system, or develop the US-Japan-ROK trilateral cooperation into a military alliance, or make an additional deployment of the THAAD system).[46] By compelling the ROK to adopt the "three no-policies" in exchange for China's de facto mitigation of sanctions, Beijing attempted to build up economic deterrence against the US-Japan-ROK missile defense cooperation.[47]

President Xi Jinping paid his first visit to North Korea just over a year after the Panmunjom Declaration in which North Korea indicated the peace regime consultations could be held without China. It recalls a situation from the previous Kim Jong Il government. North Korea suggested holding peace regime consultations without China in the Joint Declaration of the second Inter-Korean Summit (2007), and several months later, succeeded in getting China to state that the US-ROK alliance is "something leftover from the history" (May 27, 2008). This "something leftover from the history" remark from the Kim Jong Il period was reaffirmed by the nuclear diplomacy of his successor Chairman

Kim Jong Un; Chinese Vice Foreign Minister Liu Zhenmin stressed that the peace regime is prioritized because "the relevant bilateral military alliances are a product of a bygone era." A shared threat perception toward the USFK has supported North Korea's strategy of using the peace regime to elicit China into a bilateral alignment. As long as North Korea is the cause of many of the Korean Peninsula issues related to the peace regime, the country can select parties to the consultations for the resolution of the issues. China's stance toward North Korea's "denuclearization" changed incrementally the more North Korea fueled Beijing's concerns about being left out of the peace regime consultations, which could have implications for the future of the USFK. As a result, President Xi Jinping "spoke highly of" North Korea's "efforts" during his first visit to North Korea.

(3) The Ruling Power's Survival Strategy Casts a Shadow on Bilateral Activities

It should be remembered that, more than five years before President Xi Jinping's first visit to North Korea, there was an event that keenly illustrates North Korea's distrust of China: the execution of Jang Song Thaek (uncle-in-law of Kim Jong Un) in December 2013. Around two months after the execution, Chairman Kim Jong Un (then First Chairman of the National Defense Commission) remarked on the "[failure] to detect and crush in advance the modern version of factionalist group which had formed within the Party" and went on to refer to "the August 1956 factionalist group" incident.[48] It was clear Chairman Kim Jong Un considered Jang Song Thaek an internal threat, similar to the pro-China faction (known as the "Yan'an faction") that challenged the power of his grandfather, Premier Kim Il Sung, in the August 1956 incident. For several years after the power succession by Chairman Kim Jong Un, North Korea showed profound concerns that China doubted the legitimacy of a regime led by Chairman Kim Jong Un following the power succession. After some four years had passed since the execution, Chairman Kim Jong Un made his first visit to China in March 2018 that started the series of China-North Korea summit meetings.

Regarding the summit meeting during Kim's first visit, a North Korean media outlet reported the Chinese side as saying, "under the leadership of Kim Jong Un the Workers' Party of Korea would register fresh successes in steadily advancing along the socialist path," and the North Korean side responding by requesting

President Xi Jinping's "official visit to the DPRK at a convenient time."[49] North Korea requested President Xi's visit to Pyongyang after China confirmed that its counterpart, North Korea, is a regime ruled by Chairman Kim Jong Un. Following Chairman Kim's repeated visits to China, Xi Jinping's first visit to North Korea was materialized.

The above suggests that North Korea's China policy is linked to the establishment of a "monolithic leadership" system in which there can be no leader other than Kim Jong Un—something that the regime has been working hard to create. In the August incident, powerful people influenced by an ally raised doubts over the leadership of Premier Kim Il Sung. The "monolithic leadership" system that was established after the post-incident purge eliminated all leaders other than the one and only leader. The August incident led to the withdrawal and suspension of the Chinese People's Volunteer Army stationed in North Korea,[50] which had close ties to the pro-China faction.[51] As in this incident, it was seen that the bilateral alignment with China could threaten the autonomy of the regime.[52]

"Monolithic leadership" appears to reflect North Korea's intention to eliminate not only influence from the liberal democracy of its adversary, the United States, but also the risk of North Korea's alignment partner, China, supporting an alternative leader of "socialism." This led to the revision of the Constitution in April 2019. The mission of the armed forces was revised to "defend unto death the Party Central Committee headed by the great Comrade Kim Jong Un." The previous mission of the armed forces, "defend the leadership of the revolution," demanded that the military view national defense in parity with protecting a leader of a "socialist" system. The revised mission, on the other hand, defines the duty of the military in more limited terms: national defense is equivalent to protecting not only the leader of the system but a specific leader, Chairman Kim Jong Un (Article 59 of the Constitution of North Korea).

The revised constitutional text is similar to the slogan that the North Korean regime has emphasized to the Korean People's Army (KPA) in recent years. "Let us defend with our very lives the Party Central Committee headed by the great Comrade Kim Jong Un" was underscored at several military contests North Korea held two years ago,[53] i.e., 2017, a year before the summit meetings with the United States and China began. Under this ideology, there can be neither a leader who has been influenced by the United States and supports liberal democracy nor an alternative leader of "socialism" who supports China.

Preparations at the Supreme People's Assembly (SPA) to revise the Constitution to include this slogan in the provisions were undertaken in parallel with North Korea's preparations to hold the second US-North Korea Summit in Hanoi in February 2019. At the summit meetings with China before and after it, the DPRK reaffirmed the general principle of "the two parties and two countries" cooperation.[54] This is not confined to the "countries," China and North Korea, having a shared perception of the military threat of the United States. Cooperation between "two parties," both of which have a "one-party system" that competes with the United States' liberal democracy, strongly hints at a bilateral alignment for the domestic goal of regime survival. However, while North Korea required such an alignment, it had to first rule out the possibility of China using the alignment to encourage the emergence of an alternative leader.

This is suggested by a document released by the Central Committee of the Democratic Front for the Reunification of Korea, a propaganda organ of the WPK, around the time that Chairman Kim Jong Un left for the US-North Korea Summit in Hanoi. According to this document to arouse interest in the upcoming election of deputies to the SPA, North Korea manifests "people-centered philosophy," stating that power organs "always put people's interest above everything." The document urged people to engage in a struggle with "bureaucratism" that infringes the "socialist system."[55] In North Korea, criticisms of "bureaucratism" are made to instill the notion that engaging in the professional duties of organizations is equivalent to subordination under a specific leader. It originated from criticism of "*military* bureaucratism" (italics added by author). Ever since pro-China and pro-Soviet factions were removed in the August incident, Chairman Kim Jong Un's father, Kim Jong Il, Chairman of the National Defense Commission (1969 when he was Chief of the WPK Propaganda and Agitation Department; a few years before he was nominated as successor of President Kim Il Sung), lodged criticisms of "bureaucratism" in purging potential forces that could replace the regime leader. Chairman Kim Jong Il mentioned such criticisms in his address, in order to ensure that military personnel do not protest against the functional strengthening of the General Political Bureau, an organ to monitor the military on behalf of the WPK Central Committee.[56]

Criticizing "military bureaucratism" in the context of strengthening the General Political Bureau was nothing else but denying the professional autonomy of military organizations from politics. The WPK propaganda organ lodged criticisms of "bureaucratism" rooted in criticisms of "military bureaucratism," and proclaimed that military organizations should "always put people's interest above everything." The intention was likely to establish the ideology that organizations such as the military are subordinate only to Chairman Kim Jong Un, the one and only leader who represents the "people." Indeed, the aforementioned advertisement message for the SPA election interweaved extolment of "Kimilsungism-Kimjongilism" and "dear respected supreme leader Kim Jong Un."[57] Veneration for not only "socialism" but also "Kimilsungism-Kimjongilism" greatly suggests a system of political control that removes even "socialist" leaders other than Chairman Kim Jong Un. It can be conceived that the regime maintains strong wariness toward the autonomy of military organizations under the name of "bureaucratism."

Around the timing of the US-North Korea Summit in Hanoi, the *Rodong Sinmun* published a long article recalling Chairman Kim Jong Un (Marshal of the DPRK) who was out of the country. "We Miss You, Our Dear Marshal," the article said, spreading the notion that the Chairman was the one and only leader. According to this article, "the world witnesses the noble traits of Korean people who follow their leader only, reposing absolute trust in him."[58] This article, along with the election management committee's announcement made immediately after the Chairman's return to North Korea informing the status of the election of deputies to the SPA,[59] advanced the view that the people belong to "Kim Il Sung's nation and Kim Jong Il's Korea." As long as the nation and Korea seek identity from Kim Il Sung or Kim Jong Il, there can be no "socialist" system other than the Kim Jong Un regime.

Alongside this, North Korea has made it clear in its negotiations with the United States that it rejects US-style liberal democracy. In early March, shortly after returning from the US-North Korea Summit in Hanoi without a joint statement, Chairman Kim Jong Un sent a letter to the National Conference of Party Primary Information Workers. In the letter, Chairman Kim Jong Un stated that "primary information workers" must strengthen "ideological education" to protect "the Party and the state" from "imperialists and class enemies."[60] Chairman Kim Jong Un expressed similar views regarding internal control in his January 1, 2018 New Year Address, immediately before calling for North-South dialogue and engaging in the negotiations. In his address at the conference of WPK cell chairpersons held at the end of December of the previous year, Chairman Kim Jong Un noted the importance of "education by party organizations" that promotes party-wide "Kimilsungism-Kimjongilism" and stated that the United States and other countries seek to spread "non-socialist practices" in North Korea.[61] North Korea embarked on negotiations with the ROK and then with the United States upon confirming denial of US-style liberal democracy. Chairman Kim Jong Un reconfirmed this view following the US-North Korea meeting in Hanoi.

As was touched upon above, the conference of the party information workers vowed to promote the ideology of "the Party and the state," in other words, viewing and protecting the party system in parity with the state. Following the conference, activities consistent with this were observed within the military. In the same month as the conference of primary information workers, the 5th Meeting of Company Leaders and Political Instructors of the KPA was held under the leadership of Chairman Kim Jong Un. The meeting debated military-wide "Kimilsungism-Kimjongilism" under the "Korean nation-first principle" and reaffirmed national defense and subordination to political leaders.[62]

In the following month, April, the Constitution was revised at the SPA, making the national defense duties of the armed forces equivalent to defending political forces and a specific leader, i.e., the role of "defend unto death the Party Central Committee headed by the great Comrade Kim Jong Un." In his policy speech at the SPA, Chairman Kim Jong Un emphasized the nuclear crisis option, saying he "will wait for a bold decision from the US with patience till the end of this year," and at the same time, condemned "bureaucratism," or organizational autonomy of the armed forces.[63]

According to the remarks of Chairman Kim Jong Un, the simultaneous launches of SRBM and MRL in May were based on the "party's five-point policy of training revolution,"[64] and the submarine believed to operate SLBM that made an appearance in July was designed "to be capable of fully implementing the military strategic intention of the Party."[65] The "five-point policy of training revolution" was a set of guidelines deemed necessary at the aforementioned meeting of company leaders by the head of the KPA General Political Bureau for "strengthening [army-wide] companies into elite combat ranks devotedly defending the Party Central Committee."[66] North Korean discourse associated with missile and other launches repeatedly contained what was not necessarily consistent with the military rationality of the nation, requesting armed forces to act in the interests of a specific political leader.

2. South Korea: Outlook of Inter-Korean Relations and Japan-ROK Relations

(1) A Yearning for Improved Inter-Korean Relations and US-North Korea "Intermediation"

Though the US-North Korea negotiations on "denuclearization" reached a stalemate, the Moon Jae-in administration of the ROK continued to make efforts to improve inter-Korean relations aimed at easing military tension on the Korean Peninsula.

The Moon Jae-in administration places importance on mutual trust and dialogue between the two Koreas for building permanent and stable peace on the peninsula, and named the negotiations on North Korea's "denuclearization" since 2018 "the peace process on the Korean Peninsula."[67] To move this process forward, the ROK has taken steps to enhance relations with North Korea, including reducing conventional forces along the South-North Military Demarcation Line as agreed upon in 2018 and working toward providing returns corresponding with progress made in North Korea's denuclearization.

After the second US-North Korea Summit in February ended without an agreement, President Moon Jae-in squeezed in an impromptu one-night, three-day visit to the United States and held a US-ROK Summit with President Trump in April, cancelling his scheduled attendance at a ceremony commemorating the

US, ROK, and North Korean leaders meeting in Panmunjom (KCNA/Kyodo)

100th anniversary of the founding of the Provisional Republic of Korea Government. At the meeting, regarding the "denuclearization" method, the United States expressed its wish for a "big deal (complete denuclearization in exchange for the lifting of sanctions)," to which the ROK proposed a "good enough deal (dismantlement of Yongbyon facilities in exchange for the lifting of some sanctions, such as South-North economic cooperation)." Had the United States agreed to the "good enough deal," the ROK had reportedly intended to pursue further Inter-Korean Summits and US-North Korea Summits.[68] However, it appears the ROK did not receive the US response it had hoped for. With regard to South-North economic cooperation, the United States appears to have accepted the ROK's humanitarian assistance to North Korea but objected to the ROK's wish to resume operations at the Kaesong Industrial Complex and resume the Mt. Kumgang Tourism Project. Following this, the Ministry of Unification announced that the ROK government would provide humanitarian assistance worth $8 million to North Korea through international organizations, such as the World Food Programme (WFP) and the United Nations Children's Fund (UNICEF).[69] In addition, the Ministry of Unification approved a visit to North Korea by businesspeople and others who had operated plants at the Kaesong Industrial Complex, noting that the visit would be made to inspect facilities, denying direct relationship with resuming operations.[70]

Thereafter, the Moon Jae-in administration invited President Trump to visit the ROK on the occasion of the G20 Summit in Osaka in June and materialized President Trump's meeting with Chairman Kim Jong Un in Panmunjom. At the meeting, President Trump invited Chairman Kim Jong Un to the United States, and the two sides agreed to resume working-level negotiations in two to three weeks' time.[71]

As it turns out, as was mentioned in the previous section, the US-North Korea working-level consultations were not held until October. Furthermore, North Korea began to not show a positive response despite the ROK's appeasing approach, seeming to indicate a rupture in inter-Korean relations. Even the ROK's offer to provide 50,000 tons of domestic rice through the WFP as humanitarian assistance was rejected by North Korea.[72] In December, the ROK government decided to provide $5 million in humanitarian assistance through the World Health Organization; however, it is unclear whether North Korea will accept this assistance.[73] While the Agreement on the Implementation of the Historic Panmunjom Declaration in the Military Domain, agreed upon between the South and North defense ministers in September 2018, was implemented to a great extent in 2018, there still remain unachieved commitments, namely: consultations concerning the composition of the Inter-Korean Joint Military

Committee, a core part of the South-North military confidence-building; and freedom of movement for visitors and tourists in the Joint Security Area in Panmunjom, which would mark a symbolic step.[74]

(2) Adjustments in Japan-ROK Relations and the US-ROK Alliance

A succession of negative actions by the ROK side has deteriorated Japan-ROK relations. The recent downturn in relations was fundamentally caused by the decision of the Supreme Court of the ROK ordering payment of compensation to "former civilian workers from the Korean Peninsula."[75] The official view of the executive branch of the ROK had been that the issues, including payment of compensation to "former civilian workers from the Korean Peninsula," have been settled, as was set out both during the process of the negotiations of the Agreement on the Settlement of Problems concerning Property and Claims and on Economic Co-operation between Japan and the ROK—one of the agreements incidental to the Treaty on Basic Relations between Japan and the ROK concluded when relations were normalized in 1965—and in the conclusion reached by the Public-Private Joint Committee established during the Roh Moo-hyun administration in 2005 and whose meetings were also attended by the incumbent President Moon Jae-in.[76] Nevertheless, the judicial branch denied this view. The President of the ROK is the chief executive who leads the executive branch and shall represent the State vis-a-vis foreign states as the Constitution of the ROK stipulates.[77] It follows that, should differences in opinion arise between the judicial and executive branches, the President shall be responsible for settling those differences. The President, however, pushed for separation of powers and the "victim-centered approach" and has de facto neglected the issue. Moreover, notwithstanding the government of Japan's repeated requests for diplomatic consultations and establishment of an arbitration board under the Exchange of Notes concerning the Settlement of Disputes, which is included in the agreements incidental to the Treaty on Basic Relations, the ROK did not provide a substantive response.[78]

Distrust between the defense authorities of Japan and the ROK was further incited by an incident that occurred in October 2018: an MSDF destroyer was asked not to raise its flag (the Rising Sun Flag) during an international fleet review hosted by the ROK and cancelled its participation. The Rising Sun Flag was not raised as an issue by the ROK when it hosted an international fleet review in 1998 and 2008.[79] Later, when an explanation of the Rising Sun Flag was published on the website of the Japanese Foreign Ministry,[80] the ROK Foreign Ministry issued an objection statement saying that the Rising Sun Flag is "a symbol of militarism" and that Japan must face up to its history. In addition, the ROK National Assembly adopted a resolution seeking the International Olympic Committee and the Tokyo Organising Committee of the Olympic and Paralympic Games to ban people from bringing the Rising Sun Flag to the Game venues.

In particular, the incident of an ROK naval vessel directing its fire-control radar at an MSDF patrol aircraft, which became a dispute between Japan and the ROK from December 2018 through 2019, further fueled Japanese defense authorities' distrust of the ROK. On December 20, 2018, an incident occurred in which the ROK Navy's destroyer *Gwanggaeto-daewang* directed its fire-control radar (STIR-180), which is used prior to attacks, at an MSDF P-1 patrol aircraft that was flying over Japan's EEZ. In response, Japan lodged a protest and requested the prevention of recurrence to the ROK. The two sides held consultations between diplomatic authorities and working-level consultations between defense authorities but could not reach a shared opinion. Japan released footage taken from the P-1 patrol aircraft that included audio from inside the aircraft at the time of the fire-control radar irradiation.

The ROK has fully denied the fire-control radar irradiation, disclosed footage claiming that the MSDF P-1 patrol aircraft conducted "a threateningly low-altitude flight" toward an ROK destroyer engaged in a humanitarian rescue mission for a boat in distress, and requested an apology.

Subsequently, the second bilateral working-level consultations between defense authorities were held; however, the consultations once again failed to achieve an agreement regarding matters such as the method of confirming the facts of the fire-control radar irradiation. Japan then released the fire-control radar detection sound from the time of the incident.

The Code for Unplanned Encounters at Sea (CUES) adopted in 2014 at the Western Pacific Naval Symposium (WPNS) by 21 countries, including Japan and the ROK, stipulates that aiming fire-control radars is an action a commander might generally avoid. Furthermore, the ROK destroyer did not provide any response to the wireless inquiries concerning the fire-control radar irradiation made by the MSDF P-1 patrol aircraft using three types of frequencies, which, too, constitutes an unprofessional action that breaches the custom of the sea.

In contrast, the ROK's claim of "a threateningly low-altitude flight" toward a destroyer has no applicable objective standards. As has been announced by Japan, the flight method of the MSDF patrol aircraft conforms to the Convention on International Civil Aviation, which military aircraft are not obliged to comply with, and had been implemented daily for many vessels including ROK naval vessels.[81]

At the abovementioned second working-level consultation, the ROK asserted, "if the subject of the threat feels threatened, it is then a threat." On January 24, at the Navy Fleet Command, Minister of National Defense Jeong Kyeong-doo instructed the Navy to take "stern actions against threatening flybys." If the ROK felt threatened by an MSDF patrol aircraft's daily monitoring and surveillance activity, then the incident may not have been merely an incidental localized event; as discussed later, it may be hinting at changes in the threat perception of the ROK that is in a reconciliation phase with North Korea.

With regard to relations between Japanese and ROK defense authorities, Japan, the United States, and the ROK agreed to promote trilateral security cooperation at their defense ministerial meeting in June. Meanwhile, in July, Japan updated its licensing policies and procedures on exports of controlled items to the ROK, based on security concerns, and the ROK lodged a major protest. As can be seen from recent years' official documents (see Table 3.1), there has been a clear deterioration in Japan and the ROK's perception of each other's strategic importance and level of shared values, and this divergence has begun to have ripple effects on security cooperation.

Japan's update of export licensing policies and procedures drew a series of critical responses from the ROK. For example, the ruling party of the Moon Jae-in administration, the Democratic Party of Korea, established the Special Committee to Respond to Japan's "Economic Invasion" within the party. In addition, then Senior Secretary for Civil Affairs Cho Kuk of the Office of the President (later appointed Minister of Justice),

Prime Minister Abe Shinzo greeting President Moon Jae-in at the G20 Summit venue; June 28, 2019, Osaka City (Reuters/Kyodo)

Table 3.1. Changes in each other's perception observed from Japanese and ROK official documents

Year	Japan		Republic of Korea	
	Defense of Japan	Diplomatic Bluebook	Defense White Paper	Diplomatic White Paper
2014	Extremely vital / Fundamental values / Strategic interests as allies	Fundamental values / Most important neighboring country	Fundamental values	Values / Interests
2015	Extremely vital / Strategic interests as allies	Most important neighboring country		Values / Interests
2016	Strategic interests / Extremely vital / Strategic interests as allies	Strategic interests / Most important neighboring country	Fundamental values	Values / Interests
2017	Strategic interests / Extremely vital / Strategic interests as allies	Strategic interests / Most important neighboring country		n/a
2018	Future oriented	Future oriented	Partner	Future oriented
2019	Negative actions by the ROK side	Negative moves by the ROK		Future oriented

Note: The phrases similar in meaning are shown in the same color.
Source: Compiled by the author based on the documents.

who is a close associate of President Moon Jae-in, gave momentum to anti-Japanese sentiments, stating that the Japanese measure recalls the "Bamboo Spear Song" about resistance to the Imperial Japanese Army during the Donghak Peasant Revolution and asserting that anti-Japanese was patriotism. President Moon stated, "We will never again lose to Japan," at an emergency cabinet meeting that was broadcast live for the first time.[82] A pamphlet with a similar title was also published.[83] Among the people, there were widespread campaigns to boycott Japanese products and refrain from traveling to Japan.

In response to this growing public opinion, the Office of the President of the ROK announced on August 22 that it would terminate GSOMIA before the annual extension deadline. Regarding the reason for GSOMIA's termination, the

ROK stated that the government of Japan brought about "fundamental changes to the environment for security cooperation between the two countries" by removing the ROK from the so-called list of "white countries," and therefore, the ROK "decided that maintaining this Agreement, which was signed to facilitate the exchange of sensitive military information, does not serve [its] national interest."[84]

While the Japan-ROK GSOMIA is a bilateral agreement, it was considered to epitomize the strengthening of security cooperation mechanisms to deal with North Korean threats by Japan, the United States, and the ROK—comprised of Japan-US and US-ROK alliances and Japan-ROK cooperation. Thus, following the ROK's notification of GSOMIA's termination, a senior US official repeatedly expressed "disappointment," and the importance of the trilateral security cooperation was confirmed at the Japan-US-ROK defense ministerial meeting.[85] Against this backdrop, on November 22, approximately six hours prior to GSOMIA's termination, the government of the ROK suddenly announced suspension of the expiry of the agreement. In conjunction, the government announced it would suspend its WTO dispute complaint over Japan's update of export licensing policies and procedures.

At the same time, it is hard to say that the US-ROK alliance has strengthened. In order to facilitate "denuclearization" negotiations with North Korea, following on from 2018 the two countries continued to downscale US-ROK joint military exercises, which are essential for maintaining the readiness of the rotationally deployed USFK and the ROK armed forces. The Key Resolve (KR) exercise was renamed the "Dong Maeng (Alliance) 19-1" exercise, and the Foal Eagle (FE) exercise was conducted throughout the year among small units.[86] The Ulchi Freedom Guardian (UFG) exercise was named "Alliance 19-2"; however, in response to protests from North Korea, "Alliance" was deleted, and it was reportedly named "ROK-US Combined Command Post Training in the Second Half of the Year."[87]

This exercise assessed the Initial Operational Capability (IOC) of the future ROK-US Combined Forces Command (a General from the ROK armed forces will serve as the commander, and a US force personnel will serve as deputy commander), the command structure following the transfer of wartime operational control (OPCON), which the ROK aims to achieve at an early date.[88] In the Joint Communiqué of the 51st ROK-US Security Consultative Meeting (SCM) held on November 15, it states that the IOC assessment results were reported to the defense ministers of the two countries and that they agreed to proceed to the step of assessing Full Operational Capability (FOC) for the future ROK-US Combined Forces Command in 2020.[89]

As for US-ROK combined air force exercises, Vigilant Ace was not conducted in 2018, and its postponement was announced in November 2019. US and ROK air forces had planned to carry out exercises involving squadrons or smaller units; some analysts construe that such exercises were in the end postponed out of consideration for North Korea's protests.[90]

In 2019, the United States and the ROK held negotiations for concluding the 11th US-ROK Special Measures Agreement (SMA), which determines the defense costs shared between the two countries in 2020 and beyond. The previous 10th SMA consultations broke down in 2018. The conclusion of the agreement was delayed to 2019, and moreover, its effective duration was one year. In the 11th SMA negotiations, the United States demanded an increase in the ROK's cost share by approximately fivefold. The cost reportedly included that of dispatching strategic assets of the US forces and conducting US-ROK joint military exercises. The ROK objected that such costs are outside of the SMA framework.[91] The 11th SMA negotiations were held five times in 2019, but like 2018, failed to reach a conclusion by the end of the year.

As regards ROK-China relations, the souring of US-China relations has occasionally forced the ROK to choose between the United States and China in both the security and economic domains. In October 2017, the ROK announced to China that it was not considering additional deployment of THAAD, that the ROK will not join in the US missile defense system, and that the Japan-US-ROK security cooperation will not develop into a trilateral military alliance. It was believed that the THAAD issue had been shelved due to the announcement. However, recent developments, such as the raising of the issue at the ROK-China Summit held twice in 2019 and the statement in the Chinese defense white paper that THAAD has severely undermined the regional strategic balance in the Asia-Pacific, suggest that THAAD may re-arise as an issue.

In addition, to keep the ROK in check, which launched 5G service using base stations made by the Chinese company Huawei, US Ambassador to the ROK Harry Harris said in a speech that it is important for South Korean companies to choose "a trusted supplier" from a security perspective. The Office of the

President of the ROK responded that its 5G networks are separated from its military security communications network and have no impact. The remarks nonetheless suggest that the US-China competition in the economic domain might have implications for the ROK as well.

(3) The Start of Defense Reform 2.0

The Moon Jae-in administration has entered its third year. In 2018, it unveiled a national defense reform basic plan (Defense Reform 2.0) and embarked full scale on the national defense reform vision of the administration. The first defense white paper published under the Moon administration, 2018 Defense White Paper (released January 2019), deleted reference to North Korea as "an enemy" and broadened the threats to be addressed by the ROK from "North Korean nuclear and missile threats" to "omnidirectional security threats." It stressed readiness for "other potential threats," thought to refer to neighboring countries other than North Korea. In the address by President Moon Jae-in at the 71st Armed Forces Day event held at an air force base in Daegu, the President did not make reference to North Korean threats or nuclear threats as in previous years.[92] As was noted earlier, if the ROK felt threatened by an MSDF patrol aircraft's daily monitoring and surveillance activity, then it indicates a change in the ROK's threat perception and the situation may be more serious for Japan-US-ROK cooperation. This observation is substantiated by the ROK armed forces' renaming of the "Dokdo Defense Drills" held annually in waters surrounding Takeshima to "East Sea Territory Protection Exercise" immediately after the announcement of the termination of the Japan-ROK GSOMIA, and the doubling in scale of this training from previous years.

The Mid-Term Defense Plan for 2020–2024 appropriates 290.5 trillion won in total for the overall national defense budget for 2020 to 2024, equivalent to an average increase of 7.1% a year. The budget reflects the priority placed on self-reliant national defense capabilities, with improving defense forces having an even higher annual average increase of 10.3%, including building a nuclear and missile threat response system that will replace the existing "three-axis system" excluding offensive aspects.[93] The government's FY2020 national defense draft budget includes a budget for technology development related to the multipurpose large transport vessel (LPX-II) to be carried by short takeoff and landing aircraft, as mentioned in the Mid-Term Defense Plan for 2020–2024. The ROK explains that this vessel will be introduced to improve capabilities for protecting maritime interests in waters surrounding the Korean Peninsula and in open sea.[94]

On the other hand, Defense Reform 2.0 calls for troop reduction from the current number of around 600,000 to 500,000 by 2022, aiming to consolidate and curtail standing troops against the backdrop of a declining birthrate and other factors. However, 2019 saw incidents that may be attributable to personnel shortages and slackening of military discipline. They include delay in the initial response to a wooden boat that sailed to Samcheok Port on the side of the Sea of Japan for defecting purposes even though the boat had docked at the port,[95] and a false report by the military upon failing to catch an unidentified person on the premises of the Second Fleet Command in Pyeongtaek.[96]

In the area of human resources, the ROK has taken steps to increase the number of civilian officers at the Ministry of National Defense. For example, whereas nine of the 22 director-general level posts were filled by nine civilians (not including generals on reserve) in 2017, they were filled by 17 civilian officers by the end of 2018. Additionally, a female officer was promoted to major general for the first time and appointed commander of Aviation Operations Command. An air force general was also appointed commander of the Defense Security Support Command for the first time rather than an army general, breaking a custom that had been in place since the days of its precursor, the Defense Security Command. In this manner, the ROK has continued to make breakthroughs in human resources.

NOTES

1)   Thomas Schelling, *Arms and Influence*, rev. ed., Yale University Press, 2008, pp. 21-23.

2)   *Rodong Sinmun*, April 21, 2018; KCNA, May 24, 2018; NIDS, ed., *East Asian Strategic Review 2019*, Urban Connections, 2019, pp. 75-78.

3)   *Rodong Sinmun*, January 1, 2019.

4)   *Rodong Sinmun*, April 13, 2019.

5)   Scott Sagan and Kenneth Waltz, *The Spread of Nuclear Weapons: A Debate Renewed*, WW Norton & Company, 2002, pp. 59-63.

6)   Michishita Narushige, *North Korea's Military-Diplomatic Campaigns, 1966–2008*, Routledge, 2010, pp. 106-107.

7)   Ashton Carter and William Perry, *Preventive Defense: A New Security Strategy for America*, Brookings Institution, 1999, pp. 128-129; Watanabe Takeshi, "Without Incentives: North Korea's Response to Denuclearization," *NIDS Journal of Defense and Security*, No. 18, December 2017, p. 106.

8) KCNA, January 8, 2016.

9) *Rodong Sinmun*, April 18, 2019.

10) Japanese Ministry of Defense, *Defense of Japan*, 2019, p. 100.

11) *Jane's Defence Weekly*, May 5, 2019; Michael Elleman, "North Korea's Newest Ballistic Missile: A Preliminary Assessment," *38 North*, May 8, 2019.

12) Dave Majumdar, "Why Russia's Iskander Missile Is a Killer: Can It Beat Missile Defense?" *National Interest*, July 19, 2018; Michael Peck, "Meet the Iskander: Russia's Latest Navy-Killer Missile? We Take a Look," *National Interest*, May 5, 2019; "SS-26 Iskander," *Missile Threats*, Center for Strategic and International Studies, September 27, 2016 [last modified August 1, 2019]; Elleman, "North Korea's Newest Ballistic Missile."

13) Japanese Ministry of Defense, *Defense of Japan*, 2019, p. 100.

14) *Kookbang Ilbo*, May 7, 2019.

15) ROK Joint Chiefs of Staff, *Questions and Answers on the South-North Situation*, 2015, p. 55; Elleman, "North Korea's Newest Ballistic Missile."

16) ROK Joint Chiefs of Staff, *Questions and Answers on the South-North Situation*, p. 55.

17) *Rodong Sinmun*, August 1, 2019.

18) *Kookbang Ilbo*, August 2, 2019.

19) *Rodong Sinmun*, September 11, 2019.

20) Japanese Ministry of Defense, "2019 nen no Kitachosen ni yoru Hassha" [North Korea's Launches in 2019] (as of December 3, 2019).

21) *Rodong Sinmun*, November 1, 2019.

22) *Rodong Sinmun*, January 1, 2019.

23) *Rodong Sinmun*, May 9, 2019.

24) KCNA, July 16, 2019.

25) *Rodong Sinmun*, July 23, 2019.

26) Nick Hansen, "OSINT Snapshot: Images Show North Korea Building Larger Ballistic Missile Submarine," *Jane's Intelligence Review*, August 2, 2019.

27) Japanese Ministry of Defense, *Defense of Japan*, 2019, p. 100.

28) *Rodong Sinmun*, July 26, 2019.

29) *Rodong Sinmun*, August 7, 2019.

30) *Jane's Defence Weekly*, August 12, 2019.

31) Japanese Ministry of Defense, "Information on North Korea's Missile Launch," October 2, 2019.

32) KCNA, October 10, 2019.

33) *Rodong Sinmun*, January 1, 2020.

34) KCNA, December 7, 2019.

35) Chinese Ministry of Foreign Affairs, "Xi Jinping tong Chaoxian laodongdang weiyuanzhang, guowu weiyuanhui weiyuanzhang Jin Zheng'en juxing huitan" [Xi Jinping Holds Talks with Chairman of the Workers' Party of Korea (WPK) and Chairman of the State Affairs Commission Kim Jong Un of the Democratic People's Republic of Korea (DPRK)], June 20, 2019.

36) *Xinhua News*, March 28, 2018.

37)   *Xinhua News*, May 8, 2018.

38)   Chinese Ministry of Foreign Affairs, "Wang Yi tong Chaoxian waixiang Li Yonghao juxing huitan" [Wang Yi Holds Talks with Foreign Minister Ri Yong-ho of the DPRK], May 2, 2018.

39)   KCNA, May 3, 2018.

40)   *Xinhua News*, June 19, 2018.

41)   *Rodong Sinmun*, June 20, 2018; KCNA, June 20, 2018.

42)   Chinese Ministry of Foreign Affairs, "Xi Jinping tong Chaoxian laodongdang weiyuanzhang Jin Zheng'en juxing huitan" [Xi Jinping Holds Talks with Chairman of the Workers' Party of Korea (WPK) of the DPRK], January 10, 2019.

43)   *Rodong Sinmun*, June 19, 2019.

44)   Chinese Ministry of Foreign Affairs, "Jiji jianxing Yazhou anquanguan gongchuang Yatai anquan xin weilai − waijiaobu fubuzhang Liu Zhenmin zai 'Yatai diqu auquan jiagou yu daguo guanxi' guoji yantaohui kaimushi shang de zhici" [Actively Practice the Asian Security Concept and Jointly Create a New Future of Asia-Pacific Security: Remarks by Vice Foreign Minister Liu Zhenmin at the Opening Ceremony of the International Seminar on "Security Framework and Major-Power Relations in the Asia-Pacific Region"], July 9, 2016.

45)   ROK Ministry of Foreign Affairs, "Outcome of Consultations between the ROK and China on Improvement in the Bilateral Relations," October 31, 2017.

46)   ROK National Assembly Secretariat, "Minutes of FY2017 National Assembly Inspection Foreign Affairs and Unification Committee Meeting," 2017, October 30, 2017, p. 7.

47)   Watanabe Takeshi, "Mun Jein Seiken no Jishu ga Chokumen suru Fukakujitsusei: Seijikyoso to Taibeichu Kankei" [Uncertainties Faced by the Autonomy of the Moon Jae-in Administration: Political Competition and Relations with the United States and China], *"Fukakujitsusei no Jidai" no Chosenhanto to Nihon no Gaiko Anzenhosho* [The Korean Peninsula in an "Age of Uncertainty" and Japan's Foreign/Security Policy], FY2017 Ministry of Foreign Affairs Diplomacy and Security Research Program, 2018, pp. 23-24.

48)   *Rodong Sinmun*, February 26, 2014.

49)   *Rodong Sinmun*, March 28, 2018.

50)   Hiraiwa Shunji, *Chosen Minshushugi Jinmin Kyowakoku to Chuka Jinmin Kyowakoku* [The Democratic People's Republic of Korea and the People's Republic of Korea], Seorishobo, 2010, pp. 25-27.

51)   Russian State Archive of Contemporary History (RGANI), Fond 5, Opis 28, Delo 314, Listi 34-59, translated in James Person, ed., *Limits of "Lips and Teeth" Alliance: New Evidence on Sino-DPRK Relations, 1955–1984*, North Korea International Documentation Project Working Paper, Woodrow Wilson Center for Scholars, 2009, pp. 2-3.

52)   James Morrow, "Arms versus Allies: Trade-offs in the Search for Security," *International Organization*, 47 (2), 1993, pp. 213-217.

53)   *Rodong Sinmun*, April 13, 2017, photo on p. 2; *Rodong Sinmun*, June 5, 2017; NIDS, ed., *East Asian Strategic Review 2018*, Japan Times, 2018, p. 87

54)   *Rodong Sinmun*, January 10, 2019, June 19, 2019, and June 21, 2019; *People's Daily*, June 20, 2019.

55) *Rodong Sinmun*, February 26, 2019.

56) Kim Jong Il, "On Enhancing the Role of Party Organizations and Political Organs in the People's Army: Talks to Officials of the WPK Central Committee's Organization and Guidance Department and the KPA General Political Bureau," *Kim Jong Il Selected Works*, Vol. 1, Workers' Party of Korea Publishing House, 1992, p. 417; Suzuki Masayuki, *Kitachosen: Shakaishugi to Dento no Kyomei* [North Korea: Resonance of Socialism and Tradition], University of Tokyo Press, 1992, p. 107.

57) *Rodong Sinmun*, February 26, 2019.

58) *Rodong Sinmun*, February 28, 2019.

59) KCNA, March 10, 2019.

60) KCNA, March 9, 2019.

61) *Rodong Sinmun*, December 24, 2017.

62) *Rodong Sinmun*, March 27, 2019.

63) *Rodong Sinmun*, April 13, 2019.

64) *Rodong Sinmun*, May 10, 2019.

65) *Rodong Sinmun*, July 23, 2019.

66) *Rodong Sinmun*, March 27, 2019.

67) The Blue House, "Opening Remarks by President Moon Jae-in at Meeting with His Senior Secretaries," February 11, 2019.

68) *Chosun Ilbo*, March 19, 2019.

69) ROK Ministry of Unification, "ROK Government to Promote Humanitarian Assistance for North Koreans," May 17, 2019.

70) ROK Ministry of Unification, "ROK Government Approves Businesspeople's Visit to Gaeseong Industrial Complex for Property Inspection," May 17, 2019.

71) Yonhap News, June 30, 2019.

72) Yonhap News, July 24, 2019.

73) ROK Ministry of Unification, "Ministry of Unification's Inter-Korean Exchange and Cooperation Promotion Council Decides on Funding Assistance for the World Health Organization's North Korea Maternal and Child Health Program (Tentative) and Other Matters," December 9, 2019.

74) ROK Ministry of National Defense, "'9.19 Military Agreement' First-Year Status and Achievements: Easing of Inter-Korean Military Tensions and Preparing a Practical Foundation for Confidence Building," September 18, 2019.

75) Supreme Court of the ROK, October 30, 2018 Verdict, Case 2013 Da 61381, Panel Judgment.

76) NIDS, ed., *East Asian Strategic Review 2018*, p. 97.

77) "The Constitution of the Republic of Korea," Article 66, Paragraph 1.

78) Japanese Ministry of Foreign Affairs, "Background and Position of the Government of Japan concerning the Issue of Former Civilian Workers from the Korean Peninsula (Fact Sheet)," July 2019.

79) Shoji Junichiro, "The Debate over Japan's Rising Sun Flag," *NIDS Commentary*, No. 89, November 2018.

80) Japanese Ministry of Foreign Affairs, "Kyokujitsuki ni tsuite" [Rising Sun Flag], May 31, 2019.

81) Japanese Ministry of Defense, "MOD's Final Statement regarding the Incident of an ROK Naval Vessel Directing its Fire-Control Radar at an MSDF Patrol Aircraft," January 21, 2019; Japanese Ministry of Defense, "Reference Material," January 21, 2019.

82) The Blue House, "Opening Remarks by President Moon Jae-in at Emergency Cabinet Meeting," August 2, 2019.

83) ROK Government, "We Will Never Lose Again: Japan's Export Restrictions and Our Response," August 16, 2019.

84) The Blue House, "Government Announcement of the Secretary-General of NSC Secretariat," August 22, 2019.

85) Japanese Ministry of Defense, "Japan-Republic of Korea-United States Trilateral Ministers Meeting Joint Press Statement," November 17, 2019.

86) ROK Ministry of National Defense, "Telephone Talks between Minister of National Defense Jeong Kyeong-doo and US Acting Secretary of Defense Shanahan," March 4, 2019; *Joongang Daily*, March 4, 2019.

87) *Kookbang Ilbo*, August 11, 2019; *Rodong Sinmun*, August 6, 2019; *Dong-A Ilbo*, August 12, 2019.

88) ROK Ministry of National Defense, "Outcomes of the 16th Korea-US Integrated Defense Dialogue (KIDD) Meeting," September 27, 2019.

89) ROK Ministry of National Defense, "Joint Communiqué of the 51st ROK-US Security Consultative Meeting," November 15, 2019; US Department of Defense, "Joint Communiqué of the 51st US-ROK Security Consultative Meeting," November 16, 2019.

90) KCNA, November 13, 2019; Yonhap News, November 17, 2019.

91) ROK Ministry of Foreign Affairs, "Spokesperson's Press Briefing/Press Conference by Ambassador in charge of ROK-US Defense Cost-Sharing Negotiations," December 19, 2019.

92) The Blue House, "Address by President Moon Jae-in at 71st Armed Forces Day," October 1, 2019.

93) ROK Ministry of National Defense, "Mid-Term Defense Plan for 2020–2024," August 14, 2019.

94) ROK Ministry of National Defense, "Government's Draft National Defense Budget for 2020," August 28, 2019.

95) ROK Office for Government Policy Coordination, "Government Joint Briefing on Status of Small Wooden Boat from North Korea," July 3, 2019.

96) ROK Ministry of National Defense, "Investigation Findings Related to Suspicious Person at the Second Fleet Command," July 14, 2019.

Chapter 4

Southeast Asia

Challenges of Government Selection and Governance

MATSUURA Yoshihide (Lead author, Section 1)
TOMIKAWA Hideo (Sections 2 (2) and 3)
MANABE Yuko (Section 2 (1) and (3))

China's active exercise of force to defend its territorial claims in the South China Sea, including missile tests and government and fishing vessel activities in the sea, stands out among the developments in Southeast Asia in 2019. The negotiations on the Code of Conduct (COC) between the Association of Southeast Asian Nations (ASEAN) and China made progress in the drafting process. But what this actually shows is Beijing's attempt to create a framework for enclosing the South China Sea militarily and economically via ASEAN and denying the access of extra-regional countries.

There were key events that have security implications for intra-regional countries. Namely, national elections held in 2019 incited and manifested changes in existing social structures and in relations between ethnic and religious groups. In Thailand, following a general election held in March for the first time in eight years to transition to a democracy, Prayut Chan-o-cha, who was the interim head of the military government, was nominated prime minister, and the second Prayut administration was inaugurated in July. Civil-military relations in Thailand stand at a major turning point due to the enthronement of the new King Vajiralongkorn, the king's coronation in May, and the establishment of the new government. In the Indonesian presidential election in April, the incumbent candidate Joko Widodo won, and his second term commenced in October. Despite concerns that electoral agitation would cause social polarization, the nation is expected to return to calm with Widodo's rival, Prabowo Subianto, joining the cabinet.

As regards major domestic conflicts in the region, the peacebuilding process made progress, including the establishment of the Bangsamoro Autonomous Region in Muslim Mindanao (BARMM) in Mindanao in the southern Philippines and the launch of the Bangsamoro Transition Authority (BTA) in February. On the other hand, the conflict in Patani, the three southernmost provinces of Thailand, another protracted insurgency in a Muslim settlement, did not see strides toward peace.

In Southeast Asia where terrorist threats persist, fighters of the remnants of the Islamic State of Iraq and the Levant (ISIL) are working with intra-regional domestic terrorists in an attempt to set up cells in the region. Governments have stepped up their measures to deter terrorist attacks, and as part of this effort, the Philippines, Malaysia, and Indonesia established a special operations command in their respective militaries.

1. The South China Sea Issue and ASEAN

(1) Southeast Asian Countries' Struggle with China's Exercise of Force

By transforming its artificial islands into militarized outposts, China continued to strengthen its control over the South China Sea, a body of water claimed by Brunei, Malaysia, the Philippines, Vietnam, and China. From the end of June to early July 2019, China conducted several test launches of anti-ship ballistic missiles into these waters. The missiles fired were reportedly the DF-21D or the DF-26. Admiral Philip Davidson, Commander of United States Indo-Pacific Command, stated that six missiles were launched, including the JL-3 submarine-launched ballistic missile.[1] This was said to be China's first missile test in the South China Sea. A situation in which Chinese missiles could pose a threat to freedom of navigation in the sea is increasingly turning into a reality.

There were noticeable cases of Chinese fishing and government vessels clashing with other claimants in their asserted exclusive economic zones (EEZ). In Vietnam, on March 6, a Chinese maritime surveillance vessel chased and sprayed water cannons at a Vietnamese fishing vessel that was anchored near Discovery Reef of the Paracel Islands, rammed the fishing vessel into the reef, and sunk it. Beginning in mid-June, Chinese maritime surveillance vessels and Coast Guard patrol vessels were deployed to the vicinity of a gas field that Vietnam is developing through joint ventures with Russia and India in the continental shelf of Vietnam's EEZ and interfered with the activities. In addition, from early July, Chinese maritime surveillance vessels, accompanied by Coast Guard patrol vessels, carried out oil exploration activities near Vanguard Bank of the Spratly Islands and were embroiled in a standoff with Vietnamese authorities for several weeks. The Chinese side left the area in early August but resumed surveys in the middle of the month. In the Philippines, in April, a large number of Chinese fishing vessels swarmed around Thitu (Pag-asa) Island—an island that is part of the Spratly Islands and under the effective control of the Philippines. This was followed by similar intermittent incidents. On June 13, a Philippine fishing vessel sunk after colliding with a Chinese fishing vessel near Reed Bank. Protests erupted over this collision incident in the Philippines on account of the Chinese side not rescuing and abandoning the 22 Filipino fishermen who were thrown into the sea.

As these incidents reveal, other claimants lack the ability to compete with China's use of enhanced military force and law enforcement capabilities. Under such conditions, the Philippines appears to have increasing expectations for the role of the US forces under the US-Philippines alliance. On March 1, US Secretary of State Mike Pompeo, who was visiting the Philippines, provided reassurance to the country saying, "Any armed attack on Philippine forces, aircraft, or public vessels in the South China Sea will trigger mutual defense obligations under Article 4 of our Mutual Defense Treaty."[2] The joint military exercise Balikatan 2019 held in April conducted landing operation training at a naval base in Zambales Province near Scarborough Shoal that is effectively controlled by China. The amphibious assault ship USS *Wasp*, with the F-35B fighter aboard, took part in the Balikatan exercise for the first time.[3] Under the 2014 Enhanced Defense Cooperation Agreement (EDCA), facility improvements will be made at five bases of the Armed Forces of the Philippines to which the US forces are permitted access. The first projects were completed in 2018, and 12 more projects have been approved for implementation for 2019 to 2020.[4] Meanwhile, in July 2019, President Rodrigo Duterte said as follows regarding territorial issues: "If America really wants to drive away China, which I can't do, I'll ask for its help. I want the whole of the Seventh Fleet of the Armed Forces of the United States there" and "Fire the first shot, and I'd be glad to do the next."[5] The President's remarks seem to be in response to criticisms over the Philippines' weak position toward China in the fishing vessel sinking incident in June. The remarks embody a complex sentiment of his country's powerlessness, coupled with banter that the actions of the United States, the only country that can compete with China with force, are suppressive. While President Duterte's vehement criticisms of the United States since the start of the current administration have subsided, his reservations about Washington likely remain.

ASEAN-US Maritime Exercise (US Navy photo by Mass Communication Specialist 1st Class Greg Johnson)

The US Navy conducted Freedom of Navigation Operations (FONOPs) at least eight times in the South China Sea in 2019. In early May, the naval forces of the United States, Japan, India, and the Philippines held joint training in the South China Sea.[6] In September, the first ASEAN-US Maritime Exercise was carried out. This exercise, co-led by the navies of the United States and Thailand, kicked off in the Sattahip Naval Base in Thailand on September 2. During the five-day exercise that ended in Singapore, trainings such as visit, board, search and seizure (VBSS), maritime domain awareness, division tactics, and maritime asset tracking were conducted in the Gulf of Thailand and the South China Sea. ASEAN's participation consisted of vessels from Brunei, Myanmar, the Philippines, Singapore, Thailand, and Vietnam. The remaining countries of Cambodia, Indonesia, Laos, and Malaysia sent observers.[7] This exercise represented a new display of US posture to maintain presence in Southeast Asia. At the same time, for ASEAN, having held the ASEAN-China maritime exercise for the first time in October of the previous year, it was a critical event for keeping balance between the United States and China.

As far as the US forces are concerned, Prime Minister Lee Hsien Loong of Singapore, who was visiting the United States, and US President Donald Trump agreed on September 23 to extend a Memorandum of Understanding (MOU) that permits US forces' access to facilities of the Singapore Armed Forces (SAF) by another 15 years until 2030. This MOU, concluded in 1990 and renewed for the second time, enables rotational deployment of the aircraft, vessels, and troops of the US forces to SAF bases. This agreement has contributed to strengthening Singapore's defense and security by deepening military cooperation between Singapore and the United States, combined with serving as a collateral for supporting the US forces' access to Southeast Asia following the withdrawal of US bases from the Philippines. On the one hand, it is rumored that Chinese forces will establish more bases in Southeast Asia (see next subsection); on the other hand, there are limits to the recent military relations between the Philippines/ Thailand and their ally the United States. Under such circumstances, Singapore's moves have significance also for ASEAN countries in maintaining the presence of the United States for sustaining regional balance.

(2) Are ASEAN Members Leaning toward Bilateral Negotiations with China?

No significant change is seen in ASEAN's attitude on the South China Sea issue. In the initial stage of Thailand's ASEAN chairmanship in 2019, the close relations between the Thai military government and China raised speculations that ASEAN would once again shift closer to China, similar to 2017 when the Philippines was the Chair. As it turns out, ASEAN maintained a consistent posture against the backdrop of Chinese government vessel activities in the EEZs of Vietnam and the Philippines, respectively, and of China's missile tests. Regarding the South China Sea issue, the Chairman's Statement of the ASEAN Summit in Bangkok on June 23 states that ASEAN members "took note of some concerns on the land reclamations and activities in the area, which have eroded trust and confidence, increased tensions and may undermine peace, security and stability in the region."[8] The wording is the same as in the Chairman's Statement of the previous Summit in Singapore in November 2018. On the other hand, the Joint Communique of the ASEAN Foreign Ministers' Meeting in Bangkok on July 31, 2019 uses the wording, "concerns were expressed by some Ministers on the land reclamations, activities and serious incidents in the area."[9] Without explicitly saying so, ASEAN appears to have raised its level of concern over Chinese moves, such as the missile tests and maritime surveillance vessel activities that occurred following the Summit.

Later on in November, a series of ASEAN meetings were held in Bangkok. The Chairman's Statement of the ASEAN Summit dated November 3 kept the same wording as the Chairman's Statement of June.[10] In contrast, at the East Asia Summit (EAS) on November 4, countries expressed one after another a desire to rein in China's behavior in the South China Sea, and the draft Chairman's Statement mentioned grave concern over ongoing militarization, according to reports.[11] Nonetheless, the final version of the Chairman's Statement released on November 5 uses the same wording as the previous EAS Chairman's Statement of November 2018 (which is the same wording as that in the aforementioned ASEAN Summit Chairman's Statement).[12] This outcome is attributed to the Thai Chair's considerations given to China's protests.

There were developments in the negotiations for concluding the Code of Conduct in the South China Sea (COC) between ASEAN countries and China. At the ASEAN-China Foreign Ministers' Meeting in Bangkok on July 31, 2019, it was confirmed that the first reading for distilling the demands of each country was completed, based on the Single Draft COC Negotiating Text compiled in the previous year. The first reading was to be completed by the end of 2019, as of the ASEAN Summit in June. In his press conference, Wang Yi, Foreign Minister of

China, stressed that the first reading was completed early thanks to the sincerity and resolve of all parties in the consultation, and said it marks an important step toward concluding the negotiations within three years' time (as advocated by China since November 2018).[13] During the visit to China by President Duterte of the Philippines in August 2019 (discussed later), Li Keqiang, Premier of the State Council of China, stated that China hopes COC negotiations can be concluded during the Philippines' tenure as country coordinator of China-ASEAN relations (until 2021).[14] The Chairman's Statement of the ASEAN-China Summit in Bangkok on November 3 welcomed the commencement of the second reading and notes, "We welcomed the aspiration to conclude the COC within a three-year timeline as proposed by China or earlier." It suggests that the three-year target, while not official, was shared with the ASEAN side.[15]

Though the content of the negotiations has not been made public, a report cites a diplomatic source as saying: at the first reading, China advocated that the United Nations (UN) Convention on the Law of the Sea will not apply, that joint military exercises with extra-regional countries will require the prior consent of relevant countries, and that resource development will not be conducted with extra-regional countries.[16] If so, it appears China is attempting to create a framework for enclosing the South China Sea militarily and economically via ASEAN and denying the access of extra-regional countries, including the United States. In light of China's actions backed by force, such as the activities already noted, it can be inferred that China seeks to become a de facto rule-setter under this framework and establish its territorial sovereignty by the so-called nine-dash line.

The negotiations on the second and later readings will review the validity of each party's individual claims. ASEAN countries are unlikely to acquiesce to China's proposals, such as those noted above, and the drafting process is expected to face challenges. Meanwhile, it seems China is looking to use non-COC channels with ASEAN to achieve substantive benefits. Such channels refer to bilateral negotiations.

In particular, with regard to the Philippines, President Duterte visited China in August for the fifth time in his tenure. At the summit meeting on the 29th, President Duterte and President Xi Jinping agreed to launch an intergovernmental body for the implementation of their November 2018 agreement on joint natural gas development in the South China Sea. According to a statement by the

Presidential Palace of the Philippines, the two leaders held candid and open exchange of views on the South China Sea issue, including the 2016 arbitral award by the Permanent Court of Arbitration (PCA) (that denied China's territorial sovereignty over the South China Sea).[17] On September 10, after returning to Manila and speaking to reporters, President Duterte revealed Xi Jinping's offer of a 60% stake in the joint development by the Philippines if it sets aside the arbitral award and its territorial claim. Duterte did not say if he agreed to Xi's offer but said he would "ignore" the part of the arbitral award that pertains to the EEZ in order to promote economic activity. His aides were left to paper over the President's remark. The next day, September 11, Teodoro Locsin, Philippine Foreign Secretary, noted that the joint development agreement does not compromise the legal position of either side and thus the arbitral award's involvement would be unnecessary, and that the arbitral award is final and legally binding and cannot be ignored.[18] On the 12th, the presidential spokesperson said that the President has not abandoned the arbitral award.[19]

As regards Malaysia, Foreign Minister Saifuddin Abdullah visited China in September. At the foreign ministers' meeting on the 12th, the two countries agreed to establish a bilateral consultation mechanism on maritime issues to address the South China Sea issue appropriately.[20] Following the inauguration of the Mahathir administration, Malaysia reviewed its economic relations with China, including cancelling the East Coast Rail Link project, which was a large-scale economic project between the two countries. However, in July, Malaysia decided to resume this project and is reconsidering projects that it had put under review. Foreign Minister Saifuddin said in an interview that the new mechanism framework would not change Malaysia's existing position on China and that the South China Sea issue should be discussed by ASEAN as a single group.[21] As these examples attest, ASEAN parties to the territorial dispute are wavering on the strength of China's bilateral orientation.

As for Cambodia, a July news report stated that it signed a secret agreement allowing China exclusive use of the Ream Naval Base for 30 years, according to US and allied government officials.[22] The naval base is located in Sihanoukville in which China has invested heavily. Prime Minister Hun Sen of Cambodia strongly denied the report, saying that hosting foreign military bases is against the Constitution. Wang Yi, Foreign Minister of China, concurred it was fake news.[23] On the other hand, Army Brigadier General Joel B. Vowell, Deputy Director for Strategic Planning and Policy, US Indo-Pacific Command, commented it has information that China will begin construction of facilities on the base in the following year (2020).[24] If the Chinese forces acquire a new outpost in the Gulf of Thailand that connects to the South China Sea, it could have a positive impact on Chinese forces' operations in the South China Sea and on improving deployment capabilities to the Straits of Malacca, the Natuna Islands, the Sunda Strait, and elsewhere. In this regard, its implications for defense of Southeast Asian countries and regional security should be monitored closely.

As was seen above, China has sought to use economic development as a bargaining leverage to resolve substantive issues bilaterally and implement policies that are favorable to China. At the same time, such bilateral approaches may lead to softening the claims made at the ASEAN forum by other claimants to the South China Sea or other ASEAN member states. In this way, it is considered that China aims to relativize the importance of the COC and turn it into a symbolic achievement of ASEAN-China cooperation. Amidst such moves, whether or not ASEAN will be able to maintain a unified response on creating the COC will be key to reaching an agreement that is effective, i.e., contributes to maintaining regional security and freedom of navigation that is also open to extra-regional countries.

The ASEAN meetings in November put a spotlight on one more matter: the fading of the US presence. On October 29, US President Trump announced that Robert O'Brien, Assistant to the President for National Security Affairs, would attend the ASEAN-US Summit and the EAS in Bangkok as a Special Envoy, and that Trump would not attend.[25] President Trump attended the ASEAN-US Summit in Manila in November 2017 but returned to the United States just before the EAS that followed and has not attended either meeting since then. Although the 2018 meetings in Singapore were attended by Vice President Mike Pence, the 2019 meetings were attended by an official who was not at the state leader level. This is thought to have been a big disappointment for ASEAN. While no ASEAN leader officially expressed criticism, the heads of government of ASEAN countries did not attend the ASEAN-US Summit on November 4, except for Thailand, which was the Chair, Vietnam, which is the 2020 Chair, and Laos, country coordinator for the United States. This was reportedly done in retaliation for the US move, according to a Thai diplomatic source.[26]

While it is clear that President Trump has a general tendency to avoid multilateral diplomacy, there is nothing concrete suggesting that he belittles ASEAN. At the meetings, Assistant O'Brien and Secretary of Commerce Wilbur Ross who accompanied him underscored the ASEAN-US partnership under the Trump administration and the United States' commitment to ASEAN. On the other hand, the long absence of the President who leads such efforts has aroused concerns among ASEAN leaders over whether US engagement in the future is certain and whether ASEAN will be affected by the US-China deal. This is expected to compound to ASEAN's difficulties of keeping a balance between the United States and China in the face of the latter's increasing influence.

Announcement of the "ASEAN Outlook on the Indo-Pacific"

The ASEAN Summit in June 2019 adopted a document entitled, "ASEAN Outlook on the Indo-Pacific" (AOIP).[27] It was made to serve as guidelines for promoting intra- and extra-regional cooperation in the Asia-Pacific and the Indian Ocean regions. Its main principles are ASEAN centrality, inclusiveness, complementarities, a rules-based order anchored upon international law, and commitment to advancing economic engagement in the region.[28] Based on ASEAN's principles, cooperation will be implemented by making use of existing ASEAN-led mechanisms (e.g., EAS, ASEAN Regional Forum [ARF], ASEAN Defence Ministers Meeting Plus [ADMM-Plus], Expanded ASEAN Maritime Forum [EAMF], and relevant ASEAN Plus One mechanisms). Specifically, AOIP vows to promote cooperation in wide-ranging areas, including the four major areas: (1) maritime cooperation, (2) connectivity, (3) UN Sustainable Development Goals 2030 (SDGs), and (4) economic and other possible areas of cooperation.

As can be seen, AOIP did not set forth ideas or new policies which are different from ASEAN's existing ones. ASEAN in fact distilled and unveiled the Indo-Pacific concept so as to conform with the existing ASEAN framework. The Indo-Pacific concept had been driven by extra-regional countries, such as Japan, the United States, India, and Australia. AOIP's announcement of the concept had the meaning of redefining it so that it is implemented at ASEAN's initiative and further meets the interests of member states, as stated in the Chairman's Statement of the Summit: "We encouraged external partners to support and undertake cooperation with ASEAN on the key areas outlined in the Outlook as their contribution to maintaining peace, freedom and prosperity in the region."

2. Election Results and Structural Changes in Political Dynamics

(1) The Thai General Election and the Second Prayut Administration: From Interim Prime Minister to Democratically Elected Prime Minister

There were key events that have security implications for Southeast Asian countries. For one, elections were held to choose governments in Thailand and Indonesia in 2019. While the leader was not replaced in either election, the election process exposed structural political and social issues facing both countries as well as clashes over the changes in the issues. Furthermore, the armed conflicts in Mindanao in the southern Philippines and in southern border provinces of Thailand constitute critical issues for the security of intra-regional countries. Progress has varied between the two conflicts; the former made significant strides in the peace process, whereas the latter's peace talks are in a stalemate.

In Thailand, a general election was held for the first time in approximately eight years on March 24, 2019. Since 2006, Thailand has experienced a spate of political unrest and clashes between social classes. After some five years of military government, the points at issue in the election were unlike previous ones. The military coup d'état on May 22, 2014 suspended the Constitution. Over the course of the five-year military government that followed, the parliament was abolished and political party activities were banned under the rule of the National Council for Peace and Order (NCPO), whose members included military heads who led the coup d'état. The military government, which wished for stable royal succession and retention of influence after the election, postponed the general election many times. In turn, anti-military junta parties and people stepped up their calls for a general election. However, the establishment of a new Constitution and the designing of an election system were in the hands of the military junta, and issues of freedom and fairness remained in transitioning to a democratic government. As a result of the election, a new government was established by democratically elected prime minister Prayut Chan-o-cha, a retired army general who was prime minister in the military government. On July 16, 2019, the second Prayut government was inaugurated. Members of the military junta have stayed in many key cabinet posts, with Prayut himself concurrently serving as prime minister and defense minister. The cabinet was formed in alliance with 19 political parties, and this weak coalition is expected to create unstable rule.[29]

Since 2006, Thailand has seen lobbying through street protests and non-democratic means, including government overthrow by judicial intervention, as well as military coups d'état (September 2006, May 2014). Some analysts describe this situation as a "collapse of the democratic system."[30] They are conflicts between the rural population and urban lower classes, who have gained political influence in national politics due to election system changes accompanying democratization, and the urban middle and upper classes, who, conversely, lost their previous political clout. The two sides enhanced their group unity, and class cleavages deepened. Moreover, class conflicts embed cleavages over supporting election or non-institutional direct action, i.e., methods of political decision-making.[31] When the unrest could not be diffused, the military conducted political intervention.

Based on his strong rural population support, former Prime Minister Thaksin Shinawatra who was appointed to office in 2001 portrayed himself as a prime minister with a firm backing testified by elections. Achieving coexistence between democratization and the monarchy posed as a challenge. As such, previous political unrests were orchestrated over "pro-Thaksin vs. anti-Thaksin" and were conflicts between the social classes that supported the respective sides. The 2019 election, however, was unlike elections up to the previous one largely characterized by a rivalry between two major parties: pro-Thaksin political parties (e.g., Pheu Thai party) and the anti-Thaksin Democrat party. The recent election was fought between supporters and opponents of military rule. Consequently, the election result was fragmented without a clear winner, with 86.8% of the seats shared among the top five parties.

A record 80 political parties took part in the election. They can be classified mainly into three groups: pro-military rule, anti-military rule, and fence-sitting. The Palang Pracharat party (PPRP), comprised of cabinet members of the military government and others, was formed as a pro-military rule party and supported interim Prime Minister Prayut for the prime ministerial nomination. The party was named after a socioeconomic policy known as "Pracharat" implemented by the military government. PPRP aimed to gain supporters among existing Thaksin supporters through a redistributive policy for the poor, which the military government had put particular efforts into. Anti-military rule factions included pro-Thaksin parties, such as the Pheu Thai party, and the newly formed Future Forward party (FFP) and New Economics party. The Democrat party and the Bhumjaithai party adopted a fence-sitting approach and did not announce if they were pro- or anti-military rule before the election. After the election, they ultimately joined the coalition of the new government.

In the recent election, no party—not just pro-Thaksin parties that normally have a strong showing—garnered a majority. One of the reasons was the introduction of the Multi-Member Apportionment (MMA) electoral system, which was designed to keep major parties from holding most of the seats.[32] Additionally, the new Constitution set forth five-year transitional provisions stipulating that 250 NCPO-appointed Senators and 500 Members of Parliament (MP) shall jointly vote for the prime minister. This meant that PPRP only needed 126 seats in the House of Representatives to obtain the majority required to be named prime minister. Furthermore, non-PPRP parties, especially anti-military rule parties, incurred restrictions on election campaigning and dissolution rulings, which had a significant impact on the election results. On February 8, 2019, the Thai Raksa Chart party officially registered Princess Ubolratana as its prime ministerial nomination with the Election Commission (EC). Princess Ubolratana is the elder sister of His Majesty the King, and she had relinquished her royal titles. This was an unprecedented development in Thai politics. However, at late that night the King issued a proclamation stating that her nomination was "inappropriate," and the Constitutional Court's ruling to dissolve Thai Raksa Chart was followed.[33] Two days before the general election, Princess Ubolratana attended a wedding of former Prime Minister Thaksin's daughter in Hong Kong, and photos were released. On the previous night of election day, the King issued a rare statement urging Thai voters to "elect 'good people' to rule the country."[34] In Thai political context, "good people" is understood as code for anti-Thaksin groups and politicians.[35]

The election results show changes in the voting behavior of voters as well as changes in past regional voting tendencies.[36] The EC's official announcement of the general election results was mired in problems. The official election results were not released until May 8, after the King's coronation ceremony in early May, creating a void for approximately one and a half months following the election. The anti-junta camp, centered around the Pheu Thai party and FFP, announced the formation of a coalition three days after the election. Based on the seat allocation criteria announced in advance, the camp was expected to attain a majority in the House of Representatives. However, the EC abruptly unveiled a new vote calculation method. Under the new formula, anti-junta parties, primarily FFP, received seven fewer seats than the initial calculation.[37] The cap for the total number of votes obtained, which determined seat allocation in constituencies, was lowered. Accordingly, there were more than ten small parties that were granted just a constituency seat. Moreover, the EC announcement on May 28 changed the total number of votes obtained and increased the final count of total valid votes.[38] The number of parties with seats rose to 26, the most in Thailand's history. With so many small and medium parties joining the parliament, it became critical for parties to form a coalition. When it came time to name a prime minister, 254 MPs from 19 parties expressed support for Prayut, just barely exceeding the majority of the House of Representatives. This led to the emergence of internal battles over the appointment of cabinet members among PPRP and the coalition parties. A close eye needs to be kept on the administration of the National Assembly, where ruling and opposition parties contend over matters including budget deliberations conducted at the first reading on October 19.

Clashes between the government and opposition parties also merit attention. On November 20, the Constitutional Court ruled to disqualify Thanathorn Juangroongruangkit as MP for having shares in a media company when applying to become MP. Thanatorn is the leader of FFP that won the third largest number of total votes in the general election and was recommended by the opposition coalition as a challenger to Prayut in the prime ministerial nomination. On the matter of FFP's acceptance of a loan of 191 million bahts from its leader Thanatorn due to lack of campaign funding, the EC said that it would conduct hearings for alleged violation of the Organic Act on Political Parties. On December 11, the EC decided to refer the dissolution of FFP to the Constitutional Court. In response to these moves, Thanatorn called on his supporters to stage a rally in central Bangkok on December 14, and the largest anti-democracy rally since the 2014 coup d'état was held. As such examples show, the people's political activities have intensified compared to during the military rule.[39] (Addendum: On February 21, 2020, the Constitutional Court issued a ruling to dissolve FFP and ban its executives from political activities for ten years.)

In Thailand, following the demise of His Majesty King Bhumibol (King Rama IX) in 2016, His Majesty King Vajiralongkorn (King Rama X) ascended to the throne and was crowned in May 2019. The realignment of the military under King X in particular sheds light on the changing government-military relationship. Those from the 2nd Infantry Division known as "Eastern Tigers," which occupied leadership positions in the army since 2007, including executing coups d'état for protecting the monarchy under the King IX's reign, and the 21st Infantry Regiment, which is the Division's core regiment for protecting the queen, lost key posts such as Army Chief. In place of the 2nd Infantry Division, the army's 1st Division was reinstated.[40] Prime Minister and Defence Minister Prayut, Deputy Prime Minister Prawit Wongsuwon, and Interior Minister Anupong Paochinda who led the 2014 coup and the military government belonged to the 2nd Infantry Division. While they still have influence on cabinet members appointed by the military government and Senators, some analyze that their control over the armed forces is weakening.[41] Aside from inter-faction fighting, it is noteworthy that appointments to senior military positions are connected to loyalty to King X,[42] in particular, the rise of a faction known as *"kho deang."* *Kho deang* traces its origin to the shirt with a red neckline worn by members of the royal guard forces, who have completed a three-month training in the style of that of the King's Royal Rachawallop 904 Special Military Task Force (904 Special Task Force) responsible for "training officers whom the King can trust."[43] Current Army Chief Apirat Kongsompong is a former guard of the 1st Division. He concurrently serves as Commander of the 904 Special Task Force, which has enhanced *kho deang*'s influence in the military.[44] In short, political intervention for "protecting the monarchy" by an army controlled by the Eastern Tigers[45] has ended, and direct interactions between the King and the military are on the rise.

Following His Majesty King Vajiralongkorn's accession, units engaged in guarding the King were expanded and reorganized. In 2017, in placing five entities such as the Bureau of the Royal Household under the direct supervision of the King, the Royal Security Command was placed under the direct control of the King and became independent from the Ministry of Defence.[46] The Royal Security Command oversees planning, command, and all other tasks related to guarding the royal family, including the King. Its operational units are the King's close bodyguards.[47] The 1st Infantry Regiment, which is the King's Guard regiment under the 1st Infantry Division, and the 11th Infantry Regiment, are assigned as regiments of the King's close bodyguards. In April 2019, the term "*Ratchawanlop*" was specially added to the names of both regiments, and they were renamed the King's close bodyguards.[48] On September 30, 2019, it was decided by emergency decree that the two regiments' personnel and budgets would be detached from the army and transferred to the Royal Security Command.[49] Albeit opposition from the opposition party FFP, this decree was later approved by both the House and the Senate by October 20.[50] In 2017, His Majesty King Vajiralongkorn introduced a new military salute and a short hairstyle of the type worn by the King's guards in his efforts to unify disciplinary practices. Leading this effort is the aforementioned 904 Special Task Force. Those selected from around 30 brigades nationwide are required to undertake a training program supervised by the King.[51] Upon completing the training and returning to their respective duties, they must strictly adhere to the discipline, dress, hairstyle, and public demeanor which they acquired in the training.[52] There is an increasing likelihood that Narongpan Jitkaewthae, who serves as deputy commander of the 904 Special Task Force alongside Army Chief Apirat, will be appointed the next Army Chief, according to reports.[53]

The 1st Division, one of the main units of the 1st Army Area with jurisdiction over the metropolitan area, was also reorganized. According to reports, following the King's accession, key units of the 1st Division were relocated from Bangkok to neighboring provinces under Army Chief Apirat.[54] Some observers say that the relocation was meant to transfer units that orchestrated past coups d'état as well as the army's key units away from Bangkok and prevent a coup d'état against the King.[55] Meanwhile, the government reinforced the 11th Infantry Division in Chachoengsao, located east of Bangkok, in order to maintain troop strength in the metropolitan area. Furthermore, 60 M1126 Stryker armored personnel carriers procured from the United States (of which 23 were provided as a grant) are to be deployed mainly to Chachoengsao.[56] In this way, the King and the military have strengthened their ties, giving greater influence to the armed forces that are under the direct command of the King. At the same time, while it is noted that the military's support of the government has declined due to Prime Minister and Defence Minister Prayut's decreasing influence on the armed forces, Army Chief Apirat has expressed his support for the Prayut government since its initial inauguration.[57]

As examined above, while a general election for a democratic transition was held in Thailand, it was a limited transition that kept the same faces as the military government. Unlike during the military junta when military forces carried out political intervention based on a strong support base, there is now greater unity between the King and the military under a new monarch. Although backed by the King and the military, the government has lost its previous strong support base and continued attention must be paid to government-military relations. Moreover, conflicts between social classes are unresolved, and the question remains as to how the monarchy will co-exist with calls for more institutional democracy.

(2) Developments Related to Indonesia's Presidential Election Results

The Indonesian presidential election in April 2019 was a contest between incumbent Joko Widodo and Prabowo Subianto, former Commander of the Army Strategic Reserve Command (KOSTRAD). After legal amendments in 2017, the following condition was imposed in Indonesia: a party or a coalition of parties that nominates a presidential candidate must have at least 20% of the parliament seats or have won at least 25% of the votes in the most recent national election. As a consequence, the presidential election saw changes in party alignment.

Joko was backed by the Indonesian Democratic Party of Struggle (PDI-P) and its ruling coalition party. They included the Golkar Party and the United Development Party (PPP), which supported Prabowo in the 2014 presidential election. Prabowo was backed by opposition parties, such as his Great Indonesia Movement Party (Gerindra), the largest opposition party, and the Democrats Party. The opposition parties also included the National Mandate Party (PAN), which had been part of the ruling coalition party right until the start of the election campaign, and which had a ministerial seat. Thus, the political dynamics of a presidential election were extremely opportunistic; to put it another way, political compromises were feasible between parties.

In Indonesia, it is generally said that a politician's political stance is assessed based on whether he is a pragmatic nationalist or an Islamist. In this context, Prabowo projected himself as a former senior military officer with strong leadership skills and emphasized his pro-Muslim position to the masses. In the lead-up to the election, both camps engaged in negative campaigning. The General Elections Commission (KPU) declared the Joko camp's victory in the final results released in May. Dissatisfied with this result, the Prabowo camp appealed to the Constitutional Court that the election was rigged. In addition, Prabowo supporters staged street protests against the election results. Nevertheless, the Constitutional Court dismissed this case in late June due to lack of evidence. Furthermore, the violent May rallies in Jakarta, which are considered to have been instigated by members of the Prabowo camp, failed to garner broad support from the masses.[58] After the Prabowo camp had demonstrated its resistance to society, PDI-P leader Megawati Setiawati Sukarnoputri encouraged reconciliation between the Joko and Prabowo camps.

As this exemplifies, elite politicians understand the ways in which confrontation can be diffused following an intense election. The ways include allocating cabinet posts and other institutionalized methods of accommodating and distributing interests. However, the two camps' widespread use of radical rhetoric during the election campaign had the potential of creating cleavages in the civil society. Especially in times of confusion, people are exposed to a tsunami of information, making it easy to instigate the masses. Therefore, the government restricted some social media services in Jakarta when the radical rallies were held in May. The government implemented this measure out of fear that fake news and hate speech would spark public riots.

Before Joko's second term inaugurated in October, party leaders began to approach President Joko to gain a seat on the cabinet. Alongside this, they began playing a political game setting their sights on the next presidential election. This is because a president cannot be elected three times under the Constitution of Indonesia. First, in August, former President Megawati was reelected leader of PDI-P, and is thought to have enhanced her influence as kingmaker. She stressed to the people that she reconciled with Prabowo, the leader of Gerindra, and with former President Susilo Bambang Yudhoyono (SBY), who she fought against in past presidential elections and who supported the rival camp in the latest presidential election.[59] One of the objectives of such political maneuver campaigns was presumably to ensure a stable parliament administration under the next Joko administration. There was supposedly another objective: to make the name of Prananda Prabowo—Megawati's younger son and an executive member of PDI-P—known among the people and promote him as a next-generation leader candidate to succeed her.[60] As was the case for President Joko, establishing a reputation as a local political leader is one of the leading ways to become a presidential candidate. For this reason, the media has reported on several candidates for the next presidential election, including Anies Rasyid Baswedan, former Minister of Culture and Primary and Secondary Education and Governor of the Special Capital Region of Jakarta, and Ridwan Kamil, Governor of West Java Province who reformed Bandung city and led its development effort. Known as a media king, Surya Paloh, leader of the National Democratic Party (NasDem), met with Governor Anies in September and stated that he could become the next presidential candidate. This is considered part of the psychological game being played in the ruling coalition party in relation to the kingmaker.[61]

In September, the People's Consultative Assembly (MPR), which is the parliament in Indonesia, debated two bills amending the Criminal Code and the Corruption Eradication Commission (KPK) Law, respectively. The bills were subject to criticism by some citizens. Students and others staged protests around MPR. Some protestor groups clashed with public security forces, resulting in casualties. The bill to amend the Criminal Code risked impeding personal rights and freedom of the press and could stir strong opposition from President Joko's core supporters. President Joko hence requested MPR to postpone the vote. On the other hand, the bill to amend the KPK Law was revised and passed by MPR on the grounds that the existing law may be utilized for political purposes.

In October, the cabinet members of the second Joko administration were announced. President Joko identified economic growth as his top policy priority and appointed many experts to his cabinet. Meanwhile, the appointment of Prabowo, Joko's rival in the presidential election and leader of Gerindra, as defense minister came as a surprise to the media. It has been said that this appointment was made based on a request from PDI-P leader Megawati, or to have Prabowo by Joko's side to rein in Megawati's power. Either way, the largest opposition party joined the ruling party group, resulting in the ruling coalition party accounting for approximately 75% of total seats.

Such bargaining between political leaders had the effect of restraining political movements that deepen social cleavages. Nonetheless, many structural political issues remain looking at the nation as a whole. In particular, the SARA (ethnicity, religion, race, and other social divisions) matter and delays in economic development on the outlying islands or in the periphery are still not completely resolved. As an outcome, a sensitive issue related to SARA emerged in Papua. In Surabaya in the province of East Java, Papuan students were provoked by nationalists and received unequal treatment by the police. This began a series of protests by Papuans in August 2019 across the nation, including Papua province, West Papua province, and the capital city of Jakarta. In the September 23 protests in Wamena in Papua province, radical groups set government and other buildings on fire. Approximately 20 people died in this incident. The present provinces of Papua and West Papua were incorporated into Indonesia as West Irian province in 1969. Pro-independence groups questioned the legitimacy of this political process and continued to hold rallies. This area was designated the Military Operation Area (DOM) for approximately 20 years until 1998. Recently, pro-independence groups have stepped up their activities, deteriorating the security situation in this region. In December 2018, an armed group that calls itself the West Papua National Liberation Army (TPNPB), believed to be a faction of the Free Papua Movement (OPM), attacked a camp of road construction workers in Nduga regency in Papua province. This attack killed 19 workers who had come to work from other provinces and one Indonesian soldier who went to the scene. In March 2019, TPNPB attacked the Indonesian Army forces while they were on guard duty, and three Army personnel died. In response, the national armed forces deployed approximately 600 additional personnel to the region. Under these circumstances, Papuans conducted protests. The government feared that the protests would resonate with separatists or would instigate them and develop into a violent insurgency. Thus, the government immediately admitted that its response had been inappropriate.[62] The government has explored dialogue with leaders of the United Liberation Movement for West Papua (ULMWP), the political arm of pro-independence groups. However, as the government has no intention to put on the agenda an independence referendum demanded by ULMWP, a formal meeting between the two sides has not been realized.[63] Meanwhile, the government continued to restrict connections to communication services out of fear that fake news would spark public riots.

As the above analysis shows, there were concerns that the election campaign would polarize Indonesian society. Following the election, however, major political parties formed a coalition. From the outside, it looked like the second Joko administration was inaugurated based on a stable political foundation. On the other hand, the Indonesian society continues to face political issues that could turn into a security problem, including disputes in Papua. If government responses to them are inadequate, they will likely have adverse impacts on national unity and democratic practices. As far as Indonesia's foreign policy is concerned, a Chinese fishing vessel escorted by a Chinese Coast Guard patrol vessel conducted illegal operations in the EEZ claimed by Indonesia in December. This act may have implications for the country's diplomatic strategy for the South China Sea and the "nine-dash line" advocated by China. Attention is focused on how the new administration's security policy and diplomatic stance on China will or will not change.

(3) Two Domestic Conflicts and Peace Processes: Bangsamoro and Patani

This subsection discusses the conflict in Mindanao in the southern Philippines and the conflict in Patani in southern Thailand. Both are clashes between anti-government Islamic forces and the government over the expansion of an autonomous region or independence, stemming from religious and ethnic nationalism. However, in 2019, whereas the Mindanao conflict saw significant progress by way of the establishment of the Bangsamoro Transition Authority (BTA), the Patani peace process is in a stalemate.

Mindanao in the southern Philippines and Patani in the deep south of Thailand are home to armed conflicts in which prolonged daily violence has resulted in casualties, including many civilians. The death toll in Mindanao has reached at least 100,000 to 150,000 people in 40 years[64] and in Patani more than 7,000 in 15 years.[65] In Mindanao, Muslims have been marginalized under the Christian resettlement policy of the Philippine government in place since the US rule of the Philippines. In southern border provinces of Thailand, border demarcation with British Malaya led to Thailand's annexation of some territories of the former Patani Kingdom, a Malay sultanate, which was followed by the government of Thailand's implementation of an assimilation policy. Against this historical backdrop, the problems have grown more complex as national governance and the people's religions and ethnicities diverged. While nationalism was a critical element of the separatist and independence movements in both conflicts, the two cases differ with respect to the government's perception. Unlike the Malay Muslims in Patani, the Moro people are not a single ethnic group.

Mindanao plebiscite (Kyodo News)

Comprised of 13 ethnolinguistic groups in total, they are indigenous people who have existed prior to the Spanish rule of the Philippines. An existing domestic law stipulates that the Moro people have the right to identify themselves as "Bangsamoro" (meaning the lands and peoples of Moro), irrespective of whether they are of mixed or full blood.[66] On the other hand, the government of Thailand has not acknowledged the ethnic identity of Malay Muslims in Patani and the existence of insurgent groups. Both regions are geographically distant from the nation's center of power and are located at the southern tip of national territory where the central government's direct control and influence cannot reach. In addition, both are considered poor regions where development has lagged behind other parts of the nation, and separatist and independence movements have unfolded since around the 1970s. As shown, the two regions have much in common. Nonetheless, significant differences are seen in the progress of their peace processes, owing partly to the differences in the government's political will and the nature of the insurgent groups.

The Mindanao conflict made historical strides in its peace process with the holding of a referendum or plebiscite in January and February 2019. As a result of the plebiscites, a majority ratified the establishment of the Bangsamoro Autonomous Region in Muslim Mindanao (BARMM). Its predecessor the Autonomous Region in Muslim Mindanao (ARMM) was dissolved in stages, and the creation of a larger autonomous region was approved. BARMM territory was decided upon, extending over the five provinces of ARMM, Cotabato City, and 63 barangays (smallest administrative unit) in North Cotabato Province. BTA will govern the region until the Bangsamoro regional government is inaugurated upon elections in June 2022. Murad Ebrahim, Chair of the Moro Islamic Liberation Front (MILF), will serve as interim Chief Minister, and President Duterte will select the 80 members of the BTA launched in late February 2019. The Bangsamoro Organic Law (BOL) stipulates that a majority of the BTA members be appointed by the MILF.[67] The BTA held its first session on March 29, 2019. On November 30, 2019, BARMM's first budget, the budget for FY2020 equivalent to PHP (Philippine peso) 65.3 billion, was approved. In the draft budget, the education department received the largest allocation of PHP 19.0 billion, marking an important step for the sustainable development of BARMM which includes the poorest areas of the Philippines.[68] The government of the Philippines and the MILF began peace negotiations in 1997. On March 27, 2014, the Comprehensive Agreement on the Bangsamoro (CAB) was concluded under the Benigno Aquino III administration. The agreement approved the creation of an autonomous Muslim entity across a part of Mindanao, paving the way for power sharing with the MILF for autonomous governance. At this time, however, there was little political support from politicians and the public for Congress to pass the Bangsamoro Basic Law needed to implement the CAB. In particular, their opposition increased after the counter-terror operation in Mamasapano that killed over 30 police officers in 2015.[69] President Duterte, who is the first President from Mindanao and has Moro blood, has repeatedly stated that the conflict in Mindanao is the result of a "historical injustice" that the country must correct, and had demonstrated his ambition for the peace process since his presidential campaign.[70] BOL, the amended Bangsamoro Basic Law, was passed by Congress and signed by the President in July 2018 and was then passed in the plebiscites. While the peace process made remarkable strides, the start of BARMM marks no more than the beginning of the peace process. Close attention must be paid to the possibility of peace being hindered by the administrative capacity of the MILF's interim self-government authority and by violence from other decentralized insurgent groups.

In 1976, the MILF, a leading actor in the Mindanao peace process, split from the Moro National Liberation Front (MNLF), which was founded in the late 1960s, due to disagreement with the government over peace policy. The MILF needs to change itself from a "liberation front" to a political party, in order to strengthen its leadership in the peace process and reduce fighting in the new autonomous region and Mindanao. By 2022, the MILF plans to decommission the Bangsamoro Islamic Armed Forces (BIAF), an MILF unit with 40,000 combatants and 7,000 weapons. In September 2019, 1,060 combatants and 940 weapons were decommissioned under Phase 2 of the plan.[71] At the same time, the martial law in Mindanao was lifted on December 31, 2019, and accordingly, suspects can no longer be arrested without a warrant. However, application of a state of emergency to the region and deployment of the Armed Forces of the Philippines are still in effect (see Section 3). As can be observed, the peace process that includes a ceasefire agreement with armed forces is pursued in parallel with administering the interim autonomous government.

The deep south of Thailand called Patani refers to three provinces of Pattani, Yala, and Narathiwat and four districts of Songkhla province on its southern border. Insurgencies have worsened particularly from 2004 due to the Thai government's heavy-handed repression. Compounded by frequent changes in government, lack of political will for a resolution, and the structural complexity of secret insurgent groups, a formal peace process was long absent in this region. The turning point came on February 28, 2013 when Thai government representatives and the National Revolutionary Front (BRN), the largest insurgent group, agreed to commence peace talks under the Yingluck Shinawatra administration. However, the peace talks were suspended amidst political protests that were later held aimed at overthrowing the Yingluck administration. In December 2014, it was agreed that peace talks would be convened under Prayut's military government. Critical changes were made to the composition of the insurgent side. On June 5, 2015, an umbrella body of six insurgent groups known as "MARA Patani" was formed and became the principal party to the peace talks with the Thai government. Four years passed without tangible achievements in the peace talks between MARA Patani and the Thai government, which questioned the appropriateness of MARA Patani as a negotiation partner and which gave priority to a partial ceasefire agreement. In the meantime, the Malaysian government's facilitator for the peace talks was replaced following the general election in Malaysia in May 2018, and the members of the peace talks also changed. Udomchai Thammasarorat, former Commander of the 4th Army region who served as the Thai delegate to the peace talks from October 2018, was appointed Senator and was replaced with Wanlop Rugsanaoh, Secretary-General of the National Security Council, in September 2019. While Sukree Hari, who served as MARA Patani's delegate to the peace talks since 2015, is said to have announced his resignation in May 2019,[72] MARA Patani's acceptance of the resignation has been on hold. In late November 2019, amid suspended peace talks between the Thai government and MARA Patani, Thai government representatives and the BRN reportedly met in Berlin.[73] Wanlop, the Thai government's delegate to the peace talks, speaking to a press conference at the Foreign Correspondents' Club of Thailand, refrained from referring to the BRN by name but showed confidence that the insurgent group, which has significant influence on the conflict, would engage in direct talks.[74] This remark was made in light of the fact that the BRN as a whole has not joined MARA Patani, and that focus has always been paid to whether the insurgent side's delegate to the talks can command local combatants.

The number of incidents in the deep south in 2018 was the lowest ever on record since 2004, and the number has consistently decreased in recent years. However, on November 5, 2019, the largest attack since the latter half of 2001 occurred in Lam Phaya in Mueang Yala District, Yala Province, killing 15 village defense volunteers. Outside the southern border provinces, on August 2, bombs exploded in Bangkok during its hosting of ASEAN meetings, injuring five people. Thai security authorities made comments that suspected links to insurgent groups in Patani.[75] As to where the peace process in Thailand's Patani region currently stands, the key elements for resuming peace talks are: confidence building by the Thai government and MARA Patani, moves of the BRN—the largest insurgent group, and the involvement of third parties including Malaysia, the facilitator. As the above examined, while the Mindanao and Patani cases have many commonalities, there are significant differences in the progress of their peace processes. Given the difficulty of short-term resolutions, there are many lessons to be learned from individual cases for ensuring that the local civil society has space for discourse and for raising the political will of the government and insurgent groups toward making progress in the peace process.

The situations of the countries discussed in this section are intertwined with their inherent governance systems as well as with their underlying complex structural circumstances attributable to relations between ethnic and religious groups, central and local governments, and political elites and citizens. Leaders in Southeast Asia, including Indonesia, the Philippines, and Thailand, face the common challenge of addressing social polarization and prolongation of domestic conflicts by dealing with these structural issues, mitigating social instability, and implementing measures that lead to dialogue.

3. Establishment of Special Operations Commands and Enhancement of Counter-Terrorism Measures

(1) The Philippines: Increased Terrorist Activity and Strengthened Responses of the Armed Forces

Terrorist threats in Southeast Asia persisted in 2019. Remnants of the Islamic State of Iraq and the Levant (ISIL), which took a devastating blow in Syria, seek to establish outposts in areas of Southeast Asia that are not under close watchful eyes. This is thought to be strengthening ties between the globally networked

ISIL and homegrown violent extremists who are under its ideological influence. This situation is compounded by the existence of transnational terrorist and crime organizations, which in turn has further heightened the risk of terrorist attacks in this region. Governments have enhanced their counter-terrorism measures to prevent terrorist attacks and the establishment of outposts by international terrorist organizations. This section provides an overview of the cases in the Philippines, Malaysia, and Indonesia, which have recently established special operations commands as part of their institutional strengthening efforts. Whether the risk of concern is of a terrorist attack occurring in urban areas or of an organized armed uprising occurring in the periphery varies by country. The relations between the military and local communities also vary by country. This section hence focuses on the differences in the composition of the special operations command and its role and outlines the trends of terrorist organizations, the reason for reinforcing military arrangements.

The Armed Forces of the Philippines (AFP) established the Special Operations Command (SOCOM) in April 2018. The establishment was based on the lessons learned from the attack in Zamboanga in Mindanao conducted by the Nur Misuari faction of the MNLF in 2013 and from the Maute Group's siege in the Islamic City of Marawi in 2017. SOCOM is headquartered at Fort Magsaysay Military Reservation in the Province of Nueva Ecija.[76] It oversees various units in an integrated manner, including the Joint Special Operations Group under the direct control of the AFP General Headquarters, the Special Operations Wing of the Air Force, the Naval Special Operations Group of the Navy, the Army's Scout Ranger Regiment, the Special Forces Regiment, and the Light Reaction Regiment. This has created a system that can address more diverse environments and situations. Meanwhile, the terrorist and crime organization Abu Sayyaf Group (ASG) is active in the southern Philippines as well as the leftwing guerrilla group New People's Army (NPA) and the Bangsamoro Islamic Freedom Fighters (BIFF), a MILF splinter group, in an adjacent region. Therefore, continuous security operations are required in addition to responding to temporary incidents, and the Army plays a central role in carrying out constant surveillance duties.

In December 2018, to deal with ASG and other threats, the Department of National Defense of the Philippines announced that it plans to establish the Army's 11th Infantry Division in the Sulu Archipelago, where several units had been deployed previously, and that the Division will be given full capabilities by 2022. Moreover, in the same month, it was reported that the AFP activated the 1st Brigade Combat Team (BCT) capable of responding flexibly to situations, such as terrorist attacks and insurgencies.[77] The 1st BCT is expected to fulfill the role of a rapid deployable unit. Considerations have been given for the team to contribute to developing operation concepts and strategies through practice. Like SOCOM, it is headquartered at Fort Magsaysay Military Reservation and will be temporarily placed under tactical control of the Training and Doctrine Command. The 1st BCT is comprised of two infantry battalions and one mechanized, engineer combat, and field artillery battalions, respectively, as well as signal, intel, medical, and service supports as sustainment units. The 1st BCT took part in Salaknib, a joint exercise with the US forces, soon after its establishment in March 2019 and in the joint exercise Balikatan 2019 in April and enhanced its skills. In May, it was dispatched to the Sulu Archipelago as a rapid deployable unit and engaged in counter-terrorism duties.

Terrorist organizations in the Philippines conduct intense attacks in the Sulu Archipelago. At the end of July 2018, a car bomb attack occurred at a checkpoint in the suburbs of Lamitan, Basilan island. The attack, believed to involve ASG, targeted the Civilian Armed Force Geographical Unit (CAFGU) and killed at least ten people. In January 2019, just before the plebiscite on joining BARMM, bomb attacks occurred at a Catholic cathedral on Jolo island in the Sulu Archipelago, killing more than 20 people including 14 soldiers who were on guard and 2 police officers. ISIL released a statement claiming responsibility for the attacks. ASG members who pledged allegiance to ISIL are thought to have supported the terrorists behind the attacks. President Duterte visited the site and once again instructed ASG's destruction. In May 2019, it was announced that the 1st BCT consisting of 1,500 personnel would be deployed to the Sulu Archipelago. In June, the 6th Infantry Division and the Marine Corps' Battalion Landing Team 7 were also deployed to the region.

US-Philippines bilateral exercise Salaknib (US Army photo by Sgt. Ariel J. Solomon, 128th MPAD)

Nevertheless, on June 28, a terrorist group carried out a suicide bombing attack in Indanan on Jolo island against a camp where the 1st BCT's front command post is stationed. This attack killed at least 7 people, including 3 soldiers, and injured 22 people. In the case of previous suicide bombing attacks in the Philippines, the attack in Lamitan was conducted by a Moroccan and the attack at the Catholic cathedral on Jolo island was conducted by Indonesians. Accordingly, it was believed that foreign nationals carry out suicide bombings. One of the perpetrators of the June attack, however, was a Filipino national, and observers noted that the risk of homegrown terrorism had become a reality. The AFP spokesperson admitted that AFP needed to adapt its tactics. Regarding its responses going forward, he unveiled that AFP will strengthen collaboration on information sharing with countries such as Indonesia, Malaysia, the United States, and Australia, and continue to engage in the National Action Plan on Preventing and Countering Violent Extremism that includes regional development policy. At the same time, the spokesperson commented on the need to amend the Human Security Act, including extending the period of detention of suspects.[78]

(2) Malaysia: Increasingly Complex and Non-Transparent Activities of Terrorist Organizations and Role Separation between the Military and Security Authorities

In 2016, Malaysia formed the National Special Operations Force (NSOF) under the National Security Council. NSOF was composed of the armed forces, the police, and the maritime enforcement agency and specialized in combating terrorism. This force would swiftly respond to all terrorist incidents that occur in the country, according to the explanation. This reshuffle was made in response to the situation at the time, which saw the rise of ISIL and the intensifying activities of terrorist organizations that sympathize with ISIL in Southeast Asia. However, the new government that was inaugurated in June 2018 dissolved NSOF. Then, at a meeting held in January 2019, a plan was announced to establish a special operations command—a unified command of only the special units of the Malaysian Armed Forces (MAF), such as the Special Service Group (GGK), the Naval Special Warfare Forces (PASKAL), and the Royal Malaysian Air Force Special Force (PASKAU). Law enforcement functions were detached from the command. The units under the command are said to be deployed for operations to secure Malaysia's national and strategic interests, and have jurisdiction over developing special operations trainings and doctrines in cooperation with other countries. The units are equipped with not only conventional special operations capabilities to deal with sudden attacks and disturbances, but also counter-terrorism capabilities similar to NSOF, including hostage rescue. Going forward, the command is expected to be operated effectively as a function-based joint unit.

The deteriorating security situation in the Sulu Archipelago in the Philippines was a factor in Malaysia enhancing its capabilities to counter insurgencies and terrorism. There is a perceived growing risk that Sabah on the island of Borneo on the border with the Philippines will become an outpost or a transit point for terrorist organizations. Kidnappings attributed to ASG have taken place in the eastern coast of Sabah in succession in September and December 2018 and in June 2019. In response to this situation, at a National Security Council meeting held in May 2019, Defence Minister Mohamad Sabu stressed the importance of the role of the Eastern Sabah Security Command (ESSCom), which has jurisdiction over the security of Sabah's eastern coast, and proposed the strengthening of its capabilities. In addition, Chief Minister of Sabah Mohd Shafie Apdal requested the reinforcement of the military's presence by moving the Lok Kawi Army Camp located in the vicinity of Kota Kinabalu, Sabah to the eastern coast.[79]

On the other hand, the Malaysian economy actively welcomes foreign capital. Many foreign nationals travel to and out of Malaysia, including people from Arab countries, and the country has well developed infrastructure. There is thus strong likelihood that international terrorist organizations will establish logistics bases in Malaysia. For this reason, its security department continued to search proactively for terrorists. In February 2019, the Special Branch Counter-Terrorism Division (SB-CTD) announced that it detained nine terrorist suspects, including six Egyptians and one Tunisian, in the suburbs of Kuala Lumpur and Sarawak. According to reports, in March, 12 Filipino and Malaysian suspects believed to be members of ASG and the Maute Group were detained, and in September, 16 ISIL sympathizers, primarily Indonesians, who were thought to have been expanding their organization in Malaysia were detained. Such stern crackdowns have been effective; no large-scale terrorist attacks have occurred in Malaysia. However, Ayob Khan, principal assistant director of SB-CTD, states that this does not mean international terrorist organizations have diminished in strength, and warns that the risk of terrorist attacks is still high in the region.

Furthermore, ISIL continues to actively recruit members in Malaysia, even after the annihilation of ISIL forces in Syria in 2019. Recruitment methods have shifted from human solicitation to remote methods via dark web and other tools, and women and young people are among those who are targeted. As organizational structures have also transformed from groups comprised of many fighters to lone wolf-type groups consisting of one or few people who engage in radical activities voluntarily, surveillance and crackdowns by counter-terrorism units have become increasingly challenging.

(3) Indonesia: Globalized Terrorist Networks and Expanded Role of the National Armed Forces

The Indonesian National Armed Forces (TNI) also reorganized the command of its special forces that deal with terrorist attacks and insurgencies. In July 2019, air chief marshal Hadi Tjahjanto, TNI Commander, announced the establishment of the Special Operations Command (KOOPSUS). It is a unified command of the counter-terrorism special forces of the three military services, namely: the 81 Special Detachment (Gultor), which is the anti-terrorism unit of the Army Special Forces Command (KOPASSUS); the Jalamangkara Detachment (Denjaka) of the Navy's Marine Corps; and the Bravo 90 Detachment (Denbravo) of the Air Force's Special Forces Corps (Korpaskhas). KOOPSUS is to undertake specialized responses to terrorist incidents and insurgencies, including overseas missions. In other words, unlike the Philippines and Malaysia, KOOPSUS is not comprised of all special forces of the three military services but is a headquarters that commands only their counter-terrorism units in an integrated manner. As of the end of 2019, the Defence Ministry is constructing facilities for and strengthening the capabilities of KOOPSUS and the Joint Defence Area Command (KOGABWILHAN) launched in September 2019. In an interview, TNI Commander Hadi explained that KOOPSUS consists of approximately 500 personnel, around 400 of which will provide supports and around 100 of which will combat terrorist acts directly. He emphasized that for direct acts against terrorist organizations, the TNI will coordinate with the National Police and the National Counter Terrorism Agency (BNPT), and that KOOPSUS will be deployed only when necessary. There is a reason for stressing this: in the past, the TNI and its special force have conducted a counter-insurgency operation that led to human rights abuses. Some people expressed lingering concerns over the

TNI's resumption of domestic security duties, and the government needed to dispel such concerns. In fact, Presidential Chief of Staff Moeldoko had proposed the establishment of a joint command for special operations in 2015 when he was TNI Commander. However, a series of terrorist attacks occurred in 2018 (see *East Asian Strategic Review 2019*, Chapter 4, Section 3), and the proposal was reportedly not considered until the anti-terrorism law was revised. That KOOPSUS was structured to command not all special forces but only forces specializing in counter-terrorism was thought to be appropriate for obtaining the understanding of the people and the international community. On the other hand, coinciding with the TNI's expanding role in counter-terrorism, international cooperation programs have been under way for building up the capacity of Indonesia's special forces. Since 1998, the United States had declined to carry out exchanges with Indonesia's special forces due to human rights concerns, but in May 2019, sought to improve the relations. In 2020, KOPASSUS, including the 81 Gultor, and the US special forces are scheduled to conduct joint exercises related to human rights protection and emergency medical response.

In a country like Indonesia that stretches across a vast territory, it is rational to make use of the capabilities of the TNI and its counter-terrorism units for maintaining security in the face of the increasing risk of terrorist attacks. Law enforcement units, such as the special detachment of the National Police counter-terror unit (Densus 88), have taken proper responses to terrorism in urban areas. In rural areas, however, especially in jungles and mountainous areas, the Mobile Brigade Corps of the police alone cannot deal with hidden terrorist organizations and separatists. The TNI, having better emergency deployment and reinforcement capabilities, was in fact frequently requested to assist search activities and security operations in outer island areas, such as Central Sulawesi and Papua.

It has come to light that international terrorist organizations have penetrated across Southeast Asia, including Indonesia, and are developing transnational networks. In July 2019, security authorities announced findings from their investigation of a suspect detained in West Java by Densus 88. The suspect, who was plotting terrorist attacks on Independence Day, was a member of Jamaah Ansharut Daulah (JAD), an Indonesian terrorist organization influenced by ISIL. He also had links to a network of violent extremist organizations in the Philippines and was plotting to make contact with a sleeper cell of former ISIL fighters hiding in Afghanistan. In addition, investigation by intelligence has revealed that JAD's operation funds were wired from five countries by 12 people suspected to have links with ISIL. This has confirmed once again that a personnel and financing network is being formed globally among terrorist organizations. Former ISIL fighters in Afghanistan are believed to be the ones primarily behind the creation of this network, which likely supported the suspects of many recent terrorist attacks in Indonesia. The Indonesian perpetrators of the terrorist attack at the Catholic cathedral on Jolo island in the Philippines are thought to have received financial assistance from the JAD suspect.

Figure 4.1. Security situation in the Southeast Asian island region

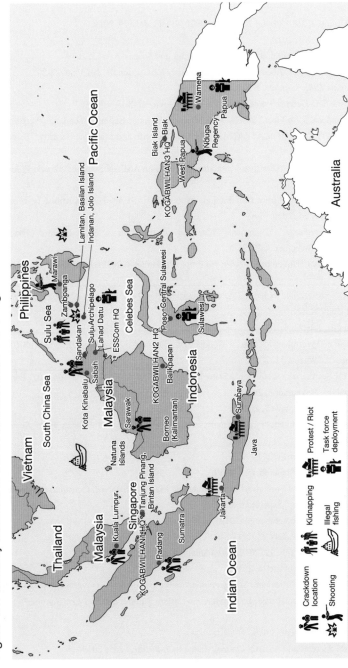

Note: ESSCom HQ (Eastern Sabah Security Command HQ), KOGABWILHAN1 HQ (Joint Defence Area Command 1 HQ), KOGABWILHAN2 HQ (Joint Defence Area Command 2 HQ), and KOGABWILHAN3 HQ (Joint Defence Area Command 3 HQ).

Source: Compiled by the author based on media reports, including *Philippine Daily Inquirer*, *Kompas*, *Benar News*, and *New Straits Times*.

NOTES

1)   CNBC, July 2, 2019; *Japan Times*, July 3, 2019; UPI, July 19, 2019.

2)   Rappler, March 1, 2019.

3)   Rappler, April 1, 2019 and April 11, 2019; *Stars and Stripes*, April 1, 2019.

4)   US Department of Defense, *Indo-Pacific Strategy Report*, June 1, 2019, pp. 28-29.

5)   *Philippine Daily Inquirer*, July 8, 2019.

6)   Maritime Self-Defense Force, "Indo-Pacific Deployment 2019 (IPD19)."

7)   Commander US 7th Fleet, "ASEAN-US Maritime Exercise Begins in Thailand," September 1, 2019; AMTI CSIS, "The ASEAN-US Maritime Exercise and Maritime Security," September 11, 2019.

8)   ASEAN Secretariat, "Chairman's Statement of the 34th ASEAN Summit," Bangkok, June 23, 2019.

9)   ASEAN Secretariat, "Joint Communique of the 52nd ASEAN Foreign Ministers' Meeting," Bangkok, July 31, 2019.

10)   ASEAN Secretariat, "Chairman's Statement of the 35th ASEAN Summit," Bangkok/ Nonthaburi, November 3, 2019.

11)   *Nikkei Shimbun*, November 3, 2019; Jiji Press, November 4, 2019; *Asahi Shimbun*, November 5, 2019.

12)   ASEAN Secretariat, "Chairman's Statement of the 14th East Asia Summit," Bangkok/ Nonthaburi, November 4, 2019.

13)   Xinhuanet, July 31, 2019.

14)   Philippine Government, "Code of Conduct Issue Raised by President Duterte with Chinese Premier Li," August 31, 2019.

15)   ASEAN Secretariat, "Chairman's Statement of the 22nd ASEAN-China Summit," Bangkok/ Nonthaburi, November 3, 2019.

16)   *Nikkei Shimbun*, August 7, 2019.

17)   Philippine Government, "Palace Reports President Duterte's Fruitful China Visit," September 1, 2019.

18)   Rappler, September 11, 2019.

19)   ABS-CBN News, September 12, 2019.

20)   Chinese Ministry of Foreign Affairs, "China and Malaysia Establish Consultation Mechanism on Maritime Issues," September 12, 2019.

21)   *Nikkei Shimbun*, September 24, 2019.

22)   *Wall Street Journal*, July 22, 2019.

23)   Voice of America, July 22, 2019; *Asahi Shimbun*, August 2, 2019.

24)   VOA Cambodia, August 26, 2019.

25)   The White House, "President Trump Announces the United States Government Mission to the United States-Association of Southeast Asian Nations Summit and East Asia Summit," October 29, 2019.

26)   Jiji Press, November 3, 2019.

27)   ASEAN Secretariat, "ASEAN Outlook on the Indo-Pacific," June 2019.

28) "Chairman's Statement of the 34th ASEAN Summit."

29) *Nikkei Shimbun*, July 17, 2019.

30) Kawanaka Takeshi, "Josho Minshushugi no Kotai: Hattentojokoku ni okeru Seiji Kiki" [Introduction Setbacks in Democratization: Political Crisis in Developing Countries], in Kawanaka Takeshi, ed., *Kotai suru Minshushugi Kyoka sareru Kenishugi* [Democratization Suffers Setbacks, Authoritarianism Strengthens], Minerva Shobo, 2018, p. 10.

31) Shigetomi Shinichi, "Dai 2 Sho Seiji Sanka no Kakudai to Minshushugi no Hokai: Tai ni okeru Minshuka Undo no Kiketsu" [Chapter 2 Increase in Political Participation and Collapse of Democracy: Consequence of the Thai Democratization Movement], in Kawanaka Takeshi, ed., *Kotai suru Minshushugi Kyoka sareru Kenishugi*, p. 67.

32) Manabe Yuko, "Tai Gunsei Shuen no Sosenkyo?" [Does the General Election End Thai Military Rule?], *NIDS Commentary*, No. 96, March 15, 2019.

33) *Bangkok Post*, February 9, 2019.

34) *Manager Online*, March 24, 2019.

35) Prajak Kongkirati, "Overview: Political Earthquakes," *Contemporary Southeast Asia*, Vol. 41 (2), August 2019, p. 164.

36) More information in Prajak Kongkirati, "Overview: Political Earthquakes," p. 165.

37) *iLaw*, May 23, 2019 (https://ilaw.or.th/node/5248).

38) Tamada Yoshifumi, "4 bun no 1 Minshushugi: Dai 2 ji Purayutto Seiken no Hassoku" [A Quarter Democracy: The Inauguration of the Second Prayut Administration], *Taikoku Joho* [Thai Information], Vol. 53, No. 4, July 2019, p. 4.

39) *Bangkok Post*, December 14, 2019.

40) Paul Chambers, "Scrutinising Thailand's 2019 Annual Military Reshuffle," *New Mandala*, September 25, 2019.

41) Paul Chambers, "What If Thailand's Junta Can't Control the Military?" *New Mandala*, March 14, 2019.

42) Paul Chambers, "Scrutinising Thailand's 2019 Annual Military Reshuffle."

43) Tamada Yoshifumi, "Gun Jinji Ido ga Utsushidasu Seigunkankei no Magarikado" [A Turning Point in Government-Military Relations as Seen from Changes in Military Personnel], *Taikoku Joho* [Thai Information], Vol. 53, No. 5, September 2019, p. 31.

44) *Matichon Sutsapda*, October 6, 2019.

45) Tamada Yoshifumi, "Dai 3 Sho Tai no Kudeta: Dokisei kara 'Tobu no Tora' e" [Chapter 3 Coup d'État in Thailand: From Classmates to "Eastern Tigers"], in Sakai Keiko, ed., *Tojokuku ni okeru Gun Seiji Kenryoku Shiminshakai: 21 Seiki no "Atarashi" Seigun Kankei* [Military, Political Power, and Civil Society in Developing Countries: "New" Government-Military Relations in the 21st Century], Koyo Shobo, 2016, p. 68.

46) *Phraratchabanyat Rabiap Borihaan Ratchakaan Nai Phraong Pho.So. 2560* (Published in Government Gazette May 1, 2017).

47) Royal Security Command website.

48) *Prakat Samnak Nayokrathamontri*, Ratchakitcha lem 136 Tonpiset 100 ngo (Published in Government Gazette April 23, 2019).

49) BBC News Thai, September 20, 2019.

50) *Prakat Samnak Nayokrathamontri*, Ratchakitcha lem 136 Tonpiset 100 kai (Published in Government Gazette October 21, 2019).

51) *Thai Post*, September 4, 2019.

52) Ibid.

53) Ibid.

54) *Nikkei Asian Review*, July 2, 2019.

55) Ibid.

56) *Nation*, August 30, 2019.

57) *Bangkok Post*, June 17, 2019.

58) *Jakarta Globe*, July 19, 2019.

59) *Tempo*, June 3, 2019.

60) *Tempo* (English edition), June 6, 2019.

61) CNN Indonesia, July 24, 2019.

62) *Jakarta Post*, August 22, 2019.

63) *Tempo* (English edition), September 25, 2019.

64) Research and Action for Peace, Project Ploughshares.

65) Deep South Watch Database.

66) *Organic Law for the Bangsamoro Autonomous Region in Muslim Mindanao*, Article 2, Section 1, Republic Act No. 11054.

67) Rappler, February 27, 2019.

68) Philippine New Agency, December 3, 2019.

69) Aljazeera, August 1, 2018.

70) *Philippine Star*, July 25, 2016.

71) *Minda News*, September 10, 2019.

72) *Benar News*, July 17, 2019.

73) *Benar News*, December 2, 2019.

74) *Benar News*, December 3, 2019.

75) *Bangkok Post*, August 3, 2019.

76) Philippine News Agency, April 8, 2018.

77) PIA, "Army Activates Brigade Combat Team vs Terrorism, Insurgency," December 18, 2018.

78) PNA, July 11, 2019.

79) BERNAMA, August 7, 2019.

Chapter 5

Russia

Termination of the Intermediate-Range Nuclear Forces Treaty from the Perspective of the Putin Administration

HYODO Shinji (Lead author, Section 2)
HASEGAWA Takeyuki (Section 1)
SAKAGUCHI Yoshiaki (Section 3)
SAWADA Hiroto (Column)

President Vladimir Putin has effectively occupied the position of supreme leader of Russia since 2000, including the time when he was prime minister. He has been under pressure to push forward social security reforms and enact strict fiscal discipline from a long-term perspective, while at the same time he is required to manage his administration carefully so as not to turn his own administration into a lame duck or provoke the destabilization of federal-regional relations. Under the strong leadership of President Putin, the Security Council (equivalent to the NSC in other countries) is playing a core role in the formulation and implementation of policies in the national security domain, including relations with Japan.

After the termination of the Intermediate-Range Nuclear Forces (INF) Treaty on August 2, 2019, the United States and Russia both officially commenced development of intermediate-range missiles, raising the possibility of a missile arms race unfolding in East Asia. There is inherent potential for fundamental changes to occur in international relations in Northeast Asia, including US-Russia relations, China-Russia relations, and Japan-Russia relations, and there is risk that the strategic environment in East Asia will be significantly impacted. Going forward, there is a pressing need to develop scenarios for Russia's deployment of intermediate-range missiles in the Russian Far East within range of Japan.

On July 23, 2019, the militaries of China and Russia carried out a joint air patrol from the East China Sea to the Sea of Japan, the first such patrol in the history of military cooperation between the two countries. Because the formation flew through airspace that had been established as the air defense identification zone of Japan and the Republic of Korea (ROK), a situation arose in which responses to airspace incursions and other measures were taken. Furthermore, in September, the large-scale exercise Tsentr-2019 (Center-2019) led by Russia and centered on the Central Military District was conducted in the form of a multilateral exercise in which members of the Collective Security Treaty Organization (CSTO) and the Shanghai Cooperation Organisation (SCO) also participated.

The "hybrid warfare" that has been actively discussed in recent years as a new form of warfare used by Russia, the "matter of degree" to which unconventional means are used, is easy to execute in some former republics of the Soviet Union due to the vulnerability of their social infrastructure. Furthermore, the dissemination of information through the mass media and the Internet is possible at an extremely small cost.

1. Issues surrounding the Leadership of President Putin and Political Stability

(1) Careful Management of Internal Affairs Required of the Putin Administration

President Vladimir Putin has effectively occupied the position of supreme leader of Russia since 2000. Including his period as prime minister, he will have ruled the Russian Federation for nearly a quarter-century by the expiration of his term in 2024. The Putin administration is characterized by political stability against the backdrop of presidential leadership and stable president-parliament relations. On the other hand, the Russian people are strongly dissatisfied with the issues of corruption, media regulation, and the economic situation. Public backlash against the administration strengthened in 2019, for example, with acts of solidarity by major media outlets in response to suspected unlawful arrests of journalists and protest demonstrations pertaining to the Moscow City Duma elections. Although Russia's political regime is based on "competitive authoritarianism," i.e., elections are regularly implemented as a formal institution, problems with fair competition are frequently reported in those elections. Based on these trends, there is a possibility that Russia's political regime will change greatly as 2024 approaches.

According to a major Russian public opinion polling agency, President Putin's approval rating had hovered in the 80% range after the annexation of Crimea in March 2014. However, triggered by the problem of pension reforms, his approval rating declined to 70% in August 2018 and 64% in March 2019, and subsequently has remained roughly in the 65% to 70% range. While this margin of decline is not expected to have a significant impact on the management of the administration immediately, it is at about the same level as during the period when the anti-Putin protests intensified from 2011 to 2012.

The basic policy direction of the current administration was indicated in the May 2018 presidential decree "On National Goals and Strategic Objectives of the Russian Federation through to 2024." The February 2019 Presidential Address to the Federal Assembly also adhered to the policy direction set out in this presidential decree, and focused on social and economic issues, including the development of the digital economy.[1] According to the three-year federal budget law for 2020–2022 approved in December 2019, the national defense budget for the single fiscal year of 2020 was 3.1 trillion rubles (approximately 4% less than in the previous year), or 2.4% of GDP.[2] In the 2021 and 2022 planned budgets as well, national defense expenditure is expected to be maintained in the 2% to 3% range with respect to GDP, and while this budget amount will remain stable, the trend toward relative restraint—as compared with immediately after the Ukraine crisis—continues.[3] On the other hand, expenditures pertaining to social policies, innovation, and the economic modernization program are growing. The administration and ruling party are expected to tackle reforms of the social security system and economic structure while paying close attention to public opinion trends as the elections for the State Duma (lower house) planned for the second half of 2021 approach.

On June 6, 2019, investigative journalist Ivan Golunov of the independent news site *Meduza* was arrested on the suspicion of attempted drug-selling. Early in the morning of the following day, June 7, a solitary picket was held in protest in front of the building of the Ministry of Internal Affairs (MIA) General Administration for the City of Moscow.[4] Moreover, on June 10, the major newspapers *Vedomosti*, *Kommersant*, and *RBK* published a joint statement on the front page of their morning editions. They pointed out the illegality of the inquiry and called for transparency in the investigation process.[5] Golunov had taken a critical attitude toward the administration in his investigative reporting, zeroing in on corruption problems related to government procurement and the actual situation regarding the enormous presidential residence on the lakefront of Lake Valdayskoye, etc.[6] The following day, June 11, as a result of the investigation, Minister of Internal Affairs Vladimir Kolokoltsev made the determination that the journalist would not be subjected to a criminal prosecution. Furthermore, the Minister of Internal Affairs petitioned President Putin to dismiss the Head of the Department for the Control of Drug Trafficking of the MIA General Administration for the City of Moscow and the Head of the Department of Internal Affairs for the Western Administrative District of the MIA General Administration for the City of Moscow,[7] and those dismissals were ordered in a presidential decree dated June 13.[8] The core of the Putin administration had aimed to put the matter to rest with a speedy response. However, as symbolized by the act of solidarity by the three major newspapers, a strong sense of distrust of the security agencies, in particular MIA, remained. In these recent incidents, the shared perceptions of media organizations and journalists with respect to the freedom of speech and the right to know guaranteed by the current Constitution of the Russian Federation were widely presented inside and outside Russia.[9] Going forward, the movement seeking to ensure accountability for the full range of the government's activities is likely to become even stronger.

During the Moscow City Duma elections, in mid-July 2019, notifications of 57 of the 233 people who intended to run for office were not accepted, with reasons given such as errors in the signatures necessary for candidate registration.[10] As a result, many of the independent candidates close to opposition leader Alexei Navalny were unable to run in the elections. For this reason, large-scale protest movements calling for fair elections were staged from late July to August, primarily in Moscow. MIA and the National Guard of the Russian Federation, which were in charge of regulating and controlling protests, responded severely to unauthorized protest movements, and on both July 27 and August 3, more than 1,000 people were temporarily taken into custody.[11] The protest movement on August 10, implemented with the permission of the authorities, was the largest since 2011; according to "OVD-Info," there were about 60,000 participants, 256 of whom were taken into custody.[12] In these series of protests, the activities of law enforcement agencies were strongly questioned once again; for example, video footage of riot police punching a female protester while taking her into custody spread on social networking services, and MIA launched an investigation.[13] Various problems related to administrative procedures and the guarantee of rights under the Constitution pertaining to public assembly and protest marches will undoubtably continue to be a focus in contemporary Russian politics.

Nationwide local elections, during which the governors and provincial assembly members of the federal subjects of Russia such as republics and oblasts are elected, were held on September 8, 2019. In some regions, the ruling party was forced into a tough battle, and advances by the opposition were seen. In the Moscow City Duma election (a total of 45 seats), the ruling party United Russia saw its seats drop from 38 held before the election to 25. On the other hand, the main opposition party, the Communist Party of the Russian Federation, increased its seats from 5 to 13, becoming the second largest party in the Duma. Furthermore, two left wing parties that had held no seats before the election, A Just Russia and the Russian United Democratic Party "Yabloko," attained third party status.[14] Opposition parties prevented from running in the nationwide local elections deployed a "smart vote strategy" to stop the ruling party forces from winning, and it is thought that this produced results to some extent, particularly in Moscow. Additionally, in the Khabarovsk City Duma elections in the Far East region, the Liberal Democratic Party of Russia (LDPR), a far-right political party led by Vladimir Zhirinovsky, won 34 of the 35 seats. In Komsomolsk-na-Amure city, the LDPR captured 24 of 25 seats.[15] The weakening of the vote-gathering machine in local areas, particularly for the ruling party United Russia, is being observed.

The trends in internal affairs surrounding the 2019 elections recall the large-scale protests about "electoral legitimacy" that took place at the time of the 2011 State Duma (lower house) elections and the 2012 presidential election. On the other hand, in the most recent 2016 lower house elections and 2018 presidential election, protest movements did not gain much momentum against the backdrop of rising approval ratings for the administration as a result of the Ukraine crisis and strengthened legal regulations and crackdowns on protest movements. The opposition, led by Navalny, called for a boycott of the elections and focused their efforts on election monitoring.[16] In the leadup to the next election cycle, including the elections of the lower house in 2021 and the presidential election in 2024, the Putin administration is under pressure to push forward social security reforms and enact strict fiscal discipline from a long-term perspective. On the other hand, President Putin is required to govern cautiously to ensure that his administration does not become a lame duck or provoke the destabilization of federal-regional relations.

In addition, it is necessary to pay attention to the discussions around constitutional reform, including amendments to the presidential term of office. At his annual end-of-year press conference held on December 19, 2019, President Putin mentioned an amendment to Article 81 of the Constitution, which stipulates the presidential term of office. Under the current system, one and the same person may not be elected President of the Russian Federation for more than two terms in a row. President Putin stated that it was possible to delete the phrase "in a row."[17] If this were realized, a prohibition on three terms for the president would be made clear. The issue of the presidential term is likely to have a large impact on the discussions around the post-Putin administration. Furthermore, discussions by Vyacheslav Volodin, Chairman of the State Duma, about constitutional amendments to expand parliamentary power are related to partial restrictions on the prime minister's authority regarding cabinet formation and the presidential authority to form federal executive organs.[18] In the leadup to the next election cycle, discussions concerning the form of the political system in Russia are expected to become even more vigorous.

(2) Policy Mechanisms in the National Security Domain and the Role of the Security Council

Under the strong leadership of President Putin, the Presidential Administration and the Security Council play a core role in the formulation and implementation of policies in the national security domain.[19] In July 2019, it was reported that the National Security Strategy of the Russian Federation would be revised in 2020.[20] This document is the most important national strategy document that presents Russia's perception of the strategic environment and stipulates the basic direction of all the major policies, from foreign policy and military security policy to the social and economic policy domains. It is revised approximately every six years based on the law on strategic planning. The current National Security Strategy was revised on December 31, 2015.[21] The Security Council, which is chaired by the president, is leading this revision work. Secretary of the Security Council Nikolai Patrushev, the top official in the Apparat of the Security Council and Putin's closest advisor, has substantial command of the revision work.

Secretary Patrushev used to work for the Komitet Gosudarstvennoy Bezopasnosti (KGB) in the Soviet era, and in 1998 succeeded Putin to serve as Deputy Chief of Staff of the Presidential Administration – Head of the Presidential Control Directorate and First Deputy Director of the FSB. Patrushev was the person responsible for the espionage and security section of the Putin administration as the Director of the FSB for approximately nine years until 2008.[22] In May 2008, a tandem administration was launched when Putin and Dmitry Medvedev swapped the posts of president and prime minister. At that time, Patrushev was appointed Secretary of the Security Council, and has since been consistently at the center of power in the Kremlin. His eldest son Dmitry Patrushev has joined the Putin administration as the Minister of Agriculture. He received training at the State University of Management, the Diplomatic Academy of the Ministry of Foreign Affairs and the FSB Academy, and is not necessarily a pure expert in agricultural policy.[23] Secretary Patrushev's second son, Andrey Patrushev, is an expert in energy who graduated from the National

University of Oil and Gas, and has also received training at the FSB Academy and the Diplomatic Academy of the Ministry of Foreign Affairs. After serving as an executive of Gazprom Neft, which is responsible for energy development in the Arctic continental shelf, he now heads the independent noncommercial organization center "Arctic Initiative."[24] The influence of Siloviki (people who used to work for the military or security agencies) remains strong in important policies related to national security, including energy development in the Arctic Circle.

On July 17, 2019, Secretary Patrushev called a meeting of the Interdepartmental Commission of the Security Council on Strategic Planning (the "Strategic Commission"). In this meeting, the importance of guaranteeing mutual connectivity between the National Security Strategy and the Russian Federation's social and economic development strategy was emphasized.[25] The Secretary of the Security Council serves as the Chair, the Deputy Secretary of the Security Council as the Vice-Chair, and the Deputy Director of the FSB as the Chief of the Secretariat in the Strategic Commission, which is comprised of the deputy director-generals of the Presidential Administration, the vice-ministers from each ministry and the Deputy Presidential Plenipotentiary Envoy to Federal District, etc. National policies at the federal level are comprehensively coordinated in the Strategic Commission before being decided in a Security Council meeting chaired by the president.

In addition to planning and deciding the national security policies, two important functions have been given to the Security Council. They are regional meetings and NSC diplomacy by the Secretary of the Security Council. In Russia, which has been faced with latent centrifugal tendencies in the federal-regional relations, the core of the administration performs direct supervision of the implementation of important policies through regional meetings. In July 2019, Yury Trutnev, Deputy Prime Minister – Presidential Plenipotentiary Envoy to the Far Eastern Federal District, Alexander

Russian Security Council Secretary Patrushev (left) and FSB Director Bortnikov (right) (Sputnik/Kyodo News Images)

Kozlov, Minister for the Development of the Russian Far East and Arctic, and other top government officials and local governors attended a regional meeting held in Amur oblast concerning urgent issues pertaining to national security in the Far East and Zabaykalsky Krai. In the meeting, various issues related to the military-industrial complex of the Far East region and counterterrorism measures were discussed. In conjunction with this, Secretary Patrushev visited the Vostochny Cosmodrome with Deputy Prime Minister Yury Borisov (in charge of national defense industries), Director General of Roscosmos Dmitry Rogozin, and other officials, and observed the launch of the Soyuz-2-1b carrying the weather satellite Meteor-M and other payloads.[26]

Furthermore, Secretary Patrushev of the Security Council frequently implemented NSC diplomacy to discuss important issues related to national security with his counterparts in other countries. When Secretary Patrushev visited Israel in June 2019, he met with John Bolton, Assistant to the President for National Security Affairs of the United States, to discuss strategic stability, arms control, the Venezuela problem, among other matters.[27] In September, in Moscow, he discussed security issues in Europe and Russian-French cooperation in the field of information security with Claire Landais, the French Secretary General for Defence and National Security.[28] In addition, on April 25, 2019, when the Russia-North Korea Summit Meeting was held in Vladivostok, Secretary Patrushev visited Seoul and met with Chung Eui-yong, Director of the National Security Office, and President Moon Jae-in.[29] On key policy issues, Secretary Patrushev continues to be entrusted to serve as President Putin's closest advisor.

Channels of dialogue are being built between the Cabinet Secretariat and the Prime Minister's Office of Japan and the Kremlin core; for example, a memorandum of cooperation was concluded between Japan's National Security Secretariat and the Russian Security Council Apparat in September 2017.[30] The establishment of channels with the Kremlin core started with the Memorandum between the Ministry of Foreign Affairs of Japan and the Russian Security Council Apparat concluded in October 2012 under the Noda Yoshihiko administration. Under the Abe Shinzo administration inaugurated in December 2012, Yachi Shotaro, Secretary General of the National Security Secretariat, and Secretary Patrushev had held eight rounds of talks by the end of 2018.[31]

In September 2019, talks were held in Tokyo with Kitamura Shigeru, the newly-appointed head of the National Security Secretariat, concerning Japan-

Russia relations and bilateral security policies and other matters, and a courtesy call was paid to Prime Minister Abe.[32] Assistant to the Secretary of the Security Council Aleksandr Venediktov, who frequently participates in talks between Japan and Russia, stated in an interview article in December 2018 that "in negotiations with our partner of Japan on the line of the Security Council, themes pertaining to Japan-US military cooperation are constantly at the center of interest,"[33] and revealed that they were discussing defense and military security issues, in particular the impact of the security treaty between Japan and the United States on Japan-Russia relations. Venediktov, who was promoted from an aide to a deputy secretary in February 2019, has a long history of working in the Apparat of the Security Council,[34] and plays a core role in the Apparat as he frequently accompanies Patrushev on his trips abroad and handles long interviews with the mass media regarding global security issues, including the INF Treaty issue.[35] The Security Council of Russia plays a large role in policies toward Japan as well, and Deputy Secretary Venediktov is seen as a key player in this context.

It can be concluded that the Presidential Administration is also a crucial state institution for implementing Kremlin-led foreign policies, in particular the delicate policies. The Presidential Directorate for Social and Economic Cooperation with the Commonwealth of Independent States Member Countries, the Republic of Abkhazia, and the Republic of South Ossetia was reorganized into the Presidential Directorate for Cross-Border Cooperation in October 2018. The matter under its jurisdiction is deemed to be that it "supports the activities of the President on cross-border cooperation with the Republic of Abkhazia, the Republic of South Ossetia and Ukraine, as well as with other neighboring states at the instruction of the President."[36] The Directorate is believed to be mainly in charge of relations with so-called unrecognized states. Vladislav Surkov, a presidential aide, commands the Directorate, and there is speculation that a division for cooperation with Ukraine has been established inside the Directorate.[37]

In April 2019, a personnel change for the Presidential Directorate for Cross-Border Cooperation was announced, and Alexei Filatov was newly appointed the head of the Directorate. Oleg Govorun, the previous head of the Directorate, was familiar with the regional economies and policies for local revitalization, having served in such roles as Chief of the Presidential Domestic Policy Directorate in the Presidential Administration, Presidential

Plenipotentiary Envoy to the Central Federal District, and Minister of Regional Development. His successor Filatov, however, reportedly commanded Russia-South Ossetia relations in the Directorate, was appointed Deputy-Head from 2018, and served as the "manager" of Donetsk and Luhansk, which have declared separation and independence from Ukraine.[38] While the situation in eastern Ukraine remains unstable, in particular with the simplification of procedures to grant Russian nationality to residents of the region, policies toward Ukraine and the unrecognized states problem are positioned as matters for the exclusive jurisdiction of the Kremlin.[39]

2. The Impact of INF Treaty Termination on Russian Diplomacy

(1) The Arms Race between the United States and Russia in Asia

On October 20, 2018, President Donald Trump declared that the United States would withdraw from the INF Treaty for the reason that Russia was in breach of the treaty. Immediately afterwards, on October 23, Assistant to the President Bolton visited Moscow on short notice and informed President Putin of the United States' intention to withdraw from the treaty. In an interview with a Russian newspaper, Assistant Bolton stated, "If Russia were to dismantle all of its equipment in violation of the treaty and China did the same, that that would be a different circumstance. I think there's zero chance of that happening."[40] Because Russia did not respond to this, the United States issued an ultimatum on December 5 to the effect that it would proceed to abrogate the treaty if Russia did not correct its violations within 60 days. The United States then officially notified Russia of its suspension of the treaty on February 1, 2019, and on March 4, President Putin also signed a presidential decree suspending observance of the treaty on the grounds that the United States was in breach of the treaty.[41] Subsequently, neither the United States nor Russia softened their stance, refusing to participate in discussions to suspend the termination unless the other party corrected their breaches of the treaty. As a result, the treaty was terminated on August 2, half a year after the United States notified Russia of its official withdrawal.

One of the reasons for the United States' withdrawal from the INF Treaty was Russia's development and deployment of new models of intermediate-range missiles in breach of the treaty. In 2014, the then Obama administration mentioned for the first time that Russia had breached the treaty when it carried out test launches of new models of missiles; subsequently, in 2018, the Trump administration revealed that those missiles were named "SSC-8" by the North Atlantic Treaty Organization (NATO) (the Russian name is "9M729"), that their flight range had extended to more than 3,000 km, and that they had been fully deployed inside Russia. According to what was revealed by then Assistant to the President Bolton, Russia commenced test launches in 2008 and had been in breach of the INF Treaty since 2013.[42]

In response to this criticism, on January 23, 2019, the government of Russia held a briefing for the foreign military attachés and press correspondents to whom it displayed the controversial 9M729 cruise missile and presented the rebuttal that the missile was a modernized version of the 9M728 cruise missile that comprises the Iskander missile system, but with an actual range of 480 km, so it does not breach the INF Treaty, which covers a range of 500 km or further.[43] On the other hand, Russia criticized the United States for breaching the INF Treaty based on Russia's understanding that the ground-based Aegis system (Aegis Ashore) that the United States had been deploying in Romania and Poland was capable of launching land-attack cruise missiles with a range of over 2,000 km. Likewise, it is for this reason that Russia has repeatedly expressed concerns about the Aegis Ashore, which Japan plans to introduce.

On August 2, when the INF Treaty was terminated, recently appointed US Secretary of Defense Mark Esper released a statement asserting that the withdrawal of the United States from the INF Treaty was the direct result of Russia's violations of the treaty over many years, and declared that beginning in 2017 the US Department of Defense (DOD) commenced research and development into ground-launched cruise and ballistic missiles within the scope of the INF Treaty, but due to its withdrawal from the treaty it would fully pursue the development of these ground-launched conventional missiles.[44] Moreover, on the following day, August 3, Secretary Esper declared his intention to swiftly deploy ground-based intermediate-range missiles in the Asia region, with an eye on China enhancing its nuclear forces. In response to this, President Putin issued a statement on August 5 denouncing the United States by saying it bore all of the responsibility for the termination of the treaty, and warning that if the United States resumed the development and deployment of intermediate-range missiles, Russia would have no option other than to engage in a full-scale effort to develop similar missiles.[45] Sergei Ryabkov, Deputy Minister of Foreign Affairs, who held a press conference on the same day, stated that "Russia will not deploy intermediate-range missiles in Europe or other regions unless the United States places armaments of the same class there," and called for self-restraint on the part of the United States not to initiate an arms race between the United States and Russia.

Nonetheless, on August 18, the US DOD launched a ground-launched cruise missile from a ground mobile launcher in California to a target more than 500 km away, making it clear that the United States had commenced development of intermediate-range missiles.[46] On the other hand, in Russia, an explosion accident occurred at a Russian military facility on August 8 after the INF Treaty termination, temporarily raising the radiation level and killing five employees. The media in Western countries speculated there had been an accident during testing of the nuclear-powered cruise missile Burevestnik, which President Putin had mentioned in his Presidential Address to the Federal Assembly in March 2018.

In the National Defense Strategy published by the US DOD in January 2018 and the Indo-Pacific Strategy Report it published in June 2019, Russia was positioned as a "strategic competitor" which is challenging the United States and its allies and undermining the international order. Subsequently, on September 18, in a meeting of the US Air Force, Secretary of Defense Esper stated that "Russia remains our greatest near-term security challenge" due to its invasion of Georgia, annexation of Crimea, sustained aggression in Ukraine, "hybrid warfare" against Europe, etc.,[47] and expressed the perception that the threat of Russia is more pressing than that of China, which "presents an even greater long-term challenge." If after termination of the INF Treaty the possibility increases of an arms race occurring between the United States and Russia over the development and deployment of intermediate-range missiles in the Asia region, the United States' perception of Russia as a threat is likely to grow further on the military front as well.

The *Ryukyu Shimpo* dated October 3 reported that, according to Russian Presidential Administration officials who spoke to a journalist from the newspaper, the United States had explained to Russia in Washington on August 26 that it intended to consult with Japan in order to deploy new models of missiles to Okinawa and other locations from the end of 2020 to 2021, that the missiles would be deployed to the four countries of Japan, Australia, the Philippines, and Vietnam, but excluded the ROK where denuclearization negotiations are proceeding, and that the measures were for the sole purpose of restraining China so it was not necessary for Russia to be concerned. Furthermore, the *Ryukyu Shimpo* dated October 19 reported that an official at the US DOD had told Tamaki Denny, Governor of Okinawa Prefecture, who was on a visit to the United States, that an announcement about where the missiles would be deployed could not be made at the current stage. In the form of a response to these media reports, in his four-hour-long, major annual press conference held on December 19, 2019, President Putin asked if there were any guarantees that the missiles would not be deployed to Japan, including the Northern Territories.[48] Vasily Kashin, senior research fellow of Higher School of Economics, a Russian military expert, has presented the outlook that the United States may deploy intermediate-range missiles in Guam and Japan, and because China already possesses many intermediate-range missiles, Russia will likely upgrade the Iskander missiles to deploy them to the Chukotka Peninsula in the Far East region facing the US state of Alaska.

Furthermore, the New Strategic Arms Reduction Treaty (New START), a nuclear arms reduction treaty between the United States and Russia that entered into force in February 2011, will expire in February 2021. Russia, which does not have the strength to engage in a nuclear arms race with the United States, repeatedly lobbied Washington to promptly commence negotiations to extend the deadline of the treaty; however, although it was agreed to commence diplomatic negotiations at the US-Russia Summit Meeting held during the G20 Osaka Summit on June 28, no concrete progress was seen in the US-Russia Foreign Ministers' Meeting held in Washington on December 10.

For the following reasons, the view that extending the deadline of the treaty will be difficult is strongly entrenched in Russia. Firstly, it is reported that when President Putin raised the problem of extending the treaty deadline in a telephone talk in January 2017 immediately after President Trump's inauguration, President Trump paused the call to ask his aides what the treaty was, and then replied that it was one of several bad deals concluded by the Obama administration. President Trump has no significant interest in the problem of arms control with Russia in the first place; moreover, he has a negative view of the policies of the previous Obama administration. Secondly, key people involved in arms control at the time of the negotiations for New START such as Rose Gottemoeller, United States Under Secretary of State, and Anatoly Antonov, Russian Deputy Minister of Foreign Affairs, are nowhere to be found; diplomatic channels between the United States and Russia are lacking due to staffing gaps at the US Department of State and the mutual expulsion of diplomats, etc. A five-year deadline extension is possible for New START, but there is little time left for the preparatory negotiations for an extension. Thirdly, as represented by Assistant to the President Bolton who contributed an opinion piece in 2011 titled "A Cold War Missile Treaty That's Doing Us Harm" to the *Wall Street Journal*, an influential US newspaper, there is the military notion that an arms reduction treaty under which only the United States and Russia are militarily constrained is not useful for responding to China's buildup of its nuclear forces. Fourthly, there are likely to be political considerations for the arms industry, one of the power bases of the Trump administration, which is attempting to expand the nuclear missile business.

Since the Ukraine crisis in 2014, Western countries have imposed economic sanctions on Russia, and this has structurally regulated the adversarial relationship between Western countries and Russia. Since the annexation of Crimea by Russia in 2014, US-Russia relations have continued to deteriorate throughout Russia's military intervention in Syria in 2015, the Russiagate problem in 2016, the attempted killing of a former Russian military intelligence agent in 2018, confrontation over the Venezuela situation in 2019, and more. If the arms control regime is lost and an arms race occurs, confrontation between the United States and Russia could escalate into military areas. Due to the Russiagate problem, US-Russia relations have become a matter of domestic politics in the United States, so it seems that a full-fledged improvement in relations is difficult for the time being.

(2) Impact on the Strategic Environment of East Asia

Concerning the inequality of the INF Treaty under which only the United States and Russia are regulated, it was in fact Russia that first raised this problem. In 2007, President Putin stated that the "INF Treaty no longer serves Russia's interests" and hinted at withdrawal from the treaty. He then cited as reasons his opposition to the deployment of the missile defense (MD) system in Europe by the United States and the fact that Russia's neighboring countries had deployed intermediate-range nuclear missiles. Subsequently, Russia proposed multilateralization of the treaty, but since there is no possibility of emerging nuclear powers such as China joining the treaty, Russia is thought to have commenced augmentation of the Iskander missiles in a manner contrary to the treaty. It is Russia, a continental state in Eurasia, that is enthusiastic about the development and deployment of ground-based intermediate-range missiles; moreover, it is reported that ground-launched missiles do not cost as much as sea- or air-launched missiles. Russia is also sensitive to the nuclear buildup of neighboring country China, with which it shares 4,300 km of international border. According to Russian military expert Aleksandr Khramchihin, more than 90% of China's missiles are capable of targeting Russia, and if the Dongfeng (DF) 26 (with a maximum range of 4,000 km) were launched from the Xinjiang Uyghur Autonomous Region, they could target nearly all of the territory of Russia except for Russia's Kaliningrad exclave.[49] Furthermore, in January 2017, China's *Global Times* reported that a new model of intercontinental ballistic missile (ICBM), the Dongfeng (DF) 41 (maximum range of 14,000 km), had been deployed to Heilongjiang Province near the Russian border. In a form of response to this, there was a series of media reports and discussions from among the media and military experts inside Russia declaring concern about China's nuclear buildup. In the current China-Russia strategic partnership, China's economic superiority has been established, but Russia's superiority is also being shaken in the military area, centered on its nuclear forces.

In September 2018, the military exercise Vostok-2018 (East-2018) was implemented in Eastern Siberia and the Far East region with the participation of approximately 300,000 troops. It was the first large-scale military exercise in 37 years, comparable to the Zapad-81 (West-81) exercise, which is reported to be the largest military exercise implemented by the Soviet Union in the Cold War period; moreover, 3,500 troops from the Chinese People's Liberation Army and the Mongolian military also participated. In this exercise, the Russian military carried out Iskander-M missile launch drills near the China-Russia border, and undertook moves that can be interpreted as being based on an awareness of China's nuclear forces. As stated earlier, the United States is criticizing these missiles for breaching the INF Treaty. Supposing missiles with a range of 2,000 km were deployed to the China-Russia border, northern China, including Beijing, and the Japanese archipelago, would also fall within their range. During the aforementioned major press conference held at the end of 2019, President

Putin repeatedly declared his sense of caution with respect to the United States, but clearly stated that he had no plan to form a military alliance with China.[50]

After INF Treaty termination, new discussions on how to deal with the emerging nuclear powers such as China also began for Russia, and from that perspective, the possibility that the confrontational phase of US-Russia relations could be alleviated cannot be excluded. Furthermore, the fact that Russia possesses intermediate-range nuclear forces with an eye on China's nuclear forces provides evidence for the existence of the "China factor" in the military policies of Russia, and there is also a possibility that this will cast a shadow over the political honeymoon between China and Russia to date. Moreover, if intermediate-range missiles appear in the Russian Far East in the future, it could have a direct impact on the security of Japan as well, as Japan would be within their range. Based on the above, there is a possibility that INF Treaty termination will lead to an arms race between the United States and Russia, and in addition, it has the potential to essentially change international relations in Northeast Asia, including US-Russia relations, China-Russia relations, and Japan-Russia relations, so in that sense there is a risk that it could have a large impact on the strategic environment of East Asia.

(3) Japan-Russia Relations from the Perspective of Security

Sharing a strong determination to resolve the issue themselves without leaving it to the next generation, at the Japan-Russia Summit Meeting in Singapore in November 2018, the two leaders agreed to accelerate negotiations for a peace treaty on the basis of the 1956 Joint Declaration, in order to resolve an issue that has remained for more than 70 years since the end of World War II, namely, resolving the territorial disputes to conclude a peace treaty. Moreover, at the Summit Meeting held in Buenos Aires during the following month of December, the two leaders agreed that the foreign ministers of the two countries would be responsible for the negotiations. At the Summit Meeting held on June 29, 2019, at the time of the Osaka G20 meeting, the two leaders welcomed the fact that the negotiations were being conducted energetically, and shared the view that they would continue to advance the negotiations. At their 27th Summit Meeting, which was held at the time of the Eastern Economic Forum in Vladivostok, the two leaders reaffirmed that they would work in a future-oriented manner, and reiterated instructions to their respective foreign ministers, who are responsible for negotiations, to advance joint work in order to find a mutually acceptable solution.[51]

Japan-Russia relations have made significant progress based on the deep relationship of trust between Prime Minister Abe and President Putin. Furthermore, we can conclude that in light of the strategic environment surrounding them, the significance of concluding a peace treaty to normalize Japan-Russia relations is shared by the two countries, although there are differences in objectives and degree.

Japan's National Security Strategy established in December 2013 states that "Under the increasingly severe security environment in East Asia, it is critical for Japan to advance cooperation with Russia in all areas, including security and energy, thereby enhancing bilateral relations as a whole, in order to ensure its security." Underlying Japan's attempt to strengthen its relations with Russia is the idea that concluding a peace treaty and normalizing relations with Russia is desirable in the context of the increasing severity of the strategic environment surrounding Japan, created by the Korean Peninsula, China, and other countries. In particular, this is the strategic idea of strengthening Japan-Russia relations so that Russia does not become a negative presence for the security of Japan, or at least of drawing Russia closer to Japan's side so that Russia does not become completely pro-China in its approach to Japan.

On the other side, the Foreign Policy Concept of the Russian Federation outlining the diplomatic strategy of Russia, which was adopted in November 2016, clearly states that Russia will "continue to build good-neighborly relations and promote mutually beneficial cooperation with Japan, including with a view to ensuring stability and security in Asia-Pacific," confirming Russia's stance of intending to place relative importance on Japan from the perspective of the security of the Asia-Pacific. Recently, the view that it is necessary for Russia to conclude a peace treaty with Japan to maintain geopolitical balance has been heard from Russian government officials as well. In a unipolar world solely dominated by the United States, Russia was fine with its stance of aiming to build a multipolar world by collaborating with China, but as Russia recognizes that a power shift from the United States to China will continue in the multipolar world that has arrived, the largest diplomatic issue for the Putin administration will be what position Russia will take between the two poles of the United States and China. In other words, the question is whether unconditional deployment of an "anti-US, pro-China policy" is desirable for Russia in the medium- to long-term.

Previously, discussions that mainly connected economic cooperation and territorial problems were mainstream. Economic cooperation is effective in bringing Russia to the negotiating table, but many observers have the view that in order to advance concrete discussions about returning the Northern Territories to Japan, it is necessary for both Japan and Russia to engage in head-on discussions of the two essential problems of historical perceptions and security. Russia is not backing away from its position that the first step of the negotiations is for Japan to recognize that the islands came under the sovereignty of Russia as a result of World War II; moreover, Russia is concerned about the possibility that the US military will deploy on the islands after they are handed over.

What value do the Northern Territories have for the security of Russia? Russia has placed military importance on the Sea of Okhotsk since the Cold War era as a nuclear launch site aimed at the United States, and as a sea area where Russia's nuclear-powered submarines equipped with nuclear weapons can navigate freely. Russia considers the Sea of Okhotsk to be an "internal sea" and "sanctuary of Russia" free of the military influence of foreign countries. Additionally, due to the creation of the Northern Sea Route, a new factor is being added, namely that the Sea of Okhotsk will become the route by which foreign ships from Asia head toward the Arctic Ocean. Therefore, in recent years, Russia has carried out military exercises repeatedly and aimed to strengthen its military presence through the modernization of its military power, etc., in order to maintain its own influence in the Arctic Ocean and the Sea

Figure 5.1. The Okhotsk Sea and surrounding areas

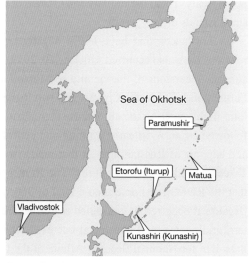

Source: Compiled by the author.

of Okhotsk. For example, it has established new military bases in the Chishima Islands on Matua Island and Paramushir Island, which are located on each side of the Northern Sea Route, in an attempt to militarily restrain foreign ships from entering the Sea of Okhotsk.

It is the Northern Territories and Chishima Islands, which Russia calls the Kuril Islands, that play the role of a fence separating the Sea of Okhotsk and the Pacific Ocean. In order to turn the Sea of Okhotsk into a "military fortress," it is necessary for the Russian military to strongly protect this fence. The Kunashiri Strait sandwiched between Etorofu (Iturup) Island and Kunashiri (Kunashir) Island is an important entranceway for the Russian Navy from the Sea of Okhotsk to the Pacific Ocean, and 3,500 members of the Russian military are stationed on both islands. The Military Doctrine outlining the military strategy of Russia states, with an eye on the territorial claims of Japan, that "territorial claims from foreign countries are a military risk for Russia," and over the last few years, Russia's moves toward military modernization have been notable, including the deployment of new models of surface-to-ship missiles to both islands and the construction of a new dual civilian-military airport on Etorofu (Iturup) Island. On the other hand, only a Border Guard Service has been deployed on Shikotan Island and the Habomai Islands, which the Japan-Soviet Union Joint Declaration concluded in 1956 clearly states are to be returned to Japan after conclusion of a peace treaty. Thus, the military importance of the two large islands and the two small islands differs greatly.

Circumstances that have had a negative impact on Japan-Russia security relations have also occurred. On June 20, 2019, Russian bombers made two short airspace incursions in the vicinity of Minamidaito island and Hachijo island.[52] Further, on July 23, two Chinese and two Russian bombers made their first ever joint flight, entering the air defense identification zones of Japan and the ROK, followed by an A-50 early warning and control aircraft engaged in the control and support of Russian aircraft that made two incursions into the airspace of Takeshima, Shimane Prefecture.[53] The ROK's Joint Chiefs of Staff announced that the ROK's Air Force fired a total of 360 warning shots in response to this. Because it occurred in a disputed region where both Japan and the ROK claim territorial rights, and because it occurred when John Bolton, Assistant to the President for National Security Affairs of the United States, was traveling from Tokyo to Seoul after visiting Japan, the move is thought to have been designed to restrain security collaboration between Japan, the United States, and the ROK. These events happened not long after May 30, when the fourth meeting of the Japan-Russia Foreign and Defense Ministerial Consultation ("2+2" Ministerial Meeting) was held in Tokyo,[54] in which Japan stated that the military build-up in the Northern Territories is inconsistent with Japan's legal positions and expressed concern about the activities of Russian military aircraft around Japan. Note that Russia has not admitted the fact of these two airspace incursions.

The surrounding countries urgently need to anticipate the possibility that after the INF Treaty termination, Russia will deploy intermediate-range missiles within the range of Japan in the Far East region, including the Northern

Figure 5.2. Joint air patrol by Chinese and Russian warplanes (July 23, 2019)

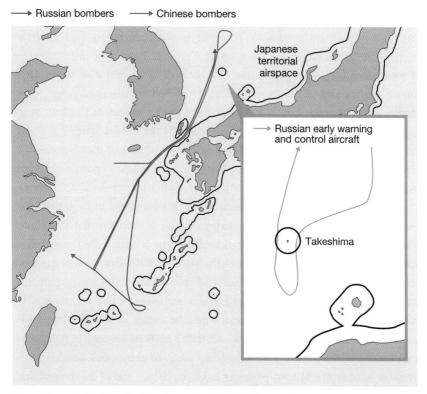

Source: Compiled by the author based on a Japan Joint Staff press release.

Territories, in the future. Since the annexation of Crimea in 2014, concerns about Russia with respect to international security have been intensifying. Nevertheless, as Russia is a neighboring country that cannot relocate, we can conclude that resolving the problem of the attribution of the Four Northern Islands in order to quickly conclude a peace treaty and normalize Japan-Russia relations has significance for alleviating these kinds of security concerns as well.

3. Discussions concerning the New Military Doctrine and Ongoing Military Reform

(1) Discussions concerning Future Warfare and the New Military Doctrine

Ever since Valery Gerasimov, Chief of the General Staff, raised the need to research new methods of warfare at the annual meeting of the Russian Academy of Military Sciences in January 2013, discussions concerning future warfare have continued in Russia. In this context, President Putin gave instructions for a revision of the Military Doctrine in December 2018, and discussions about future warfare and the Military Doctrine intensified in 2019 in response. Three major points of contention in the discussions can be indicated. The first, in the context that the perception of the threat posed by the United States and NATO has become more severe, is the evaluation of that threat and the response to it. The second is the evaluation of the outcomes of the military operation in Syria. And the third is the discussion about the best approach to strategic deterrence.

During the meeting of the Defence Ministry Board held in February 2019, Sergei Shoigu, Defence Minister, expressed the perception that the United States and NATO are a large threat. Specifically, he criticized the strengthening military presence of NATO in the Baltic states and the Eastern and Southern European countries, the growing scale of its exercises, and the participation of even non-NATO nations such as Ukraine and Georgia in the exercises. He stated that in response to this, Russia would be forced to respond adequately, combining strategic deterrence measures with a planned increase in the combat capabilities of the formations and military units. At the annual meeting of the Russian Academy of Military Sciences in March 2019, Chief of the General Staff Gerasimov reported on the major directions in the development of a military strategy based on the characteristics of future warfare.[55] In the report, Chief of the General Staff Gerasimov expressed the same perception as Defence Minister Shoigu that the United States and its allies are a large threat, and raised the "strategy of active defense" as the response of Russia. Firstly, Chief of the General Staff Gerasimov warned that the United States and its allies are increasingly deploying aggressive military operations, pursuing invasive diplomacy in which they use the color revolutions approach and soft power to aim for regime change in other countries, and dubbed this the "Trojan Horse" strategy by the United States and its allies. The essence of this strategy is to use domestic fifth-column protest potential against the administration of the country in which they wish to intervene to invite internal chaos, while at the same time using long-range precision guided weapons to attack strategically important facilities of that country. The "strategy of active defense" refers to taking various measures to preemptively neutralize the invasive actions of the enemy in order to ensure that this kind of threat does not extend to Russia. In relation to this strategy, Chief of the General Staff Gerasimov also made clear that the General Staff Headquarters had established a defense plan to respond to both military and non-military (hybrid) invasive actions. It can be considered that the establishment of this kind of plan hints at the intention of the Russian leadership to use the military to suppress all domestic riots that the Russian leadership sees as being supported by the West.

Next, Chief of the General Staff Gerasimov mentioned the "strategy of limited actions" based on the lessons learned from the military operation in Syria. This is a strategy aiming to defend and enhance the national interests of Russia outside the territory of Russia. He said that just as a group of troops based on units of the Russian Aerospace Forces showed high mobility and capability to execute assigned missions in the operation in Syria, the formation of a highly capable group of troops with the units of one service at its core is important in order to realize this strategy, and that it was essential to secure and maintain superiority in the realm of intelligence in terms of operation preparedness, command and logistics, and the covert deployment of units. Moreover, regarding the anticipated scope of military operations outside the territory of Russia, he indicated that Russia would not aim for power projection on a global scale; rather it would be oriented toward limited actions taking into consideration the economic and military constraint that Russia is facing.

Further, Chief of the General Staff Gerasimov touched on strategic deterrence, a key role of military power, and mentioned the importance of providing for nuclear deterrence and non-nuclear deterrence in the military strategy. The military operation in Syria verified the effectiveness of Russia's precision guided weapons and demonstrated the high capabilities of conventional forces, and as a result, Russian military experts share the idea that it is appropriate to provide for non-nuclear deterrence in the Military Doctrine. The focus of attention will be how these issues are provided for in the new Military Doctrine.

(2) Ongoing Military Reform and the Strengthening of the Military Posture

Equipment upgrades by the Russian military continue to progress, and the strengthening of the military posture in the Military Districts and joint strategic command is ongoing. In March 2019, at the expanded meeting of the Defence Committee of the State Duma of the Federal Assembly, Defence Minister Shoigu gave a detailed report on the results of military reform since he became Defence Minister in 2012.[56] As a result of progress made in procurement of the latest armaments, possession of the latest armaments, which was 16% as of 2012, had risen to 61.5% (by service and branch, Ground Forces: 48.3%, Aerospace Forces: 74%, Navy: 62.3%, Strategic Missile Forces: 82%, Airborne Forces: 67.3%) by the beginning of 2019, and it is looking increasingly likely that the goal of raising this percentage to 70% by the end of 2020 will be achieved. In particular, the introduction of precision guided weapons has progressed rapidly, with ground, sea, and air-deployed long-range precision guided transporters increasing more than twelve-fold and precision guided cruise missiles increasing more than thirty-fold. Of course, the Minister is aware of some challenges. According to the report by Defence Minister Shoigu, to further stabilize development of the military, the Activity program of the Defence Ministry for 2019–2025 was newly approved, and it was decided to aim for the realization of more than 50,000 measures. These measures will be executed based on the provisions of the State Armament Program for 2018–2027.[57]

Placing importance on the Strategic Missile Forces and Aerospace Forces and giving priority to precision guided weapons are recognized in the modernization and strengthening of armaments. This has been reflected in the large-scale (strategic nuclear) exercise Grom-2019 implemented in October 2019. This large-scale exercise was implemented with the objective of verifying the rapid reaction capability of all of the ground-deployed, sea-deployed, and aircraft-deployed strategic deterrent forces under the threat of an invasion. The units of the Strategic Missile Forces, the Aerospace Forces long-range aero-transport forces, the units of each Military District, the Northern Fleet, the Pacific Fleet and the Caspian Flotilla participated in the exercise and ballistic missiles and cruise missiles were actually launched.[58] Furthermore, in December of the same year, the Russian Defence Ministry announced that the state-of-the-art hypersonic missile Avangard had been fully deployed for the first time. The Avangard is a nuclear-capable missile that has been reported in the media to be capable of breaking through all missile defense systems, including those of the United States.[59]

Defence Minister Shoigu's report went on to explain the progress in recruitment for the military. All regiments and brigades are formed from three battalions (two battalions comprised of the contract service and one battalion comprised of conscripted soldiers), and the conscripted soldiers are not involved in combat missions. Currently, the Russian military is formed from 136 battalion tactical groups comprised of the contract service, and it is able to handle the execution of any mission. It is reported that all of the Military District commanders, joint troops of branches commanders, Air Force and air defense forces commanders, division commanders, as well as 96% of the commanders of the joint brigade of branches and regiments have combat experience. Judging from the content of this report, it can be seen that the upgrading of military armaments has been going on as planned and that the recruitment of troops and their capability improvements have been made steadily.

In addition, Defence Minister Shoigu's report mentions the Crimea, Mediterranean Sea, and Arctic regions as areas where military posture has been strengthened. The strengthening in Crimea is to defend the territory of that peninsula and Russia's interests in the Black Sea. A pelagic operation command was established in Crimea in order to command the activities of ships in the Mediterranean Sea, including the Navy ships dispatched to Syria. We can conclude that these moves are intended to check the moves of the United States and NATO, who have been intensifying their military activities on the western strategic front of Russia.

Development of military infrastructure in the Arctic is also progressing.

In the Arctic overall, a total of 475 military facilities have been built on the Kotelny Islands, Zemlya Aleksandry Islands, Vrangel Island and Cape Schmidt since 2012. Their total area is approximately 710,000 m^2 and the stationing of soldiers and the installation of armaments is being carried out at these facilities. The attitude of the Russian leadership, which places importance on the Arctic from the perspectives of securing future economic interests and military security, has led to moves to strengthen the posture of the Northern Fleet which has jurisdiction over this region (the Northern Joint Strategic Command). Every year, the Northern Fleet implements large-scale exercises in the Arctic Ocean and the adjacent marine areas, and in April 2019 it carried out a large-scale exercise off the coast of Norway. This exercise is evaluated as having been larger in scale than the Trident Juncture exercise implemented by NATO in the summer of 2018. In August 2019, it was revealed that there was a plan to upgrade the status of the Northern Fleet to Northern Military District.[60] It is said that the Russian leadership expects that upgrading the status of the fleet to that of a Military District and strengthening its administrative authority will make decisions in the operational missions of the Northern Fleet easier. In addition to the units of the Northern Fleet, several units belonging to the Central Military District and the Eastern Military District will also be included under the jurisdiction of the new Military District command. Furthermore, it is reported that the units located in the Arctic islands and Cape Schmidt will be incorporated into the joint tactical group responsible for military security in the Arctic region, which had already been formed in October 2014. Moreover, these units will be equipped with the latest armaments such as the coastal missile system Rubezh.

The military posture in the Eastern Military District and the Central Military District also continues to strengthen. In May 2019, Ruslan Tsalikov, First Deputy Defence Minister, carried out an inspection of the Eastern Military District and the Central Military District.[61] In the Eastern Military District, he inspected the units and the status of the construction of military facilities in the Kunashiri (Kunashir) and Etorofu (Iturup) Islands in the Northern Territories and in Khabarovsk. In the Central Military District, he also visited Omsk, the location of the command of the 33rd Army, one of the three armies in the Strategic Missile Forces, and inspected the units and the status of the construction of military facilities. In particular, the First Deputy Minister Tsalikov's inspection of the training center of the Airborne Forces is seen as related to the large-scale exercise

Tsentr-2019 in September. This kind of inspection of units and military facilities by top officials in the Defence Ministry is carried out regularly, and is a move aimed at strengthening the military posture on the eastern strategic front and Central Asian strategic front in the same way as on the European front.[62]

Strengthening of the military posture in the Eastern Military District is proceeding in two respects: organizational measures and armaments upgrades. The main organizational measures are formation of the aero-combined division and surface-to-air missile brigade for improvement of the air defense capability in the Amur-Sakhalin direction, and formation of the coastal missile division that deployed the coastal missile system Bastion. Moreover, it can be seen that 26 battalion tactical groups were deployed in the Eastern Military District overall by the end of 2019. Concerning armaments procurement, Russia plans to introduce 1,744 of the latest armaments in order to replace the armaments of 139 units based on the State Armament Program, which will raise the percentage of the latest armaments possessed by this Military District overall to 53%. Concerning the strengthening of the Pacific Fleet, the Petropavlovsk-Kamchatsky, the first diesel-electric submarine (Project 636.3), was commissioned in November 2019. The Project 636.3 submarines have a high degree of silence and long-range target detection capability and carry the cruise missile Kalibr. Russia plans to deploy six of these submarines overall.[63]

The Central Military District contains the Central Asian strategic front and faces the threats of intensifying international terrorism and expanding Islamic extremism, so consistent measures to improve the combat capability of the units of this Military District are being adopted. Due to procurement of the latest armaments, the percentage of the latest armaments possessed by this Military District overall is expected to increase to 53% or greater by the end of 2019. One of the comprehensive measures for strengthening the posture of the Central Military District is the implementation of Tsentr-2019. This exercise took the form of a multilateral exercise in which members of the CSTO and the SCO also participated, and it was implemented with the objective of ensuring the security of the Central Asia region through this kind of military cooperation.[64] Tsentr-2019 was a large-scale exercise that involved not only the units of the Central Military District, but also the Caspian Flotilla of the Southern Military District, the units of the Eastern Military District, the Airborne Forces, and the long-range aero-transport forces of the Aerospace Forces, and mobilized

Figure 5.3. The Tsentr-2019 exercise, mainly held in the Central Military District

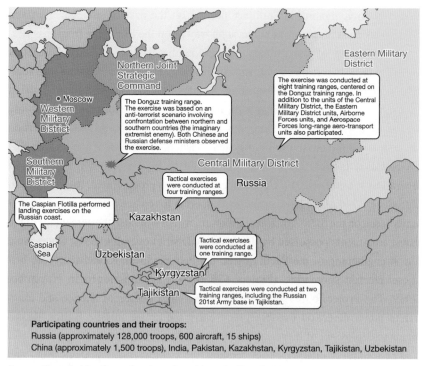

Eastern Military District

The exercise was conducted at eight training ranges, centered on the Donguz training range. In addition to the units of the Central Military District, the Eastern Military District units, Airborne Forces units, and Aerospace Forces long-range aero-transport units also participated.

Northern Joint Strategic Command

The Donguz training range. The exercise was based on an anti-terrorist scenario involving confrontation between northern and southern countries (the imaginary extremist enemy). Both Chinese and Russian defense ministers observed the exercise.

Moscow
Western Military District

Southern Military District

Central Military District

Russia

Tactical exercises were conducted at four training ranges.

The Caspian Flotilla performed landing exercises on the Russian coast.

Kazakhstan

Caspian Sea

Uzbekistan

Tactical exercises were conducted at one training range.

Kyrgyzstan

Tajikistan

Tactical exercises were conducted at two training ranges, including the Russian 201st Army base in Tajikistan.

Participating countries and their troops:
Russia (approximately 128,000 troops, 600 aircraft, 15 ships)
China (approximately 1,500 troops), India, Pakistan, Kazakhstan, Kyrgyzstan, Tajikistan, Uzbekistan

Source: Compiled by the author based on *Krasnaia Zvezda*, November 15, November 18, and November 20, 2019.

128,000 troops and more than 20,000 armaments, including approximately 600 aircraft and 15 ships. Moreover, in addition to the Russian military, units from China, India, Pakistan, Kazakhstan, Kyrgyzstan, Tajikistan, and Uzbekistan also participated in this exercise. Furthermore, besides the scale of the participating troops and mobilized armaments, the exercises were implemented across a wide range of locations including eight training ranges, centered on the Donguz training range in Orenburg oblast, and the Caspian Sea, while related tactical exercises were implemented on four training ranges in Kazakhstan, one training range in Kyrgyzstan, and the 201st Army base stationed in Tajikistan. The main exercise of Tsentr-2019 was implemented from September 16 to September 21 at the Donguz training range. The scenario of the exercise was that the "Southern

Army," an armed group and attack unit of an international terrorist organization, would invade the territory of the "Northern Country," and in response, the "Northern Army" would form an anti-terrorism coalition army with the armies of other countries to carry out a defense operation, and then go on the offensive to restore its impregnable defense posture in the occupied border area. Following China's participation in Vostok-2018 in the previous year, approximately 1,500 troops from China were allowed to participate in Tsentr-2019, and, for example, Wei Fenghe, Defense Minister, inspected the exercise at the Donguz training range, which demonstrated the strengthening of China-Russia military cooperation. At the China-Russia Defence Ministers Meeting held during the exercise, Defence Minister Shoigu stated that he expected that these kinds of exercises would be continued going forward.

(3) Strengthening of Military Cooperation and Arms Exports Aimed at Expansion

In the context of greater tension in its relationship with the United States and NATO, it is becoming more vital for Russia to step up its strategic cooperation with China, and military cooperation between the two countries is being raised to an even higher level.[65] In May 2019, the two countries carried out the naval joint exercise Maritime Cooperation-2019 in the East China Sea off the coast of Qingdao. Fifteen ships, ten aircraft, and marine units from the two militaries participated in the exercise, which was implemented with the objective of improving the command level of the joint defense operation at sea.[66]

As stated earlier, on July 23, 2019, the militaries of China and Russia carried out a joint air patrol from the East China Sea to the Sea of Japan, the first such patrol in the history of military cooperation between the two countries.[67] A formation comprised of two of Russia's Tu-95MS strategic bombers and two of China's H-6K strategic bombers, as well as Russia's A-50 early warning and control aircraft and China's KJ-2000 early warning and control aircraft, flew from the East China Sea over the Sea of Japan, following a predetermined route. According to an announcement by the Russian Defence Ministry, the objectives of this flight were to deepen and develop the comprehensive partnership of China and Russia, further improve the level of mutual collaboration between the two militaries, improve the joint operation executing capability of the two militaries, and strengthen global strategic stability. Moreover, the Ministry explained that the action was based on the 2019 military cooperation plan between the two countries and was not directed against any particular third country. This formation flew into airspace established as the air defense identification zones of Japan and the ROK, which led to a situation in which measures such as a response to the airspace incursions were taken. Regarding this, the Russian Defence Ministry explained that freedom of flight exists in air defense identification zones, unlike in sovereign airspace; moreover, based on objective data, there were no airspace incursions.

As already mentioned, the Chinese military participated in the Tsentr exercise conducted in Russia, and Wei Fenghe, Defense Minister, inspected the site of the exercise. In addition to the meeting here between Defence Minister Shoigu and Defense Minister Wei, the top military officials of China and Russia held meetings, and moves aiming to strengthen the military cooperation and military-technical cooperation between the two countries were recognized. In June 2019, a meeting between the Russian General Staff and Chinese Joint Staff Department was held and was attended by Chief of the General Staff Gerasimov and Shao Yuanming, Deputy Chief of the Joint Staff Department in the Chinese People's Liberation Army.[68] Moreover, in September 2019, the 24th meeting of the Russia-China Inter-governmental Joint Committee on military-technical cooperation was held in Moscow. The meeting was attended by Defence Minister Shoigu and Xu Qiliang, Vice Chairman of the Central Military Commission, and a series of documents concerning cooperation in this area were signed.[69] In response to these recent developments in China-Russia military cooperation, Defence Minister Shoigu expressed the evaluation that military cooperation between the two countries had entered a new phase. It has been reported that in his keynote speech at a meeting of the Moscow-based think-tank Valdai Discussion Club in October 2019, President Putin stated that Russia is cooperating with China in the construction of their missile early-warning system; this will attract attention as a new development in bilateral military cooperation between China and Russia.[70]

In addition, in its East Asia policies, the Russian military leadership is re-acknowledging the importance of military cooperation with North Korea. In July 2019, Alexander Fomin, Deputy Defence Minister in charge of international military cooperation, visited Pyongyang and held meetings with top officials of the Korean People's Army, including No Kwang-chol, Minister of People's Armed Forces. At the meeting, Deputy Minister Fomin confirmed the importance of friendly, good-neighborly and cooperative relations between the military authorities of Russia and North Korea and discussed the direction of a joint plan for the development of military cooperation between the two countries.[71]

Russia is continuing to strengthen military cooperation among the CSTO countries, which it has positioned as a priority matter in its military cooperation. Two points can be made concerning the direction of enhanced cooperation. The first is how to improve the military's capability to respond to the expansion of terrorism and Islamic extremism. The second is how to strengthen the joint air defense system, which is an issue in the strengthening of cooperation in the aerospace area.

In May 2019, joint sessions of the Councils of Defense Ministers of the CSTO and SCO were held in Bishkek, Kyrgyzstan.[72] During these sessions, joint responses to a wide range of security issues within the area of responsibility of the two organizations, expansion of the implementation of antiterrorism exercises, exchanges of experiences in antiterrorism operations, and the establishment of a robust communication mechanism for coordinating defense operations and responses to changing military situations were considered. In these sessions, Russia's Defence Minister Shoigu invited the units of the SCO countries to participate in the Tsentr exercise. In addition, in his meeting with the Kyrgyzstan military leadership, Defence Minister Shoigu mentioned the importance of strengthening military cooperation and military-technical cooperation between the two countries in order to strengthen the combat capabilities of the Kyrgyz military, which is directly threatened by an unstable Afghanistan.

In October 2019, CSTO's joint exercise Nerushimoe Bratstvo-2019 (Indestructible Brotherhood-2019) was conducted in Tajikistan, during which an anti-terrorist joint operation exercise was conducted by the Collective Rapid Reaction Forces, the Central Asia region units of the CSTO. Prior to this, Alexander Lapin, Commander of the Central Military District, inspected the status of the unit at the Russian military's 201st Base stationed in Tajikistan, a major constituent unit of the Collective Rapid Reaction Forces.[73]

The joint air defense system of the CSTO countries was founded as the CIS joint air defense system and has been maintained as such, but currently it is comprised of the CSTO members and Uzbekistan only. For Russia, the issue is building an impenetrable air defense network in the areas surrounding its own country by strengthening this system. In September 2019, the CIS joint air defense system's exercise Boyevoye Sodruzhestvo-2019 (Combat Cooperation-2019) was conducted at the Ashuluk training range in Astrakhan oblast and at the Sary-Shagan training range in Kazakhstan. Each country dispatched air defense units to the exercise; for example, Russia dispatched the S-400 surface-to-air missile system units of two surface-to-air missile divisions. The exercise was implemented with the goal of repelling an attack by unmanned aerial vehicles and cruise missiles, drawing from the combat experience in Syria.[74] At the same time as this exercise, the Joint Air Defense Coordination Committee of the CIS Defense Ministers' Council was held, during which the establishment of a future plan for strengthening the bilateral and multilateral joint air defense system and budget problems, etc., were considered. A proposal concerning the joint preparedness measures of the air defense units in 2020 was also approved.[75]

Russia's arms exports are expanding, with total exports in 2018 reaching approximately $13.7 billion.[76] At a time when the importance of aerospace attack weapons in military operations is growing, awareness of the importance of air defense weapons to respond to those weapons is also on the rise. It is reported that of the percentage of the total orders received by Russia's military industrial companies, aircraft account for approximately 40% and air defense weapons account for 35%. Leading in the area of air defense weapons is the aerospace defense company Almaz-Antey, which produces surface-to-air missile systems such as the S-400, S-300PMU, Buk-M2E, and Tor-M2, and total orders for these systems have reached approximately $14.0 billion.

In 2019, the issue of the transfer of the S-400 surface-to-air missile system to Turkey, a NATO member, became a particularly large focus of attention. A contract for this export had already been concluded in 2017, but the United States and NATO opposed its transfer from the perspective that it would obstruct the building of the NATO joint air and missile defense network and the F-35 combat aircraft joint project. However, Turkey decided to accept the transfer, and in July 2019, the first S-400 surface-to-air missile system was installed in Myurted air base near Ankara. Furthermore, the first personnel were already dispatched to Russia in May for training in using this system.[77] If disagreements grow between Turkey and the United States in particular, and also with other members of NATO, there is a possibility that Turkey's closeness to Russia in terms of weapons will strengthen, leading to the further expansion of weapons exports to Turkey.

It has also been pointed out that Russia has already proposed to Turkey the option of adopting the Su-57 stealth fighter instead of the F-35 combat aircraft. Moreover, the strengthening of friendly relations with Turkey is important in terms of military strategy. This is because Turkey controls the Bosporus and Dardanelles straits, the entrances to the Mediterranean Sea from the Black Sea, and it is thought that if Turkey becomes a friendly state, navigation of this strategic route will become easier for Russia, as will the activities of the Russian Navy in the Mediterranean Sea with opposition to NATO in mind.

Comprehending Russian "Hybrid Warfare"

The definition of "hybrid warfare," which has recently been discussed as a new form of warfare by Russia, differs slightly among analysts, but it can be roughly summarized as "a set of activities that: (1) combine unconventional means such as information warfare with conventional forces; (2) utilize nonstate proxy actors; (3) adopt covert and deniable techniques to avoid escalation into war; and (4) are aimed at achieving political goals."[78] In fact, these kinds of methods are not a new form of warfare that suddenly appeared in recent years. Moreover, making large-scale changes to the status quo while avoiding escalation into war, say, a Crimea-like fait accompli, has been more widely observed historically than changes to the status quo through coercive diplomacy and war.[79] Therefore, we can conclude that modern "hybrid warfare," rather than being a truly new phenomenon, is a "matter of degree" to which unconventional means are used.[80]

Furthermore, the term "hybrid warfare" is used in Russia almost only when analysts refer to such discussions in the West or when they discuss unconventional ways of fighting by Western countries.[81] For this reason, the concept of "hybrid warfare," rather than being an original approach of Russia, actually can be understood as a passive concept, namely, specifically as "a response to the West which Russia believes had an impact on the series of color revolutions" or an "adaptation to the trends in new forms of warfare." Furthermore, it is important to note that researchers in the West also present this perspective. This fact suggests the need for a dispassionate analysis of the novelty of "hybrid warfare."[82]

Nonetheless, there is no doubt that the methods of fighting called "hybrid warfare" are at least characteristic of modern Russia (even if not unique to it). If we suppose that the rise of modern "hybrid warfare" is no more than a "matter of degree" accounted for by unconventional means, then why has the "degree" become larger? Firstly, in some of the post-Soviet states, there can exist social vulnerabilities that make it easier to use "hybrid" techniques. There is a sizable population of ethnic Russians living in these states that became independent when the Soviet Union dissolved. Of course, this kind of diversity in itself does not immediately make the society vulnerable to "hybrid warfare." However, there is a possibility that some of the population who are of Russian origin could be utilized as proxy actors in a crisis. In addition, the population of ethnic Russians itself can be a reason for Russia's political or military interventions in these states in the name of protecting its citizens.[83]

Secondly, the dissemination of information through the mass media and the Internet requires very little resources. Governments that adopt "hybrid" tools can transmit disinformation through social media and government-affiliated mass media, and this tactic does not require any military assets. Therefore, if the transmission of disinformation can have a political effect, then it is a convenient tool from the perspective of cost-effectiveness.[84] Of course, as the effect of information dissemination by Russia in Western countries is small, there is large room for discussion about the size of the effect of propaganda using such media. On the other hand, in former Soviet republics such as Estonia and Latvia that have a sizable population of Russian speakers, the Russian-affiliated media is used on a daily basis and can have a political impact to some degree.[85] Furthermore, recent empirical studies reveal that biased media can (1) encourage mass mobilization of the recipients of biased information in times of conflict and (2) strengthen the political preferences the recipients initially have.[86] These effects can possibly exacerbate political polarization in society.

NOTES

1)   Prezident Rossii, Poslanie Prezidenta Federalnomu Sobraniiu, February 20, 2019.

2)   *Rossiiskaia Gazeta*, December 6, 2019.

3)   TASS, October 1, 2019.

4)   *Meduza*, June 15, 2019.

5)   *Vedomosti*, June 9, 2019.

6)   *RBK*, July 13, 2016.

7)   Ministerstvo Vnutrennikh Del RF, Ofitsialnaia informatsiia (website), June 11, 2019; *Rossiiskaia Gazeta*, June 11, 2019.

8)   Ukaz Prezidenta RF, June 13, 2019, No. 271, *Sobranie Zakonodatelstvo Rossiiskoi Federatsii (SZRF), June 17, 2019, No. 24, Art. 3074.*

9)   Chast 1, 4 i 5, Stati 29, Konstitutsii Rossiiskoi Federatsii.

10) *Vedomosti*, July 16, 2019.

11) *Nezavisimaia Gazeta*, August 4, 2019.

12) OVD-Info, August 10, 2019.

13) *Guardian*, August 13, 2019.

14) *Kommersant*, September 9, 2019.

15) *Lenta.ru*, September 9, 2019.

16) Aburamoto Mari, "Puchin Seiken to Senkyo no Seitosei" [Elections and Legitimacy in Putin's Russia], *Kaigai Jijyo* [Journal of World Affairs], July/August 2018, pp. 44-58.

17) Prezident Rossii, Bolshaia press-konferentsiia Vladimira Putina, December 19, 2019.

18) Hasegawa Takeyuki, "Russian Presidential Power in the Putin Era and the Recent Discussion on Constitutional Revisions," *Briefing Memo*, NIDS, January 2020.

19) Hasegawa Takeyuki, "Puchin Seikenka no Gendai Roshia ni okeru Daitoryo no 'Kenryoku Shigen': Daitoryofu ni yoru Juyo Seisaku no Shikikantoku" [A Study on Resources of the Russian Presidential Power under Putin: the Presidential Administration of Russia as Directive and Supervisory Authority], *Roshia Yurashia no Keizai to Shakai* [Russian Eurasian Economy & Society], No. 1037, 2019, pp. 2-19.

20) TASS, July 17, 2019.

21) Punkt 1, Stati 18, Federalnyi Zakon RF, June 28, 2014, No. 172-FZ, *SZRF, No. 26, 2014, Art. 3378*; Ukaz Prezidenta RF, December 31, 2015, No. 683, *SZRF, No. 1 (Chast 1), Art. 212.*

22) *Lenta.ru*, "Patrushev Nikolai" (website).

23) Hasegawa Takeyuki, "Commencement of the New Putin Administration and its Strategy," *NIDS Commentary*, No. 83, August 2018.

24) Interfax, November 27, 2019.

25) Sovet Bezopasnosti RF, July 7, 2019.

26) Sovet Bezopasnosti RF, July 5, 2019.

27) Sovet Bezopasnosti RF, June 24, 2019.

28) Sovet Bezopasnosti RF, September 9, 2019.

29) Sovet Bezopasnosti RF, April 25, 2019.

30) Sovet Bezopasnosti RF, September 5, 2017; Japanese Ministry of Foreign Affairs, "Gemba Gaimu Daijin to Patorushefu Roshia Renpo Anzenhoshokaigi Shoki to no Kaidan" [Meeting between Minister for Foreign Affairs Gemba and Secretary of the Security Council of the Russian Federation Patrushev], October 23, 2012.

31) Sovet Bezopasnosti RF, Vse Novosti.

32) Japanese Ministry of Foreign Affairs, "Patorushefu Roshia Renpo Anzenhoshokaigi Shoki ni yoru Abe Soridaijin Hyokei" [Courtesy Call on Prime Minister Abe by Secretary of the Security Council of the Russian Federation Patrushev], September 17, 2019.

33) RIA Novosti, December 19, 2018.

34) TASS, February 22, 2019; Ukaz Prezidenta RF, February 21, 2019, No. 60, *SZRF, 2019, No. 8, Art. 768*; Sovet Bezopasnosti RF, VENEDIKTOV Aleksandr Nikolaevich (website).

35) *Rossiiskaia Gazeta*, June 16, 2019; RIA Novosti, December 19, 2018.

36) Ukaz Prezidenta RF, October 2, 2018, No. 559, *SZRF, October 8, 2018, No. 41, Art. 6223.*

37) *Vzgliad*, April 17, 2019.

38) *Kommersant*, April 5, 2019.

39) Ukaz Prezidenta RF, April 24, 2019, No. 183, *SZRF, 2019, No. 17, Art. 2071.*

40) US Embassy & Consulates in Russia, "APNSA John Bolton Interview with Elena Chernenko, Kommersant," October 22, 2018.

41) President of Russia, "Executive Order Suspending Russia's Compliance with the USSR-US INF Treaty," March 4, 2019.

42) US Embassy & Consulates in Russia, "APNSA John Bolton Press Conference at Interfax," October 23, 2018.

43) Ministry of Defence of the Russian Federation, "Russian Defence Ministry Briefs Military Attaches with Presentation of 9M729 Missile of Iskander-M Complex," January 23, 2019.

44) US Department of Defense, "Statement from Secretary of Defense Mark T. Esper on the INF Treaty," August 2, 2019.

45) President of Russia, "Statement by the President of Russia on the Unilateral Withdrawal of the United States from the Treaty on the Elimination of Intermediate-Range and Shorter-Range Missiles," August 5, 2019.

46) US Department of Defense, "DOD Conducts Ground Launch Cruise Missile Test," August 19, 2019.

47) US Department of Defense, "Remarks by Secretary Esper at the Air Force Association's 2019 Air, Space & Cyber Conference, National Harbor, Maryland," September 18, 2019.

48) President of Russia, "Vladimir Putin's Annual News Conference," December 19, 2019.

49) *Nezavisimaia Gazeta*, January 25, 2017.

50) President of Russia, "Vladimir Putin's Annual News Conference," December 19, 2019.

51) Japanese Ministry of Foreign Affairs, "Japan-Russia Summit Meeting," September 5, 2019.

52) Japanese Ministry of Defense and Self-Defense Forces, "Roshiaki ni yoru Ryokushinpan ni tsuite" [Airspace Incursions by Russian Aircraft], June 20, 2019.

53) Joint Staff, "Chugokuki oyobi Roshiaki no Higashishinakai oyobi Nihonkai ni okeru Hiko ni tsuite" [Flights by Chinese Aircraft and Russian Aircraft in the East China Sea and Sea of Japan], July 23, 2019.

54) Japanese Ministry of Foreign Affairs, "Japan-Russia Foreign and Defense Ministerial Consultation," May 30, 2019.

55) *Krasnaia Zvezda*, March 4, 2019.

56) *Krasnaia Zvezda*, March 13, 2019.

57) *Krasnaia Zvezda*, March 13, 2019.

58) *Krasnaia Zvezda*, October 16, 2019.

59) *Krasnaia Zvezda*, December 25, 2019.

60) *Rossiiskaia Gazeta*, August 7, 2019.

61) *Krasnaia Zvezda*, May 6, 2019.

62) *Hezavisimoe Voennoe Obozrenie*, No. 32, September 6-12, 2019.

63) *Krasnaia Zvezda*, May 27, 2019.

64) *Krasnaia Zvezda*, September 23, 2019.

65) Hilary Appel, "Are Xi Jinping and Vladimir Putin Partners? Interpreting the Russia-China Rapprochement," *PONARS Eurasia Policy Memo*, No. 603, July 2019.

66) *Rossiiskaia Gazeta*, May 1, 2019.

67) *Krasnaia Zvezda*, July 24, 2019.

68) *Krasnaia Zvezda*, July 24, 2019.

69) *Rossiiskaia Gazeta*, September 4, 2019.

70) *Jane's Defence Weekly*, October 16, 2019, p. 9.

71) *Krasnaia Zvezda*, July 5, 2019.

72) *Krasnaia Zvezda*, May 6, 2019.

73) *Krasnaia Zvezda*, October 4, 2019.

74) *Krasnaia Zvezda*, September 6, 2019.

75) *Krasnaia Zvezda*, September 4, 2019.

76) *Hezavisimoe Voennoe Obozrenie*, No. 30, August 23-29, 2019.

77) *Kranaia Zvezda*, July 19, 2019.

78) Williamson Murray and Peter R. Mansoor, eds., *Hybrid Warfare: Fighting Complex Opponents from the Ancient World to the Present*, Cambridge University Press, 2012; Andrew Radin, *Hybrid Warfare in the Baltics: Threats and Potential Responses*, RAND Corporation, 2017; Alexander Lanoszka, "Russian Hybrid Warfare and Extended Deterrence in Eastern Europe," *International Affairs*, Vol. 92, No. 1, 2016, pp. 175-195.

79) Murray and Mansoor, eds., *Hybrid Warfare*; Dan Altman, "By Fait Accompli, Not Coercion: How States Wrest Territory from Their Adversaries," *International Studies Quarterly*, Vol. 61, No. 4, 2017, pp. 881-891.

80) Mark Galeotti, "Hybrid, Ambiguous, and Non-linear? How New Is Russia's 'New Way of War'?" *Small Wars and Insurgencies*, Vol. 27, No. 2, 2016, pp. 282-301.

81) Charles K. Bartles, "Getting Gerasimov Right," *Military Review*, January-February 2016, pp. 30-38.

82) Kier Giles, *Russia's "New" Tools for Confronting the West: Continuity and Innovation in Moscow's Exercise of Power*, Chatham House, 2016, pp. 9-12; Radin, *Hybrid Warfare in the Baltics*, pp. 11-12.

83) Lanoszka, "Russian Hybrid Warfare and Extended Deterrence in Eastern Europe."

84) Linda Robinson, Todd C. Helmus, Raphael S. Cohen, Alireza Nader, Andrew Radin, Madeline Magnuson, and Katya Migacheva, *Modern Political Warfare: Current Practices and Possible Responses*, RAND Corporation, 2018, pp. 61-64.

85) Ibid., pp. 66-69.

86) David Yanagizawa-Drott, "Propaganda and Conflict: Evidence from the Rwandan Genocide," *Quarterly Journal of Economics*, Vol. 129, No. 4, 2014, pp. 1947-1994; Leonid Peisakhin and Arturas Rozenas, "Electoral Effects of Biased Media: Russian Television in Ukraine," *American Journal of Political Science*, Vol. 62, No. 3, 2018, pp. 535-550.

Chapter 6
The United States

Implementing the "Great Power Competition" Strategy

ARAKAKI Hiromu (Lead author, Section 1)
KIRIDORI Ryo (Section 2)

The National Security Strategy (2017 NSS) expressed that the United States will respond to strategic competitions with its challengers. China and North Korea, alongside Russia, Iran, and transnational threat organizations, were named as the challengers that the United States faces. The Trump administration has strengthened its competitive stance against Beijing not only in the military field but also in economic and social fields. On the other hand, while relations with North Korea, which is continuing its nuclear weapons and missile development, improved from the initial tensions through to the US-North Korea Summit Meeting, this has not led to seeing any specific progress toward "complete denuclearization of North Korea."

In the National Defense Strategy (NDS) unveiled in January 2018, the Trump administration raised "long-term, strategic competition" with China and Russia as the highest priority, and described a policy of focusing on an approach to force suitable for the age of competition among major powers, especially strengthening force capability including modernization. The fiscal year (FY) 2020 defense budget request shows a stance of mainly investing in the capability highlighted in the NDS, including that in space and cyber domains. On the other hand, the Army and Navy have worked on restoring and expanding force capacity since the beginning of the Trump administration. While the efforts for enhancing force capability are remarkable, further developments should be closely monitored.

In addition, in the era of great power competition, US forward operational bases and other military facilities are to be put in contested environments once a conflict occurs, and thus building operationally credible forward forces, not "presence for its own sake," is urgently needed. Based on this, the US military is testing concepts that swiftly deploy forces to areas within the range of threats and create strategic and operational dilemmas for adversaries in the western Pacific region.

1. The Policies for the Indo-Pacific Region

(1) China's Military and Economic Statecraft and Hardened US Attitude

A confrontational, competitive view toward China is growing in the Trump administration. The 2017 NSS states that China wants to "shape a world antithetical to US values and interests" and positions China as a strategic competitor that aims to reorder the Indo-Pacific region in its favor.[1]

The Indo-Pacific Strategy Report issued in June 2019 also expresses a critical view of China, stating that it has exploited the economic benefits of the rules-based international order while eroding its values and principles. The report assesses China's motives as being to seek "Indo-Pacific regional hegemony in the near-term and, ultimately global preeminence in the long-term" while continuing its economic and military ascendance.[2]

The report specifically raises China's actions that warrant concern as being (1) strengthening discriminatory treatment of Muslims living in China, (2) China's cyber theft targeting confidential business and technological information at companies in the United States and other countries, (3) China's placement of anti-ship cruise missiles and long-range surface-to-air missiles on the Spratly Islands and its militarization of manmade islands in the South China Sea by deploying paramilitary forces, (4) China's ongoing enhancement of its military capabilities while its forces simultaneously carry out dangerous actions that could cause accidents, and (5) China's coercive use of non-military methods, including economic methods, in the "gray zone."[3]

What has garnered attention is the Trump administration's growing concern about China's aim to use economic methods and influence public opinion in target countries as ways to alter those countries' actions to fall in line with China's agenda. The Indo-Pacific Strategy Report points out that "China is using economic inducements and penalties, influence operations, and implied military threats to persuade other states to comply with its agenda."[4] This concern is also identified in the Annual Report to Congress: Military and Security Developments Involving the People's Republic of China 2019 (Chinese Military Report) issued in May 2019.[5]

In a speech at the Wilson Center on October 24, 2019, Vice President Michael Pence depicted China as a strategic and economic rival of the United States and criticized China's

President Trump meeting with President Xi Jinping at the G20 Osaka Summit (Reuters/Kyodo)

military expansionism, its diplomacy approach assessed as a "debt trap," its repression of religion within the country, its construction of a surveillance state including strengthening of monitoring of minorities as well as its overseas transfers of surveillance technology, and China's many policies inconsistent with free and fair trade as being "harmful to America's interests and values."[6]

The speech raises China's theft of intellectual property as well as military-civilian fusion concerning technology in the form of forced transfers of private companies' technologies to the military as specific issues. Vice President Pence stated, "To protect intellectual property rights and the privacy of our citizens and our national security, we've taken strong steps to curtail illegal behavior of Chinese companies like Huawei and ZTE [telecommunications equipment companies]."

Moreover, in his speech, Vice President Pence referenced the efforts by the Chinese Communist Party to influence public debate in the United States by stating that it is "continuing to reward and coerce American businesses, movie studios, universities, think tanks, scholars, journalists, and local, state, and federal officials." Vice President Pence had also expressed concerns about China's activities to influence public opinion in the United States before this speech. In a speech at the Hudson Institute on October 4, 2018, he expressed strong wariness about China's actions not only concerning the United States' policies and politics, but also China's "steps to exploit its economic leverage, and the allure of their large marketplace, to advance its influence over American businesses."[7]

In addition, Vice President Pence criticized that China's military action "has also remained increasingly provocative," including creating and militarizing unlawful artificial islands in the South China Sea, deploying maritime militia, and sending Chinese Coast Guard ships into the waters around the Senkaku Islands.

This severe view of China is also affecting policy dialogues between the United States and China as well as military-to-military relations between the two countries. In place of the Strategic and Economic Dialogue, a comprehensive working-level consultation framework of the Obama administration, the Trump administration established four frameworks: (1) the US-China Diplomatic and Security Dialogue (D&SD), (2) the US-China Comprehensive Economic Dialogue, (3) the US-China Law Enforcement and Cybersecurity Dialogue, and (4) the US-China Social and Cultural Dialogue. Although all of the dialogues were held in 2017, the D&SD was held only once in 2018, and none of the dialogues had been held as of 2019.[8] In regard to military exchanges, through bilateral exchanges in the form of mutual visits by high-level officials of both countries as well as policy dialogues between high-level

The USS *Ronald Reagan* aircraft carrier deployed to the South China Sea (US Navy photo by Mass Communication Specialist 2nd Class Kaila V. Peters)

officials, the Trump administration aims to prevent international crisis and to build and strengthen processes necessary for control and defense in the event that an international crisis does occur.[9] However, there was a downward trend in exchanges, as the 30 exchanges held in 2016 fell to 19 in 2017, 14 in 2018, and 12 in 2019.[10]

The Trump administration is also strengthening relations with Taiwan. The Indo-Pacific Strategy Report names Taiwan as an important partner alongside Singapore, New Zealand, and Mongolia. The Report also states that the United States "has a vital interest in upholding the rules-based international order, which includes a strong, prosperous, and democratic Taiwan" and specifies that the United States will strengthen relations with Taiwan and faithfully implement the Taiwan Relations Act.[11]

The Report also states that the United States will continue its arms sales to Taiwan with the objective of ensuring that "Taiwan remains secure, confident, free from coercion, and able to peacefully and productively engage the mainland on its own terms." The report cites as the background for this China's development and deployment of advanced military capabilities without renouncing the option of the use of military force for unification with Taiwan. As of the end of December 2019, the Trump administration had conducted 11 cases of foreign military sales to Taiwan. A total of four cases were notified to Congress in 2019, including sale of training, maintenance, and logistical support for F-16 pilots in April, sale of 108 M1A2T Abrams battle tanks and anti-aircraft missiles in July, and sale of 66 F-16C/D Block 70 fighter aircraft in August.[12]

(2) Response to the North Korea Nuclear Problem

As North Korea continues its ongoing nuclear weapons and missile development, the Trump administration continues to maintain the goal of "complete denuclearization of North Korea." Since the inauguration of the administration, "maximum pressure" policies have been raised aiming for denuclearization of North Korea through strengthening economic sanctions implemented by the United States and the United Nations. These policies have had the same direction as the Barack Obama administration's policies on North Korea that were known as "strategic patience." However, the Trump administration's initial stance was characterized by focus on the role of China's diplomatic and economic pressure on North Korea as well as eliminating the possibility of the use of military force by North Korea.

The focus of the initial policies was economic pressure, and the United Nations' sanctions and the United States' independent sanctions served as the two pillars in support of that. The United Nations' sanctions began with the UN Security Council Resolution 1718 that was adopted in October 2006 in response to the first nuclear test implemented by North Korea. Against the backdrop of North Korea's repeated nuclear weapon and ballistic missile tests, sanctions have been adopted 10 times through to Resolution 2397 adopted in December 2017. In addition to prohibiting the transfer and procurement of supplies related to nuclear weapons and missiles with North Korea, the United Nations' sanctions regime freezes the assets of individuals and organizations subject to sanctions, prohibits entry into ports as well as takeoff and landing of North Korea's ships and aircraft as well as ships and aircraft that are suspected of carrying prohibited goods, prohibits financial transactions, and places an embargo on coal, iron, lead, and marine products. Furthermore, Resolution 2375 and Resolution 2397 respectively adopted in September and December 2017 drastically reduced the upper limit established for the supply volume of refined petroleum products such as gasoline and diesel oil to North Korea.[13]

In addition to these United Nations' sanctions, the United States also strengthened its sanctions against North Korea. In 2017, the Trump administration returned North Korea to the list of state sponsors of terror. Based on President Trump's executive order, the US Department of the Treasury announced implementation of sanctions against North Korea's financial institutions and individuals related to the country's development of weapons of mass destruction and ballistic missiles, prohibition of transactions with the Bank of Dandong due to its involvement with money laundering for North Korea, and the freezing of assets under US jurisdiction of North Korean high government officials, among other announcements.

Against the backdrop of North Korea's ICBM tests in 2017 (on July 4 and November 29) as well as its sixth nuclear test (on September 3), US-North Korea relations following the establishment of the Trump administration deteriorated to a situation in which there were fears that the United States might use military force against North Korea. However, entering 2018, tensions eased in US-North Korea relations against the backdrop of North Korea's appeals to the United States as well as the improvement in Republic of Korea (ROK)-North Korea relations.

After receiving North Korea's request for a US-North Korea Summit Meeting to be held, which was conveyed by the ROK's special envoy delegation when it visited Washington DC in early March 2018, President Trump agreed to a meeting with Chairman Kim Jong Un of the Workers' Party of Korea. The first US-North Korea Summit Meeting was held on June 12 in Singapore. The joint statement issued after the meeting indicated that there was agreement (1) to build new US-North Korea relations overcoming tensions and hostilities, (2) to work to build a lasting and stable peace regime on the Korean Peninsula, (3) that North Korea would work toward complete denuclearization of the Korean Peninsula, and (4) that the remains of US soldiers who died in the Korean War would be returned.

Following this, the second US-North Korea Summit Meeting was held in Hanoi in February 2019. However, there were major differences of opinion concerning the terms of agreement, as the United States sought progress in North Korea's efforts toward denuclearization and North Korea sought lifting of economic sanctions. President Trump left his seat midway through the Summit Meeting, and it ended without an agreement. Contrasting with the United States' request for North Korea to abandon all its nuclear weapon programs as a condition for lifting sanctions, North Korea indicated its position of offering to dismantle its Yongbyon nuclear facility as a condition for revoking the specific clauses in the UN Security Council resolutions to impose economic sanctions adopted in 2016 and 2017. Although President Trump and Chairman Kim met again later in Panmunjom on June 30, a specific agreement was not reached toward denuclearization. A working-level meeting was held between both countries in Stockholm on October 3, but there was no progress.

2. Exploring Force Posture in the Age of Great Power Competition

(1) The National Defense Strategy and Rebalancing Force Capability and Capacity

In the summary of the NDS issued in January 2018 by the Department of Defense (DOD), the Trump administration positioned "long-term, strategic competition" with China and Russia as the highest priority issue and indicated that less priority would be placed on responding to so-called "rogue states," terrorism, and the like.[14] As pillars of advancing this competition, the NDS raises building a more lethal Joint Force, strengthening alliances and attracting new partners, and reforming the DOD's business practices for greater performance and affordability. However, as the NDS was formulated at the order of the Trump administration in the context of "rebuilding the military," the main pillar is the first one of strengthening the Joint Force.

To strengthen the Joint Force, the NDS reconsidered the approach adopted by the US military in the post-Cold War era. During the unipolar age of American primacy from the 1990s to the 2000s, as seen in the Gulf War and the Iraq War, the United States could deploy large-scale forces when and where necessary and execute operations with the necessary means. On the other hand, during the current age of great power competition, the military forces of the "great powers" like China and Russia are highly modernized, and they pose serious challenges to the US military to maintain its overwhelming superiority in all the ground, maritime, air, space, and cyber domains. Such changes in the strategic environment are the background for the need to build a more lethal force.

Accompanying the United States' defense priority shifting from responding to "rogue states" to "great power competition," it is also necessary to change the post-Cold War force construct that mainly presumed conflict with "rogue states." Since the DOD formulated the Bottom-Up Review in 1993, the United States had built up the force based on the force construct of being able to respond to two major theater wars (2MTW) nearly simultaneously, mainly envisioning ones occurring in the Middle East and the Korean Peninsula. Although the Obama administration's 2012 Defense Strategic Guidance shows a force construct at a so-called "1.5" MTW standard to defeat and deny two invasions by nation states, high officials such as Secretary of Defense Leon Panetta and Deputy Secretary of Defense Ashton Carter suggested that the basic idea of 2MTW would remain unchanged. In short, the basic principle of 2MTW was continued for over 20 years until the latter half of the 2010s.[15] Because of this, more focus was put on ensuring force capacity including personnel and assets to enable 2MTW than on investing in force capability.[16]

However, as seen in the Third Offset Strategy that laid out conventional deterrence against China and Russia from around 2014 by the Obama administration, the DOD had gradually begun to explore optimizing the capability of the US military in the era of great power competition. The 2018 NDS specifies the shift from the 2MTW concept to prioritizing capability of "defeating aggression by a major power" and "deterring opportunistic aggression elsewhere."[17] Accompanying this, Secretary of Defense James Mattis specified that building capability would be given priority over force capacity.[18]

In regard to specific capabilities to be strengthened, the NDS raises eight fields: nuclear forces; space and cyberspace capabilities; command, control, communications, computers and intelligence, surveillance and reconnaissance (C4ISR); missile defense; joint lethality; forward force maneuver and posture resilience; autonomous systems; and resilient and agile logistics. The DOD placed importance on these priority fields in the FY2020 defense budget proposal which requests $718.3 billion (4.9% higher than the previous fiscal year). Above all, the budget request asks for $14.1 billion (19.5% higher than the previous fiscal year) and $9.6 billion (12.9% higher than the previous fiscal year) for the unclassified space and cyberspace programs, respectively.[19] In addition, if one looks at FY2020 acquisition programs, the funding for all categories of missiles and ammunitions (including strategic missiles), space systems, C4I systems (including cyberspace capabilities), and missile defense—each of which can be classified in the first four (nuclear, space and cyberspace, C4ISR, missile defense) of the above eight priorities—maintains or exceeds the level of FY2019. They marked an even more drastic increase compared to the FY2016 defense budget proposal under the Obama administration (Table 6.1).

Table 6.1. Main weapon systems procurement in the Obama and Trump administrations (Unit: $ Billion, nominal values)

Weapon System		Obama Administration	Trump Administration		
		FY2016	FY2019	FY2020	Growth Rate Compared to FY2016
Missiles and Munitions		11.9	20.7	21.6	+81.5%
	Strategic Missiles	2.4	3.3	3.5	+45.8%
Space Systems		7.1	9.3	11.9	+67.6%
C4I Systems		7.4	10.0	10.2	+37.8%
	Cyber Capability	n/a	2.6	2.8	n/a
Missile Defense		8.8	12.0	11.6	+31.8%

Source: Compiled from the FY2016, 2019, and 2020 editions of the *Program Acquisition Cost by Weapon System* by the Office of the Under Secretary of Defense (Comptroller)/CFO.

In recent years, there has been steady progress in improvement of standoff missiles, whose utility is widely recognized. In the testimony at the Senate Committee on Armed Services in January 2019, Elbridge Colby, who led the NDS as Deputy Assistant Secretary of Defense for Strategy and Force Development, raised specific munitions names such as Joint Air-to-Surface Standoff Missile-Extended Range (JASSM-ER) and Long-Range Anti-Ship Missiles (LRASM), and asserted that these types of munitions are essential for building a combat-credible force.[20] The DOD has indicated that it will produce these two types of missiles at maximum capacity in the same production line, in order to acquire as quickly as possible the capabilities needed in the severe strategic environment.[21]

On the other hand, balancing capability and capacity in each service is crucial for executing the NDS within the budget limits. Although President Trump has promoted "rebuilding our military" since his inauguration, this has meant quantitative increases in force in many settings. The Army, which had planned a reduction of active duty military personnel to 440,000-450,000 people due to the reduced budget under the Obama administration, was one of the services that has received the largest benefit under the Trump administration's plan to increase force capacity.

In regard to active duty personnel, the Army requested 476,000 people in the FY2018 budget and 487,500 in FY2019, and the FY2019 Future Years Defense Program (FYDP) presented a plan for 495,500 by FY2023. The logic behind the increase was that the Army's operational tempo in areas like the Middle East outpaced the force capacity, which made it difficult to maintain a sufficient level of readiness. Nevertheless, from the viewpoint of the NDS or that of great power competition, an emphasis is placed more on strengthening force capability, including modernization, than on simply expanding capacity.

In that sense, the FY2020 budget request indicates that the Army is gradually in line with the NDS. According to Undersecretary of the Army Ryan McCarthy, the ratio between modernization and legacy systems in the Army will improve from the current 20:80 to 50:50 by FY2024.[22] In 2017, the Army put Long Range Precision Fires (LRPF) on the top of the list in its "Modernization Priorities." The Army reflected this priority in the FY2020 proposal asking for $164.2 million (a 3% increase over the previous year) as well as $848.7 million as part of the FYDP for research, development, testing and evaluation (RDT&E) of LRPF.

Additionally, the Army also emphasizes tactical air and missile defense that protects ground targets including command posts, supply bases, and airfields. In particular, the Army's RDT&E requests for the mobile short-range air

Table 6.2. The US Army's six modernization priorities and major efforts

Modernization Fields	Major Efforts
Long Range Precision Fires (LRPF)	Strategic Fires, Precision Strike Missiles, Extended Range Cannon Artillery
Next Generation Combat Vehicles	Optionally Manned Fighting Vehicles, Armored Multi-Purpose Vehicles, Mobile Protected Firepower, Robotic Combat Vehicles
Future Vertical Lift	Future Attack Reconnaissance Aircraft, Future Long Range Assault Aircraft, Future UAS, Modular Open Systems Architecture
Network	Unified Network, Command Post Common Environment, Joint Interoperability/Coalition Accessible, Command Post Mobility/Survivability
Air and Missile Defense	Army Integrated Air and Missile Defense, M-SHORAD, IFPC, LTAMDS
Soldier Lethality	Next Generation Automatic Rifle, Next Generation Rifle, Enhanced Night Vision Goggles, Integrated Vision Augmentation System

Source: US Army, *2019 Army Modernization Strategy: Investing in the Future*, October 2019, p. 7.

defense (M-SHORAD) missiles and lower tier air and missile defense sensors (LTAMDS) were $262.1 million and $427.8 million, which were respectively about double and quadruple the amounts in the previous fiscal year's request. The service is also planning to reach the operational capability of Indirect Fire Protection Capability (IFPC) by FY2023, and requested Israel's Iron Dome air defense system as an interim measure to keep up air defense capabilities until that year. The IFPC is a system capable of dealing with an extensive range of aerial threats from rockets, artillery and mortar (RAM) to unmanned aircraft systems (UAS) to cruise missiles. However, some experts point out that the more the M-SHORAD addresses threats from aircraft, UAS, and RAM, the more available the IFPC is to deal with higher-end threats such as cruise missiles.

Another characteristic of the Army's FY2020 budget proposal is the deceleration of expansion of force capacity. The budget's request for 480,000 active duty military members was a reduction of 7,500 people compared to the previous request. In addition, the Army's goal is 488,000 soldiers for FYDP through FY2024, setting a lower number compared to the FY2019's goal of 495,500 soldiers by FY2023. Although this change can be perceived positively as a sign of the Army shifting its focus to modernization, whether this purely stems from such a shift needs to be dug deeper.

According to the Army, financial problems and the worsening employment environment due to factors such as the low unemployment rate are principal reasons for the slowing pace of expansion of Army personnel. Particularly in regard to the latter reason, it has become difficult to achieve the targeted end strength while maintaining hiring standards. This is mainly due to the newly-introduced deployability policy started in October 2018, which discharges officers who have not been deployed for over one year due to such reasons as illness, injury, or imprisonment.

In fact, the Army has been facing a challenge to recruit people who sufficiently meet employment standards. It became difficult for the Army to achieve the end strength of 487,500 active soldiers indicated in FY2019, and the estimated number of personnel (as of the FY2020 budget request in March) was revised downward to 478,000 people. It is highly likely that the Army, taking into consideration the severe employment condition, adjusted the target number of personnel to a more realistic one. It is thus too haste to conclude that the slowing pace of the personnel expansion came from the Army's focus on capability.

From the perspective of balancing the force, the Navy's structure is also an important issue. The Force Structure Assessment (FSA) unveiled by the Navy in December 2016 raised the target number of battle force ships from 308 to 355. Thereafter this 355-ship fleet became an indicator for Navy shipbuilding. However, the outlook on when this will be achieved has changed. The Navy formulated its accelerated fleet plan in 2017 and reported that the number would be reached by 2030 by extending the service life of vessels in conjunction with accelerating the pace of construction. However, the 30-year shipbuilding plan (FY2019-FY2048) submitted to Congress in February 2018 estimated the figure of 355 ships to be reached in the first half of the 2050s. The 30-year shipbuilding plan (FY2020-FY2049) issued in March 2019 now reveals an ambitious plan, in which the 355-ship force-level goal is to be achieved by 2034, about 20 years earlier than the report from the previous year.[23]

However, there are challenges with the Navy's new shipbuilding plan. The latest FY2020 plan shows that even after the 355-ship architecture is achieved, some types of ships, including attack submarines, will not reach the number that was targeted in the 2016 FSA. In addition, although the FY2020 shipbuilding plan aims to achieve the 355-ship goal up to 20 years earlier than the FY2019 plan, there is only a slight increase of three ships in the actual number of ships to be constructed under the 30-year shipbuilding plan, with 301 ships in the FY2019 plan and 304 ships in the FY2020 plan.

The main reason for the drastic acceleration of shipbuilding pace in the FY2020 plan is the service life extensions for certain ships. Above all, the service life of all Arleigh Burke-class destroyers was extended from the normal 35–40 years to 45 years. Although this greatly contributes to maintaining and expanding the total number of ships, it does not necessarily help promote force modernization. The Navy under the Trump administration has placed an emphasis on quickly reaching the target number of ships and focused on expanding force capacity. The Navy faces a conundrum of promoting a more lethal and modernized fleet suitable for great power competition while simultaneously expanding capacity.

Amidst this, the Navy is revising the 2016 FSA (as of the end of December 2019). The surface combatant force architecture is considered to be one of the main components of this revision. In the 2016 FSA objective, there are to be 104 large surface combatants (LSC) such as cruisers and destroyers and 52 small surface combatants (SSC) such as littoral combat ships and frigates (a 2:1 ratio), without taking into consideration the number of unmanned surface vehicles. This architecture would be reversed in a new FSA, resulting in a 1:2 ratio of LSC to SSC, plus a larger number of large- and medium-sized unmanned surface vehicles.[24]

The rationale behind this potential fleet architecture is that it would enable the Navy to maximize the efficacy of operations particularly in the western Pacific region at a lower cost than that of the existing composition. Deploying more relatively inexpensive SSC rather than utilizing a small number of expensive LSC, for example, is expected to complicate the enemy's targeting process, to minimize the effect of loss of one ship on entire fleet capability, and to help deploy (unmanned) surface combatants to highly risky theaters during conflict. The Navy's new FSA based on a series of strategic documents formulated under the Trump administration will play a pivotal role in showing size and composition of the force as well as capacity-capability balance that the Navy demands for great power competition.

In this way, the efforts to strengthen US military force qualitatively are remarkable. In addition to these efforts, the establishment of the Space Force in December 2019 initiated by President Trump reflects the administration's awareness of the changing nature of military threat. On the other hand, the administration has another important project to recover and expand force capacity. Unless the current US financial condition dramatically improves, the issue of tradeoff between capacity and capability will continue to be discussed.

(2) Efforts for Building a More Effective Forward Force

Important components for strengthening the capabilities of the US forces comprehensively and maintaining effective deterrence and war-fighting capability include not only force modernization and substantive reinforcement, but also force deployment, training, and employment in accordance with the strategic environment. Although the US forces deployed in the western Pacific region play an important role for deterrence and defense in the region, there is also a dilemma faced by the forward-deployed forces.[25] Namely, although the visible forward presence of the US armed forces as a symbol of deterring regional conflicts and commitment since the Cold War continues to have vital importance, China's so-called anti-access/area denial (A2/AD) system has the potential to pose a threat to military assets such as bases, harbor facilities, and surface vessels within the first island chain especially from Kyushu to Okinawa, and to Taiwan, the Philippines, and Borneo Island (Kalimantan Island). This issue, which is also known as the visibility-vulnerability dilemma, imposes challenges that are impossible to ignore for the forward-deployed US forces.

The Trump administration stipulates policies of enhancing force quality while maintaining a forward military presence, including maintenance of a favorable balance of power as well as a forward military presence in order to deter and defend against conflicts as outlined in the NSS, and the strengthening of forward posture of US forces accompanying the rise of great power competition as outlined in the NDS. As concepts concerning more specific employment, the NDS describes dynamic force employment in order to enhance flexibility and unpredictability of force employment, and a Global Operating Model comprising four layers (contact, blunt, surge, and homeland) concerning the ideal force posture.

As shown in Table 6.3, forward force plays important roles for everything from competition and deterrence in peacetime to actual war fighting. In other words, what is needed is not simply a symbolic "presence for its own sake" by the US forward forces (former Deputy Assistant Secretary Colby). On the contrary, it is presumed that forward base facilities and other military assets will be placed in contested environments in the event of armed conflict, and it is necessary to have a forward posture that can deny enemy military actions while swiftly deploying troops.[26]

The Army's efforts in recent years are noteworthy for denying enemy forces on the front lines. In particular, Multi-Domain Operations (MDO) continuously tested and revised under the Army's initiative is one of the most important concepts for responding to the future strategic environment. MDO deters military escalation while competing from an advantageous standpoint with mainly Russia and China, and, if deterrence fails, implements operations nearly simultaneously in multiple domains, namely land, sea, air, space, cyberspace, and electromagnetic spectrum. This concept is designed to provide diverse options to the United States and also create operational dilemmas for enemy operations.[27]

The Army plans to realize MDO by 2028. In 2017, the Multi-Domain Task Force (MDTF) was introduced centered on the 17th Field Artillery Brigade that possesses a High Mobility Artillery Rocket System (HIMARS). Through the MDTF, the US Army has tested the necessary specific components of the concept

Table 6.3. Global Operating Model

Layer [Force]	Main Tasks	Notes
Contact Layer [Forward Force]	· Responds to situations in the "gray zone" jointly with allies · Ensures national interests in competitive spaces below the threshold of armed conflict	· Delays, degrades, and denies enemy operations as the blunt layer when competition escalates to conflict
Blunt Layer [Forward Force]	· Prevents achievement of a fait accompli · Endures until arrival of the surge force · Delays, degrades, and denies enemy maneuvers	· "Blunts" enemy operations through stand-off strikes and forward-deployed and combat forces · Essential to have a resilient, dispersed basing posture with sufficient stockpiles of logistics items and a command and control network
Surge Layer [Homeland Forces and Forward Forces in Other Regions]	· Dispatch and deployment of war-winning force · Escalation control · Ends conflict with preferable terms	· Exploits creation of operational and political leverage by the blunt force · Expects to be contested while dispatching and deploying forces · Essential to maintain such capabilities as command and control, artillery, mobility, logistics to penetrate A2/AD systems
Homeland Layer [Homeland Force]	· Deters and defeats attacks on the US homeland	· Maintains consistency with forward operations and manages escalation favorably

Sources: DOD, *Summary of the 2018 National Defense Strategy of the United States: Sharpening the American Military's Competitive Edge*, January 2018, p. 7; Elbridge A. Colby, "Testimony Before the Senate Armed Services Committee," p. 6; Robert B. Neller, "Statement of General Robert B. Neller Commandant of the Marine Corps as Delivered to Congressional Defense Committees on the Posture of the United States Marine Corps," April 20, 2018, pp. 2-3.

in the western Pacific region. According to US Army Pacific Commander Robert Brown, the MDTF enables penetration of A2/AD multi-layered defenses which had previously proven difficult in training and war games.[28] The Army plans to additionally adopt the first MDTF in Europe and the second MDTF in the Indo-Pacific region going forward.

The MDTF already plays a major role related to testing surface-to-ship missiles. The MDTF implemented sinking exercises (SINKEX) jointly with Japan's Ground Self-Defense Force using HIMARS during the Rim of the

Pacific Exercise (RIMPAC) in 2018, and surface-to-ship missile exercises using HIMARS during the Japan-US joint military exercise Orient Shield held in September 2019. Through such exercises, the MDTF advanced efforts to enhance not only readiness, but also interoperability with partner countries in joint operations.

The operational advantages of ground-based missiles like HIMARS include the relatively higher survivability—particularly when using a mobile launcher—and higher responsiveness that makes it possible to strike adversary assets, both at sea and on land, from within the theater. While the concept of deploying ground forces on the first island chain and denying enemy maneuvers from land is becoming a mainstream discussion concerning A2/AD, the MDTF initiative embodies this concept.

At the same time, capability strengthening is also being undertaken for so-called "new domains" of MDTF. The Intelligence, Information, Cyber, Electronic Warfare and Space (I2CEWS) battalion launched by the US Army in January 2019 is an important component of MDTF alongside the 17th Field Artillery Brigade. The I2CEWS battalion is composed of four companies each specialized in a respective domain of intelligence; information; cyber and electronic warfare; and space capabilities and signals, and plays a role to ensure US information advantage not only during conflicts but also in the phase of competition. In relation to cooperation with the artillery brigade, the long range sensing section enables precision fires and supports artillery, air and missile defense capabilities. Within the process from targeting to shooting through the adoption of the sensing section, the task force greatly expands domains capable of independent execution. Furthermore, the MDTF first conducted a practical test of methods and capabilities necessary for executing I2CEWS functions during Cyber Blitz 2019. Through this as well, MDTF activities will probably provide important indicators to confirm the extent of progress of MDO going forward.

Movements by the Air Force to actively participate in MDO can also be seen. Chief of Staff of the US Air Force David Goldfein highly evaluates MDO as a concept that "will change the character of modern warfare."[29] He raises multi-domain command and control (MDC2) as a maximum priority field during his tenure and indicates the objective to enhance capabilities to grasp situations extending over multiple domains, the speed of decision-making, and employment of force. The Air Force sets examination of operational concepts, adoption of advanced technologies, and training and education as the three pillars of future MDC2-related efforts. The Shadow Operations Center, which examines applications of innovative advanced technology, was established at Nellis Air Force Base in Nevada in 2017, and MDC2 efforts switched from the consideration stage to the execution stage, including starting the "13 Oscar" career field to train human resources in 2019.

In addition, the paper co-written by Commander David Perkins of the US Army Training and Doctrine Command (TRADOC) and Commander James Holmes of the Air Combat Command (ACC) in 2018 admitted that various branches of the military had separately examined tactical operations over the past 30 years and indicated that TRADOC and the ACC would work to harmonize their concepts and capabilities while cooperating in order to create multi-domain capabilities.[30] Such progress within the Air Force and with another branch not only polishes operations and detects problem areas, but also has significance as a signal to promote further unification of the US military as a whole.

On the other hand, there has also been specific cooperation on operations between the Air Force and Army. One example is HIMARS rapid infiltration (HI-RAIN) implemented mainly between the Army and the Air Force throughout the 2010s. HI-RAIN further extends the strike range of HIMARS by having transport aircraft swiftly carry and deploy this system forward. Usually one or two HIMARS systems as well as personnel needed for operation, command and control vehicles, and the like are embarked on C-17 or C-130 transport aircraft.[31] During the US-Australia joint exercise Talisman Sabre in 2019, there was a transport and deployment exercise for implementing HI-RAIN in which the Marine Corps HIMARS unit embarked on Air Force MC-130J aircraft and the Army MDTF on the Marine Corps KC-130J aircraft. The scale of cooperation based on the concept expanded, including with the conducting of a live-fire exercise under the command and control of the Australian military.

Nonetheless, it must be noted that although air superiority is essential for executing HI-RAIN in conflict situations with airlift to the theater, ensuring air superiority would be a highly-difficult task in the age of great power competition. Therefore, when and how HI-RAIN is in fact to be executed in the face of an opponent's counter-air capabilities, is a crucial question to further advance this concept.

Furthermore, the Air Force is advancing efforts for continuous employment of aircraft in the contested environment. Agile combat employment (ACE) is one such concept that the Air Force is focusing on. It entails employment of multiple fighter aircraft packaged with transport aircraft carrying the minimum level needed of maintenance supplies and personnel and aims to quickly execute provision of supplies and maintenance in an austere base environment. ACE follows the basic concept of "Rapid Raptor," an operational concept for F-22 fighter aircraft unveiled by the US Air Force in 2013. On the other hand, there have been notable developments in ACE from the previous concept. For instance, testing of employment of fighter aircraft besides F-22s, such as F-15s and F-16s, has been carried out

A live-fire demonstration performed during Exercise Talisman Sabre 2019 (US Army Pacific Public Affairs Office; Photo by Senior Airman Ashley Maldonado-Suarez)

in recent years. The US Air Force has also embarked on cooperation with like-minded countries, including by creating opportunities for exchanges of views and explanatory meetings concerning ACE with US allies and partner countries.

The US Air Force tested this concept from various viewpoints in 2019. In April, fighter aircraft such as F-22s, F-15s, and F-16s and transport aircraft such as C-130s and C-17s moved from major bases in the Pacific region to gather at Andersen Air Force Base in Guam, in order to carry out a dispersal exercise in which the aircraft were deployed to various areas throughout Micronesia. This exercise had not only the military aspect of enhancing readiness, but also the more strategic aspect of strengthening partnerships with countries in Micronesia. Also, during the RED FLAG exercise held in August in Alaska, four maintenance personnel completed ammunitions and fuel replenishment for two F-15 fighter aircraft in less than one hour. One of the worst conceivable scenarios in the A2/AD environment is aircraft being unable to land and take off due to strikes on base facilities. However, as seen in the above-mentioned exercise, the US Air Force's efforts to reduce the operational risks are noteworthy.

The United States is also working on expeditionary advanced base operations (EABO) that quickly seize and sustain land-based forward locations from the water. The concept, being examined by the Marine Corps, aims to support and complement friendly surface forces by deploying sensors, missiles, and the like to temporarily-secured forward locations, and seize the strategic initiative. According to the Marine Corps, the heart of this concept is to create an opportunity to "turn the sea denial table" on the competitors.[32] EABO are mutually complementary to the Navy's distributed maritime operations (DMO) concerning operations in littoral areas. Going forward, creating networks of sea-based and land-based sensing and strike capabilities will be an urgent task.

In this way, branches of the US military are testing and advancing operational concepts designed to deal with A2/AD in the Pacific region. Among others, it is worth noting that through the above-mentioned exercises and trainings, the United States seeks not only to enhance the readiness of its forward forces but also to promote interoperability and partnerships with allies and partners in the region. This is fully in line with the United States' strategic guidelines of building a more effective force posture while maintaining its presence in the Indo-Pacific region. On the other hand, the US forces do not have a joint operational concept at the present point, and how these various operational concepts result in a wider concept of the US Joint Force remains to be seen. In addition, many of the above-mentioned operational concepts seem to focus on forward deployment, that is, deployment within the territory of allies and partner countries of the United States. This makes cooperative relations with regional partners particularly important during peacetime, including in the case of accessing base facilities in these countries.

NOTES

1) The White House, *National Security Strategy of the United States of America*, December 2017, p. 25.

2) Department of Defense, *Indo-Pacific Strategy Report*, June 1, 2019, p. 7.

3) Ibid., p. 8.

4) Ibid., p. 9.

5) Department of Defense, *Annual Report to Congress: Military and Security Developments Involving the People's Republic of China 2019* (May 2, 2019), p. 112.

6) The White House, "Remarks by Vice President Pence at the Frederic V. Malek Memorial Lecture," October 24, 2019.

7) The White House, "Remarks by Vice President Pence on the Administration's Policy toward China," October 4, 2018.

8)   CRS Report R45898, "US-China Relations" (updated September 3, 2019), pp. 11-12.

9)   Department of Defense, *Indo-Pacific Strategy Report*, p. 10; Department of Defense, *Annual Report to Congress 2019*, p. 107.

10) CRS Report, "US-China Relations," September 3, 2019, p. 38.

11) Department of Defense, *Indo-Pacific Strategy Report*, p. 16; Department of Defense, *Annual Report to Congress: Military and Security Developments Involving the People's Republic of China 2018*, May 16, 2018, p. 126; Department of Defense, *Annual Report to Congress 2019*, pp. 118-119.

12) CRS Report, "US-China Relations," p. 38.

13) CRS Report, "North Korea: US Relations, Nuclear Diplomacy, and Internal Situation," July 27, 2018, pp. 6-7; CRS Report, "North Korea: What 18 Months of Diplomacy Has and Has Not Achieved," August 5, 2019; CRS, "US-North Korea Relations," *In Focus*, August 13, 2019.

14) Department of Defense, *Summary of the 2018 National Defense Strategy of the United States of America: Sharpening the American Military's Competitive Edge*, January 19, 2018.

15) Fukuda Takeshi, "Obama Seiken ni yoru Kokubo Yosan Sakugen no Doko: Kyoseisakugen no Hatsudo to Kokubosenryaku Heiryokukeikaku no Shusei" [Reduction of Military Spending under the Obama Administration: Sequestration and Reviews of Defense Strategy and Force Planning], *Refarensu* [The Reference], No. 793, February 20, 2017, pp. 70-71; Jim Mitre, "A Eulogy for the Two-War Construct," *Washington Quarterly*, Vol. 41, No. 4, pp. 15-16.

16) Mitre, "A Eulogy," pp. 8-9.

17) Department of Defense, *Summary of the 2018 National Defense Strategy*, p. 6.

18) Department of Defense, "Remarks by Secretary Mattis on the National Defense Strategy," January 19, 2018.

19) Office of the Under Secretary of Defense (Comptroller), *Defense Budget Overview: United States Department of Defense Fiscal Year 2020 Budget Request*, March 2019, p. 1-5.

20) Elbridge A. Colby, "Testimony before the Senate Armed Services Committee: Hearing on Addressing China and Russia's Emergence as Great Power Competitors and the Implementation of the National Defense Strategy," January 29, 2019, p. 10.

21) Office of the Under Secretary of Defense (Comptroller), *Program Acquisition Cost by Weapon System: United States Department of Defense Fiscal Year 2020 Budget Request*, February 14, 2019, pp. 5-6, 5-11.

22) Ryan McCarthy and Lt. Gen. Thomas Horlander, "Department of Defense Press Briefing on the President's Fiscal Year 2020 Defense Budget for the Army," March 12, 2019.

23) Office of the Chief of Naval Operation, *Report to Congress on the Annual Long-Range Plan for Construction of Naval Vessels for Fiscal Year 2020*, March 2019, p. 5.

24) Unknown, "Navy Force Structure and Shipbuilding Plans: Background and Issues for Congress," *Congressional Research Service*, RL32665, June 19, 2019, pp. 4-5.

25) Department of Defense, *Annual Report to Congress: Military and Security Developments Involving the People's Republic of China 2019*, pp. 54-58; Elbridge Colby and Jonathan F. Solomon, "Avoiding Becoming a Paper Tiger Presence in a Warfighting Defense Strategy," *Joint Forces Quarterly* (JFQ), 82, 3rd Quarter 2016; Mark Gunzinger and Bryan Clark, *Winning*

the Salvo Competition: Rebalancing America's Air and Missile Defenses, Center for Strategic and Budgetary Assessments, 2016, p. 1; Stephen Biddle and Ivan Oelrich, "Future Warfare in the Western Pacific: Chinese Antiaccess/Area Denial, US AirSea Battle, and Command of the Commons in East Asia," *International Security*, Vol. 41, No. 1, Summer 2016, pp. 7-48.

26) Colby, "Testimony," p. 8.

27) Training and Doctrine Command, *The US Army in Multi-Domain Operation in 2028*, December 6, 2018, pp. viii-ix, 24-26, GL-7; Andrew Feickert, "The US Army and Multi-Domain Operation," *CRS Insight*, January 17, 2019.

28) Quoted in Sydney J. Freedberg Jr., "Army's Multi-Domain Unit 'A Game-Changer' in Future War," *Breaking Defense*, April 1, 2019.

29) US Air Force, "Goldfein Stresses Promise of Multi-domain Operations, Calls It 'the Single Most Critical' Tool for Winning Future High-end Fights," July 18, 2019.

30) Amy McCullough, "The Future Fight Must Be Truly Joint," *Air Force Magazine*, January 24, 2018; David G. Perkins and James M. Holmes, "Multi-domain Battle: Converging Concepts toward a Joint Solution," *JFQ*, 88, 1st Quarter 2018, pp. 54-57.

31) Air Mobility Command, "Mobility Airmen and Artillery Soldiers Combine Strengths," July 1, 2019.

32) US Marine Corps, "Expeditionary Advanced Base Operations," US Marine Corps Concepts & Programs website; US Marine Corps, *Expeditionary Advanced Base Operations (EABO) Handbook: Considerations for Force Development and Employment: Version 1.1*, June 1, 2018, p. 45.

Chapter 7

Japan

Initiatives for a Free and Open Indo-Pacific

SATAKE Tomohiko

In recent years, Japan has been strengthening whole-of-government initiatives toward maintaining and bolstering an open maritime order based on the rule of law and freedom of navigation under the "Free and Open Indo-Pacific" (FOIP) concept. The Ministry of Defense (MOD)/the Self-Defense Forces (SDF) have also been promoting various initiatives toward realizing FOIP as shown by the National Defense Program Guidelines for FY 2019 and beyond (2019 NDPG). The 2019 NDPG stressed: "in line with the vision of free and open Indo-Pacific, Japan will strategically promote multifaceted and multilayered security cooperation, taking into account characteristics and situation specific to each region and country."

If maintaining and strengthening the international order based on the principles of the rule of law and freedom of navigation are the main objectives of FOIP, then FOIP is certainly not a new concept, but rather a goal that Japan has consistently pursued since the Cold War era. At the same time, due to India's rise and China's strengthening its maritime advances since the latter half of the 2000s, FOIP has been characterized by unprecedented focus on maritime security and strengthening cooperation with democratic countries with ocean borders. Together with being a concept led by the United States aimed at maintaining and strengthening the existing order, FOIP has also emphasized expanding roles of non-US countries including Japan and has a potential to become a vision for a new order in an age of "multipolarization."

From the above perspective, in recent years the MOD/SDF, centered on the Maritime Self-Defense Force (MSDF), have been expanding their presence and strengthening partnerships in the Indo-Pacific region (hereafter the Ground Self-Defense Force, the Maritime Self-Defense Force, and the Air Self-Defense Force are referred to as GSDF, MSDF, and ASDF, respectively). In addition, the MOD/SDF are strengthening initiatives to provide capacity building assistance with other countries in the region as well as multilateral security cooperation. Nevertheless, amidst the ongoing severe financial situation and personnel shortages, there are some views that further project expansion would be difficult.

As budget and personnel constraints become increasingly tight going forward, it is becoming more important to develop a whole-of-department approach as well as to strengthen cooperation with other ministries and agencies in order to promote defense exchanges and cooperation. Additionally, to review individual projects and set an order of priority for these projects, it is essential to draft a long-term strategy for defense cooperation and exchanges in the Indo-Pacific. Considering the placement of the Republic of Korea (ROK) and China in FOIP is also an important pending issue.

1. About the "Free and Open Indo-Pacific" Concept

(1) FOIP as an Order Concept

FOIP is synonymous with an objective or "vision" of Japanese diplomacy that denotes a regional order desirable to Japan.[1] The objective or vision is for Japan to make the region extending from the Pacific Ocean to the Indian Ocean free and open as "international public goods," such as by "ensuring rules-based international order including the rule of law, freedom of navigation and overflight, peaceful settlement of disputes, and promotion of free trade," and thus promote the peace, stability, and prosperity of the region.[2]

The principles of the rule of law and freedom of navigation are essentially the "operational code" of the liberal international order aimed for by Western countries centered on the United States following World War II. If FOIP is an attempt to make these principles and this order take root in the region extending from the Pacific Ocean to Africa, it is not new for Japan to have this kind of order concept. Rather, the concept of FOIP that aims at promoting an order based on the liberal values of the rule of law and market economies should be considered the goal or "parameters" that post-war Japanese diplomacy has consistently pursued.[3]

Particularly following the Cold War, as Japan has striven for a new role in the international community, maintaining and strengthening the liberal order have been more explicitly raised as the goals of Japanese diplomacy and the Japan-US Alliance.[4] Japan's Official Development Assistance (ODA) Charter unveiled in 1992 lists as one of the "four principles" for implementing assistance, "Full attention should be paid to efforts for promoting democratization and introduction of a market-oriented economy, and the situation regarding the securing of basic human rights and freedoms in the recipient country."[5] In addition, while developed countries' interest in Africa weakened due to the end of the Cold War, Japan first held the Tokyo International Conference on African Development (TICAD) in 1993, and strengthened initiatives toward the development and democratization of Africa.[6] Furthermore, under the Partnership for Democratic Development (PDD) unveiled by the Ministry of Foreign Affairs in 1996, Japan has been providing assistance not only to Asian countries, but also to countries in Eastern Europe and Africa, including support for elections, cooperation toward domestic efforts to establish the rule of law, strengthening of civil society, and cooperation toward expanding participation in politics by women.[7]

Cooperation with India and Australia, the frequent focus of FOIP, also did not begin recently. Especially from the beginning of the 2000s mainly against the backdrop of the rise of China, Japan has been strengthening strategic relations with Australia and India. As a result, the Joint Statement: Towards Japan-India Strategic and Global Partnership was issued in December 2006 and the Japan-Australia Joint Declaration on Security Cooperation was issued in March 2007, confirming further promotion of relations with both countries, including for defense and security cooperation.

Prime Minister Abe Shinzo's speech titled "Confluence of Two Waters" in front of the Parliament of India in 2007 has been often cited in literature as a prototype for FOIP. Furthermore, the National Security Strategy unveiled in 2013 clearly placed maintaining and protecting the international order "based on rules and universal values, such as freedom, democracy, respect for fundamental human rights, and the rule of law" as being in Japan's national interest, and raised as a goal strengthening relations with not only the United States, but also countries that share values with Japan: the ROK, Australia, ASEAN countries, and India. In this way, protecting liberal values and cooperation with Australia and India as emphasized in FOIP did not suddenly appear with the advent of the second Abe administration, but rather had been continuously strengthened amidst Japan's increasing engagement in shaping the regional order following World War II, particularly following the Cold War.

That being said, usage of the new regional concept of "Indo-Pacific" took root from the 2010s. It is true that the term FOIP emerged reflecting the new trend of developments in the region, including the rise of India. One development in this new trend has been the rise in importance of maritime security particularly since the latter half of the 2000s.

For example, the "Arc of Freedom and Prosperity" concept, which was unveiled by the first Abe administration and is often pointed out to resemble

FOIP, broadened the liberal order along the outer rim of the Eurasian continent in the same way as FOIP, but emphasized engagement in the continent's regions of Central Asia and the Caucus, Turkey, as well as Central and Eastern Europe, and the Baltic countries.[8] By contrast, FOIP brings to the forefront enhancing connectivity with ocean-facing countries in Southeast and Southwest Asia to the coastal countries of East Africa, as well as infrastructure support, defense cooperation, and the like related to these countries.[9]

Needless to say, the backdrop for this included China's expansion of its maritime advances from the latter half of the 2000s. In particular, China not only rapidly expanded its military actions both qualitatively and quantitatively in maritime areas, but also sought to unilaterally change the status quo by force through increasing its government vessels and military operating around the Senkaku Islands as well as its actions to construct artificial islands in the South China Sea. China's military movements threaten freedom of navigation and the stable use of sea lanes, and have thus come to be perceived as a serious threat to Japan. In an essay published in 2012 by Prime Minister Abe, he harshly criticized China for attempting to make the South China Sea into the "Lake of Beijing," and indicated plans to maintain and strengthen the rules-based order by strengthening cooperation with the United States as well as Australia and India, which are all democratic maritime countries.[10]

Nevertheless, FOIP does not aim to "contain" China. On the contrary, since its establishment in December 2012, the Abe administration has consistently worked to repair relations with China that had deteriorated due to the boat collision incident near the Senkaku Islands in 2010. As a result, while recognizing that both countries have different views on what led to tensions in the East China Sea, including the Senkaku Islands, through dialogue and consultations, the "Four Points Consensus" was reached between Japan and China in November 2014 and confirmed that deterioration of the situation should be prevented. In addition, consultation resumed toward building a maritime communication mechanism between Japan and China in January 2015, and the mechanism became operational in June 2018. During Prime Minister Abe's visit to China in October 2018, it was agreed to advance cooperation between Japan and China in many fields including economic fields and maritime security. During the Japan-China Summit Meeting in June 2019, in addition to confirming that "Japan-China relations have gotten back on a normal track and that there have been new developments in the relations," Prime Minister Abe and President Xi shared determination to carve out a "new era of Japan-China relations."[11] In August of the same year, the vice-ministerial level Japan-China Strategic Dialogue was resumed after not being held for about seven years.

In this way, Japan has been strengthening cooperation with the United States, its allies, and other countries in the region under the FOIP concept on the one hand, while leveraging such relations on the other hand to improve relations with China. If FOIP's ultimate objectives are the various principles of the liberal order of ensuring rules-based international order including the rule of law, freedom of navigation, peaceful resolution of disputes, and promotion of free trade, then China can be positioned as one important country within FOIP as long as it respects and adheres to these principles.

To that extent, FOIP does not have the objective of opposing any particular country. Rather, it is a concept that aims to form a rules-based, inclusive order by including all countries in the region. It should be understood that it is within the above context that the Abe administration places importance on engagement concerning China while aiming for a balance of power with China through Japan-US-Australia-India cooperation. These are not contradictory policies. Instead, they are positioned as mutually essential components for realizing an inclusive FOIP order concept.

(2) Seeking a New Order in the Age of Multipolarization

Another reason FOIP is garnering attention as an order concept is that there is unprecedented necessity for Japan to strengthen cooperation with countries besides the United States. As many Asian countries achieve rapid economic growth, not only China but also India, the ROK, and other Southeast Asian countries have a growing presence in the region, and this trend is expected to continue going forward (Figure 7.1). To incorporate the dynamism of countries with remarkable growth and to realize a FOIP, it is essential for Japan to strengthen cooperation not only with the United States but also with emerging nations expanding in the region as well as other countries inside and outside the region.

From the above perspective, Japan has been diversifying its strategic partnerships for both security and economic aspects particularly since the 2000s. For the security aspect, Japan is strengthening the rules-based Indo-Pacific order by strengthening defense exchanges with Australia, India, and the

Figure 7.1. Trends in the GDP growth rate (projected)

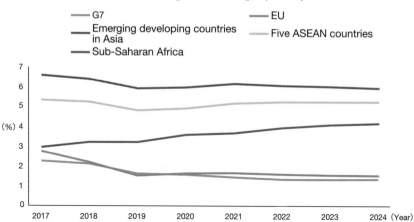

Notes: Figures are real GDP. Figures shown for after 2019 are estimates. The emerging developing countries are 30 countries including China, Southeast Asian countries, South Pacific countries, and Pacific Island countries. The five ASEAN countries are Indonesia, Malaysia, the Philippines, Thailand, and Vietnam.

Source: International Monetary Fund, *World Economic Outlook Database*, October 2019.

Indo-Pacific countries of ASEAN, as well as promoting initiatives that actively leverage defense capabilities, such as joint training with the United Kingdom and France as well as defense equipment and technology cooperation with other countries (Figure 7.2). Japan has also been strengthening interoperability between the SDF and the militaries of other countries by concluding the General Security of Military Information Agreement (GSOMIA) and the Acquisition and Cross-Servicing Agreement (ACSA) (Table 7.1). Japan has also advanced negotiations on the Reciprocal Access Agreement (provisional name) to improve administrative, policy-related, and legal procedures for reciprocal visits by the SDF, the Australian Defence Force, and the British Armed Forces, further streamlining joint operations and exercises.

The diversification of security cooperation does not diminish the importance of the Japan-US Alliance, but rather leads to strengthening of the Alliance. Although Japan has strengthened security cooperation with several countries besides the United States, this could not become a "substitute" for the alliance with the United States under the current circumstances. On the contrary, Japan is taking on part of the United States' role toward maintaining the regional order by

Figure 7.2. Number of cases of defense exchanges and cooperation (2008–2018)

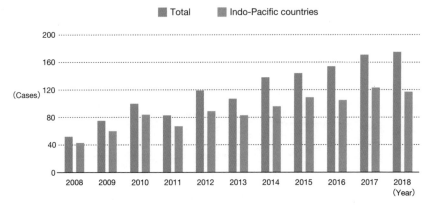

Notes: Excludes the United States. Defense exchanges and cooperation include high-level exchanges among leaders such as summit leaders and defense ministers, regularly-held consultations among defense authority officials, exchanges between military units, and trilateral trainings (such as Japan-US-Australia or Japan-US-ROK trainings).
Source: Compiled by the author based on each year's edition of the *Defense of Japan* by the Ministry of Defense.

strengthening cooperation with US allies and partner countries. This lightens the burden on the United States, and as a result provides bottom-up reinforcement of the United States' alliance system in the region, including the Japan-US Alliance. In other words, as the United States' clearly unipolar system in the "Asia-Pacific" wavers, Japan is complementing the United States' role through cooperation with diverse actors in a wider region, thus maintaining or strengthening the order mainly led by the United States.

Nevertheless, it is unrealistic to think that the United States' leadership will continue forever. If the United States' relative power continues to shrink, it will become necessary for Japan, together with other democratic countries, to substitute for part of the role taken by the United States thus far. As a result, it cannot be denied that a more multipolar order could develop in the future, different from the bipolar structure between the United States and the Soviet Union (or the United States and China) during the Cold War and from the unipolar structure with the United States following the Cold War. This has active significance as the concept of a new order replacing the "New Cold War"

Table 7.1. Security agreements concluded with countries in the region

	Joint security declarations/ statements	Foreign and Defense Ministerial Meetings (2+2)	Acquisition and Cross-Servicing Agreements (ACSA)	General Security of Military Information Agreements (GSOMIA) / Information Security Agreements (ISA)	Bilateral joint training	Agreements concerning Transfers of Defense Equipment and Technology
Australia	○ (2007)	○ (2007-)	○ (2010)	○ (2012)	○ (Ground, maritime, and air forces)	○ (2014)
United Kingdom	○ (2017)	○ (2015-)	○ (2017)	○ (2013)	○ (Ground, maritime, and air forces)	○ (2013)
India	○ (2008)	○ (2019)	△	○ (2015)	○ (Ground, maritime, and air forces)	○ (2015)
France	×	○ (2014-)	○ (2018)	○ (2011)	○ (Maritime forces)	○ (2015)
Canada	○ (2010)	×	○ (2018)	×	○ (Maritime forces)	×
ROK	×	×	△	○ (2016)	○ (Maritime forces)	×
Indonesia	×	○ (2015-)	×	×	○ (Maritime forces)	△
Philippines	×	×	×	×	○ (Maritime forces)	○ (2016)

Notes: Years in parentheses are the years of announcement, commencement, or conclusion. The △ symbol indicates ongoing negotiations.
Source: Compiled by the author based on each year's edition of the *Defense of Japan* by the Ministry of Defense.

between the United States and China. Thus, together with being a means to maintain the existing order, FOIP also potentially has significance as a new order concept toward an era of multipolarization.

2. Initiatives by the MOD/SDF

(1) Strengthening Japan's Maritime Presence and Partnerships

As discussed in the previous section, ensuring maritime security and freedom of navigation is a central component of FOIP. This is why the MSDF has been expanding its presence and partnerships in the Indo-Pacific region in recent years. Since the 2000s, the MSDF has perceived its maritime operations areas as extending to the Middle East and Africa due to the rise of non-traditional threats such as terrorism and piracy as well as changes in the regional power balance. From this viewpoint, the MSDF has strengthened its efforts to ensure the security of sea lanes over 1,000 nautical miles (1,852 km) (which Japan had raised as the extent of its sea lane defense in the 1980s).[12]

It is necessary to understand the regional characteristics and environment in order to ensure stable maritime transportation routes. Additionally, because it is impossible to defend sea lanes in the vast maritime areas alone, it is necessary to strengthen interoperability regularly with the United States, other friendly nations, and coastal countries through enhanced cooperation. To demonstrate Japan's determination to engage in the region, moreover, it is essentially important to maintain the regular presence of SDF vessels in the South China Sea and the Indian Ocean.

From the above perspective, since 2017 the MSDF has been carrying out the long-term deployment of vessels, including the JS *Izumo* and JS *Kaga* large

Figure 7.3. Indo-Pacific Deployment 2019 (IPD19) activities

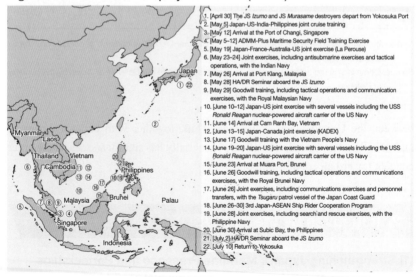

1. [April 30] The JS *Izumo* and JS *Murasame* destroyers depart from Yokosuka Port
2. [May 5] Japan-US-India-Philippines joint cruise training
3. [May 12] Arrival at the Port of Changi, Singapore
4. [May 5–12] ADMM-Plus Maritime Security Field Training Exercise
5. [May 19] Japan-France-Australia-US joint exercise (La Perouse)
6. [May 23–24] Joint exercises, including antisubmarine exercises and tactical operations, with the Indian Navy
7. [May 26] Arrival at Port Klang, Malaysia
8. [May 28] HA/DR Seminar aboard the JS *Izumo*
9. [May 29] Goodwill training, including tactical operations and communication exercises, with the Royal Malaysian Navy
10. [June 10–12] Japan-US joint exercise with several vessels including the USS *Ronald Reagan* nuclear-powered aircraft carrier of the US Navy
11. [June 14] Arrival at Cam Ranh Bay, Vietnam
12. [June 13–15] Japan-Canada joint exercise (KADEX)
13. [June 17] Goodwill training with the Vietnam People's Navy
14. [June 19–20] Japan-US joint exercise with several vessels including the USS *Ronald Reagan* nuclear-powered aircraft carrier of the US Navy
15. [June 23] Arrival at Muara Port, Brunei
16. [June 26] Goodwill training, including tactical operations and communications exercises, with the Royal Brunei Navy
17. [June 26] Joint exercises, including communications exercises and personnel transfers, with the *Tsugaru* patrol vessel of the Japan Coast Guard
18. [June 26–30] 3rd Japan-ASEAN Ship Rider Cooperation Program
19. [June 28] Joint exercises, including search and rescue exercises, with the Philippine Navy
20. [June 30] Arrival at Subic Bay, the Philippines
21. [July 2] HA/DR Seminar aboard the JS *Izumo*
22. [July 10] Return to Yokosuka

Note: The numbers in the map indicate the approximate locations where activities took place.
Source: Compiled by the author based on the Ministry of Defense website.

destroyers, each year in the Indo-Pacific region. In April 2019, the JS *Izumo* and JS *Murasame* destroyers departed from Yokosuka under the Indo-Pacific Deployment 2019 (IPD19). The vessels visited and made port calls at various locations in Southeast Asia and the Indian Ocean over about three months. In addition to conducting goodwill events with countries in the region, these ships conducted joint training in various locations with friendly nations including the above countries as well as the United States and Australia (Figure 7.3).

Besides these operations, there were frequent port calls at countries in the region, joint trainings, and other such exercises conducted by destroyers dispatched for anti-piracy operations, the MSDF Training Squadron, and others. From September 2019, the MSDF Mine Division first began long-term cruise trainings from the Asia-Pacific to the Indian Ocean over about three months (International Maritime Exercise at Indian Ocean). The unit, composed of the JS *Bungo* minesweeper tender, the JS *Takashima* minesweeper, and about 180 crew members, made port calls in Vietnam, the Philippines, Malaysia, Bangladesh, the Maldives, and India during its voyage, and conducted training, including for minesweeping and diving, with the navies of various countries in several locations.[13]

With the increased operations of the MSDF in the Indo-Pacific region, there have been an increasing number of opportunities for joint trainings including with the militaries of other countries in the region, the United States, and friendly nations. The JS *Izumo* and JS *Murasame*, which were dispatched under the IPD19 from western Kyushu to the South China Sea in May 2019, implemented joint cruise training for the first time with navy vessels from the United States, India, and the Philippines. In the same month, the JS *Izumo* and JS *Murasame* conducted joint training for the first time with the French Navy's *Charles de Gaulle* nuclear-powered aircraft carrier in the Indian Ocean near western Sumatra, Indonesia, and, by adding vessels from the Australian and US navies, joint training for the first time between Japan, France, Australia, and the United States. Furthermore, in the same month, the JS *Ariake* and JS *Asahi* destroyers participated in the Pacific Vanguard joint training held by Japan, the United States, Australia, and the ROK in maritime and aerial areas from southern Honshu to the island of Guam. The MSDF also participated for the first time in the Talisman Sabre 2019, practical training held by the United States and Australia in locations such as Shoalwater Bay in Queensland, Australia in June.

Additionally, in recent years not only the MSDF, but also the GSDF, the ASDF, and the Japan Coast Guard are actively participating in exercise activities in the Indo-Pacific. For example, the GSDF's Amphibious Rapid Deployment Brigade, which was newly formed in March 2018, participated in the IPD19 for the first time, and participated in goodwill events and other activities with countries in the region. The ASDF has also been contributing to strengthening the SDF's presence in the region through participation in bilateral and multilateral joint trainings, overseas transport operation trainings, and more. Furthermore, the joint training between the MSDF and the Japan Coast Guard was also held for the first time in June 2019 in the South China Sea.

In addition to the above, Japan has strengthened its engagement with Pacific Island countries as part of the new trend in recent years. Compared to Southeast Asian and South Asian countries, engagement by the MOD/SDF in South Pacific countries was extremely limited, with the exception of some capacity building assistance projects. This is partly because only three countries—Papua New Guinea, Fiji, and Tonga—have militaries in the region. However, in recent years as China has been strengthening its economic, political, and military clout in the region, strengthening engagement in the region is being raised as an important issue.

In August 2019 on the journey back to Japan after the Talisman Sabre 2019 ended, the MSDF's JS *Ise* helicopter destroyer and the JS *Kunisaki* transport vessel stopped at Port Moresby, the capital of Papua New Guinea, deepening goodwill with its defence force. In the same month, the MSDF's Training Squadron made port calls in French Polynesia and Fiji. Furthermore, in September, three personnel were dispatched from the Joint Staff Office and the Joint Staff College to Equateur 2019, a multilateral joint exercise concerning humanitarian assistance and disaster relief (HA/DR) hosted by the French armed forces in New Caledonia. In October, GSDF, MSDF, and ASDF personnel, who were participating in U-4 multi-purpose support aircraft overseas utilization training by the MSDF's Training Squadron and the ASDF, joined together to visit Palau and participated in a ceremony to commemorate the 25th anniversary of the establishment of diplomatic relations between Japan and Palau. In addition, the ASDF participated in Christmas Drop, an HA/DR joint training implemented annually by the air forces of the United States, Australia, and New Zealand in the Federated States of Micronesia.

In addition to these activities, based on the Government Initiatives to Ensure the Security of Ships Related to Japan in the Middle East approved by the National Security Council and the Cabinet on December 27, 2019, the anti-piracy forces' P-3C fixed-wing patrol aircraft were utilized and the JS *Takanami* destroyer was dispatched for information-gathering activities by the SDF in the Middle East. The geographic scope of the information-gathering activities by the SDF was the Gulf of Oman, the northern Arabian Sea, and international waters in three maritime areas of the Gulf of Aden on the side of the Bab-el-Mandeb strait (including the exclusive economic zones of coastal countries). The period for activities is planned until December 26, 2020.[14]

In this way, as the SDF's activities have rapidly expanded in the Indo-Pacific, there are concerns inside the MSDF about a shortage of personnel, including the number of vessels, crew, and logistics personnel.[15] Also, if the security environment surrounding Japan becomes more tense in the near future, reducing the operations in the Indo-Pacific can be considered because it would be necessary to deploy many vessels and patrol planes to conduct surveillance and missile defense in the areas surrounding Japan. The MSDF reduced the number of destroyers deployed for anti-piracy operations from two to one, and also reported in 2019 that it was considering withdrawing from Antarctic exploration activities that had been continued since 1965 due to the personnel shortage.[16]

Based on this situation, the MOD has begun working to more efficiently execute duties by allocating funds for equipment aspects of building new smaller, more multifunctional destroyers compared to the conventional destroyers as well as introducing patrol vessels, and introducing "manpower saving" and "multi-crew shiftwork" (a system of operating vessels by having crews alternate between several vessels, rather than having a crew only for one certain vessel).[17] In addition, from the perspective of further strengthening the human resources base supporting the SDF's activities, the MOD raised the fixed retirement age for SDF personnel in the Early Retirement System and has promoted further activities by female SDF personnel.[18]

Amidst concerns about further worsening of the personnel shortage due to the declining birth rate going forward, securing adequate personnel and maintaining their skills are urgent issues. In addition, to establish a system for support such as supplies and maintenance for MSDF vessels docked in foreign countries, it is necessary to advance cooperation among the entire government, not just the MOD, as well as public-private cooperation including with private airline companies. In addition to these points, it is required to expand a more efficient and effective presence and partnerships in the Indo-Pacific by strengthening cooperation with the United States, the United Kingdom, and other countries that have overseas bases and facilities.

(2) Capacity Building Assistance

In 2011, the Capacity Building Assistance Office was established within the International Policy Division of the Bureau of Defense Policy of the MOD in 2011. Since then, the MOD/SDF have strengthened capacity building assistance activities for Southeast Asia. In recent years, there has been a trend of expanding assistance with target countries and fields. As of July 2019, assistance is being provided in extensive fields to 15 countries and one organization (Table 7.2).

Table 7.2. Capacity building assistance implemented by the MOD/SDF (number by country and project)

Country / project	Oceanography	International aviation law	Defense medicine	Civil engineering	Unexploded ordnance disposal	Search and rescue	PKO	Aviation safety	Military band training	HA/DR	Vehicle maintenance	Vessel maintenance	Underwater medicine	Aerial rescues	Cyber	Aviation meteorology	Japanese language education	Total
Brunei										1								1
Cambodia				8	1													9
Indonesia	7	1																8
Kazakhstan			2															2
Laos					1					5								6
Malaysia		1								3								4
Mongolia			5	9														14
Myanmar		1								5			5		2	8		21
Papua New Guinea									12	1								13
Philippines		1	2	1						2		2						8
Sri Lanka			1			2												3
Thailand		1					2	2										5
Timor-Leste				1							11							12
Uzbekistan			2															2
Vietnam		1			1		4	4		1			8	3			2	24
ASEAN										3								3
Total	7	6	12	19	3	2	6	6	12	21	11	2	13	3	2	8	2	135

Note: As of July 2019.
Source: Compiled by the author based on the Ministry of Defense website.

As stated above, engagement with Pacific Island countries is one major theme of capacity building assistance. The MOD/SDF have provided HA/DR and assistance for the military music unit of Papua New Guinea since 2014. Musical techniques instruction was provided to the Papua New Guinea Defence Force Band, which participated in the Royal Edinburgh Military Tattoo, a military music festival held by the United Kingdom in Australia in October 2019.

The MOD/SDF have held many seminars aimed at capacity building. In March 2019, an underwater medicine seminar was held aimed at the Vietnam People's Navy. Medical officers from the National Defense Medical College, the JMSDF Underwater Medical Center, and the Japan Self Defense Forces Hospital Yokosuka worked on capacity building together with medical officers from the US Navy in the underwater medicine field of the Vietnam People's Navy. In the same month, 15 cybersecurity personnel from the Vietnam People's Armed Forces were invited to attend the Cyber Security Seminar, which was held for the second time after first being held in 2017. During the seminar, instructors from the GSDF Signal School taught about passwords, authentication, firewalls, and intrusion detection systems, and private lecturers also provided instruction concerning incident responses. In May, an HA/DR seminar was held for 45 people related to the Malaysian Armed Forces aboard the MSDF's JS *Izumo* destroyer, which was visiting Malaysia (Port Klang).

In addition, as emphasized in the "Vientiane Vision" unveiled by the MOD in November 2016, one trend in recent years has been not only assistance to individual countries, but also strengthening assistance for ASEAN as a whole. For example, during the 2nd Japan-ASEAN Invitation Program on Humanitarian Assistance and Disaster Relief held in Tokyo from January–February 2019, a tabletop exercise (TTX) concerning HA/DR was held at the National Institute for Defense Studies (NIDS) as part of the Program, and there were active discussions among the participants from ASEAN and the GSDF. In July, the First Professional Airmanship Program was held inviting participants (lieutenant colonels and majors) from all ASEAN member states and the ASEAN Secretariat, which promoted confidence-building and shared understanding concerning international law among the air forces of Japan and ASEAN. In addition to strengthening Japan-ASEAN cooperation and ensuring ASEAN's unity, holding such seminars and TTX holds important significance for spreading the basic principles and standards of freedom of navigation and the rule of law that Japan places importance on.

On the other hand, only holding a one-off seminar or TTX does not necessarily lead to continuous capacity improvement of the recipient country. Ideally, it is essential to have initiatives for concentrated capacity improvement for target countries in specific fields by drafting long-term plans including seminars and TTX. A good precedent is the training for the Papua New Guinea Defence Force Military Band held 12 times over four years from 2015. Even though this was a small program, it was the first example of direct engagement by the MOD/SDF in forming and strengthening an organization of a foreign country's military. In addition, when conducting proper follow-up on the effects of capacity building assistance, studying local coverage and reactions about the project based on assistance from external organizations can be considered.

In the longer-term, it is required to draft long-term plans in order to determine the priority levels of countries receiving assistance and projects. As stated above, although there is a rising trend of expanding capacity building assistance projects with target regions and fields, there has also been a trend in which Japan frequently has vague plans and objectives in terms of assistance targets and priority levels. This is because projects have basically been conducted based on the ad hoc needs of target countries. While the first stage of expanding projects and target countries has been completed, some argue that the MOD needs to formulate long-term plans focusing on the next three to four years. For this, based on the rapidly-changing security environment surrounding Japan, the Japanese government should clarify projects truly necessary for Japan and decide their priority level by reexamining the significance of capacity building assistance, reviewing past projects, and other efforts. This suggests that capacity building assistance projects by the MOD/SDF have reached a new stage following their "dawn" in 2011.

(3) Multilateral Security Cooperation

Since the establishment of the ASEAN Regional Forum (ARF) in 1994 following the Cold War, there has been a growing tendency for strengthening multilateral security frameworks focusing on confidence-building and preventive diplomacy among countries in the Asia-Pacific (Indo-Pacific) region. The East Asia Summit (EAS) was established in 2005 through increasing discussions toward the East Asian Community from the beginning of the 2000s. In addition to

Northeast Asian countries and ASEAN member states, India, Australia, and New Zealand were added (as well as the United States and Russia later on), which created a discussion framework at the summit level on initiatives for shared regional issues, including security issues faced by countries in the Indo-Pacific region.

Nevertheless, these initiatives were created with countries' diplomacy departments as the main players. It was thus required to have frameworks centered on defense departments for more practical cooperation toward dealing with regional security issues. Amidst this, bearing in mind the establishment of the ASEAN Community in the future, the ASEAN Defence Ministers' Meeting (ADMM) was established in 2006, and the ASEAN Defence Ministers' Meeting-Plus (ADMM-Plus) was established in 2010 with the addition of non-ASEAN countries (Japan, the United States, Australia, New Zealand, India, China, the ROK, and Russia). This created the first multilateral security framework centered on defense departments in the Indo-Pacific region. Six Experts' Working Groups (EWGs) (later expanded to seven) were established under the minister-level meetings and the high-level consultation meetings of the ADMM-Plus, and discussions, exercises, and other activities are implemented by the participating countries primarily concerning non-traditional security issues.

Because the ADMM-Plus is also the only official defense ministers' meeting that includes non-ASEAN countries in the Indo-Pacific region, the MOD/SDF have constantly placed importance on it. Although the Defense Ministers' Meeting was planned to be held once every three years in principle at the start, it was held once every two years from 2013, and since 2017 has been held annually. The 5th ADMM-Plus was held in Thailand in November 2019. Defense Minister Kono, who attended the meeting, announced the "Vientiane Vision 2.0," the updated version of the Vientiane Vision guidelines for Japan-ASEAN defense cooperation unveiled in 2016, as the start of initiatives to further accelerate momentum for Japan-ASEAN defense cooperation. The updated Vision inherits the direction of cooperation that stresses three key areas of realizing the "rule of law," strengthening maritime security, and dealing with non-traditional threats such as natural disasters. In addition, under the "Three Principles for Japan's Defense Cooperation with ASEAN" of "Heart-to-heart Cooperation," "Tailored and Lasting Cooperation," and "Equal and Open Cooperation," it aims to strengthen ASEAN's resilience through more practical defense cooperation and thus contribute to ASEAN centrality and unity. The Vision also stressed that the principles of openness, transparency, and inclusivity outlined in the ASEAN Outlook on the Indo-Pacific "share the same bases" with those of Japan's vision for FOIP.[19]

Rather than being a new initiative, strengthening the centrality, unity, and resilience of ASEAN as outlined in the Vision has been something Japan has consistently pursued since becoming an ASEAN Dialogue Partner in the 1970s. During the Cold War period, such efforts were mainly conducted through diplomatic and economic means. Following the end of the Cold War, defense-related contact between Japan and ASEAN began to gradually expand due to the rise of non-traditional security issues. The Vientiane Vision of 2016 and the Vientiane Vision 2.0 of 2019 can be assessed as clear means for Japan's cooperation with ASEAN as defense exchanges and cooperation with ASEAN have been expanding.

The MOD/SDF are also actively participating in other multilateral frameworks besides the ADMM-Plus. In January 2019, the Chief of Staff of the Joint Staff participated for the first time in the Raisina Dialogue in India, which was being held for the third time. He discussed maritime security in the Indo-Pacific with then US Indo-Pacific Command Commander Harry Harris, Chief of Navy Timothy Barrett of Australia, and Chief of Naval Staff of the Indian Navy Sunil Lanba. In June, then Defense Minister Iwaya attended the annually-held Asia Security Summit (Shangri-La Dialogue), and called for the participating countries' endorsement of the FOIP vision. Furthermore, the Japan-ASEAN Defense Vice-Ministerial Forum was held in October. The Forum has been held 11 times as of this year. At the Forum, there was an exchange of views among the participants regarding three themes: "the Regional Security Situation," "Visions for the Indo-Pacific: Towards the Free and Open Regional Order," and "ASEAN's Initiatives for Regional Defense Cooperation."

In this way, as multilateral frameworks concerning security issues become increasingly active, the issue of how Japan should approach such cooperation frameworks is coming into question. For example, among the seven EWGs of the ADMM-Plus, which field should Japan work on as a priority item in addition to the EWG on PKO for which Japan serves as co-chair country along with Vietnam since 2020? Also, as the importance of the "new domains" of cyber and space further rises for security, how should that reality be reflected in multilateral security cooperation? Additionally, how should the MOD/SDF be involved with multilateral frameworks led by China, which China has been exerting efforts for in recent years as seen with the Xiangshan Forum? As it has become more difficult to continue to expand projects in the manner thus far due to budget and personnel constraints, now is the time for the MOD/SDF to reexamine their long-term strategies in the same way as capacity building assistance based on multilateral security cooperation, international circumstances, and changes in Japan.

3. Challenges for a Free and Open Indo-Pacific

(1) Toward More Efficient and Effective Defense Exchanges and Cooperation

As already shown, although the MOD/SDF are rapidly expanding activities in the Indo-Pacific region to realize FOIP as an order concept, there are many budget and personnel shortage constraints. The Japanese government has consistently increased the defense budget since the beginning of the second Abe Cabinet, but the growth rate remains at a low level compared to other major countries. In addition, although utilization of Official Development Assistance (ODA) for the militaries of other countries that was first approved through the Development Cooperation Charter in 2015 can be considered for providing larger-scale capacity building assistance in the Indo-Pacific region, the objective of the ODA is limited to non-military uses such as disaster relief. There is still reluctance toward providing ODA to militaries.

Amidst this, it was reported that the Japanese government began coordination to provide life-saving systems used by the SDF to the Philippine Army utilizing ODA in September 2019.[20] If this project is realized, it would be the first example of provision of equipment used by the SDF to the military of a foreign country through ODA. It is required to closely cooperate with other ministries and agencies, including the Ministry of Foreign Affairs and the Ministry of Economy, Trade and Industry, as well as the National Security Secretariat in order to carry out more strategic defense cooperation such as for equipment provision, including with the utilization of ODA.

In addition, as examined in the previous section, it is necessary to constantly

Figure 7.4. Changes in defense budgets in major countries (2009–2019)

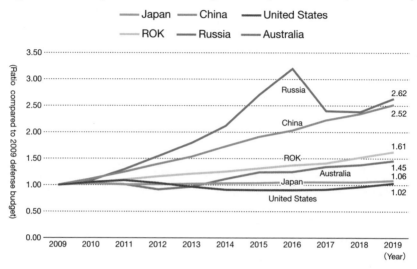

Note: The ratios (rounded to two decimal places) of respective countries' officially publicized defense budgets for FY2010 onward when considering their defense budgets for FY2009 as 1.
Source: Ministry of Defense, *Defense of Japan*, 2019, p. 244.

review the policies and strategies of defense exchanges and cooperation in the Indo-Pacific in order to make projects of capacity building assistance and multilateral security frameworks more efficient. Based on this recognition, the Japan-ASEAN Defense Cooperation Committee was once held at the MOD with the State Minister of Defense sitting as the chair to discuss consideration concerning Japan-ASEAN defense cooperation as well as the future approach.[21] Within the MOD, it was exceptional that a cross-organizational committee was established regarding defense cooperation with certain countries and regions. Going forward, establishing the same kind of committee or some sort of review system targeting various Indo-Pacific countries can be considered as a direction.

(2) Toward Strengthening Further Cooperation with Indo-Pacific Countries

To deepen cooperation with Indo-Pacific countries going forward, it is necessary to further strengthen interoperability between the SDF and the militaries of partner countries through joint trainings, concluding agreements, and other efforts. A particularly urgent issue is strengthening cooperation with countries in important locations within the Indo-Pacific region: Australia, India, and Indonesia.

In September 2019, six Australian FA18 fighter aircraft visited Japan, and the joint training known as "Bushido Guardian" was held with the ASDF for the first time. With India, in addition to annually-held joint trainings such as Malabar, bilateral cooperation between the MSDF and the Indian Navy is being advanced in the field of maritime situational awareness, including by starting utilization of information-exchanges such as information on vessels, under the "Implementing Arrangement for Deeper Cooperation between the Japan Maritime Self-Defense Force and the Indian Navy" concluded in October 2018. In November 2019, the first Japan-India 2+2 Foreign and Defence Ministerial Meeting (2+2 Ministerial Meeting) was held. Both countries' ministers welcomed tremendous progress in negotiations toward concluding the ACSA between Japan and India, and expressed their wish to finish negotiations soon. With Indonesia, strengthening relations is being promoted such as through implementation of joint trainings between the MSDF, which visited Indonesia in May, and the Indonesia Navy.

The Legislation for Peace and Security, which was approved by Cabinet decision in September 2015 and entered into force in March 2016, also contributes to strengthening relations between Japan and other countries in the region. In particular, permission for the partial use of the right of collective self-defense in a "survival-threatening situation" enabled Japan to exercise the right to self-defense under certain conditions in the event of an armed attack against not only the United States, but also third-party countries with close relations with Japan. On the other hand, because exercising the right to self-defense is limited to a situation that "threatens Japan's survival and poses a clear danger to fundamentally overturn people's right to life, liberty and pursuit of happiness," there is a view that the possibility of recognizing an attack on a country besides the United States that is an ally of Japan as a "survival-threatening situation" would actually be considerably limited.[22] This will probably become one obstacle to Japan promoting security cooperation at a deeper level with countries in the region in the future.

In addition, the issue of how to position the ROK and China in the FOIP vision has not seen progress in discussions despite its importance. In regard to the ROK, issues with negative effects on Japan-ROK defense exchanges and cooperation have occurred, including the ROK's negative response concerning the SDF vessel flag for the international naval review conducted by the ROK in October 2018, and the incident involving fire-control radar lock-on to an MSDF patrol plane by a ROK Navy destroyer that occurred in December of the same year. On the other hand, due to the ally relationship with the United States and the geopolitical importance of the Korean Peninsula to Japan, there is no change to the fact that cooperation with the ROK is extremely important strategically for Japan. Moreover, the ROK has been strengthening engagement in Southeast Asia and India through its "New Southern Policy." Actively utilizing such opportunities and promoting defense cooperation in broad fields with the ROK through multilateral cooperation frameworks and other means will probably become an important component for realizing a FOIP.

By contrast, defense exchanges with China have increased since 2012 due to improvement in Japan-China relations in recent years. In April 2019, the MSDF's JS *Suzutsuki* destroyer visited China, which was the first visit by an MSDF vessel in about seven years, and participated in the International Fleet Review held by China to commemorate the 70th anniversary of the establishment of the Chinese People's Liberation Army Navy. In addition, the MSDF Chief of Staff, who visited China for the first time in about five and a half years, attended a high-level symposium held on the sidelines of the Fleet Review, and held exchanges of views with participating navy officials including from the Chinese navy. Furthermore, in October, the Chinese navy's missile destroyer *Taiyuan* made the first visit by a Chinese navy vessel to Japan in 10 years. Joint training was held with the MSDF's JS *Samidare* destroyer in an area south of Tokyo Bay, including forming column and line formations and signal correspondence.

As reviewed in the first section, FOIP is not a concept that excludes China. On the contrary, it ultimately intends to welcome China as an important component country. As this is the case, advancing such defense exchanges with China also represents an important initiative to realize FOIP as an order concept. On the other hand, China is further increasing, rather than diminishing, the operations by its government vessels in the waters around Japan including the Senkaku Islands. Entering 2019, official Chinese vessels have been approaching the waters near the Senkaku Islands on a nearly daily basis, and frequently entering Japan's territorial waters. In addition, as it centralizes its power, the Xi Jinping administration has strengthened actions counter to the principles of FOIP, including suppressing freedom of speech, religion, and learning as well as minorities, strengthening social monitoring systems, and other actions.

Based on the above situation, it is necessary to share the FOIP principles and vision with other countries in the region to further advance bilateral and multilateral defense cooperation and exchanges going forward. In addition to "hard" cooperation in the form of joint trainings and equipment cooperation, "soft" exchanges in the form of accepting and dispatching international exchange students are an important component for this. For example, Australia, which is strengthening its engagement in the Indo-Pacific like Japan, has been accepting over 700 military-related people as exchange students annually from various countries, mainly from Southeast Asian and Pacific Island countries, under its Defence Cooperation Program.[23] Because many of these exchange students occupy important positions in the militaries of their countries once they return, acceptance of exchange students is an invaluable method for Australia's defence-related engagement with other countries.

Japan is also generally accepting over 100 people from the militaries of various countries annually as exchange students to the National Defense Academy, the JMSDF Command and Staff College, the NIDS, and its other educational institutions. Although there are issues such as language problems, it is necessary to strengthen and expand such cooperation going forward. Additionally, rather than just welcoming students, there should also be consideration of actively dispatching MOD human resources to educational institutions, including military universities and commanding officer courses of Indo-Pacific countries. Such human resources exchanges and education can be implemented at relatively low costs compared to cooperation utilizing material resources such as joint trainings and defense equipment provision. It also appears that this will be increasingly important going forward for expanding the ideas and principles of FOIP in the region.

NOTES

1)   Ministry of Foreign Affairs, "Free and Open Indo-Pacific," November 21, 2019.

2)   Ministry of Foreign Affairs, "Free and Open Indo-Pacific."

3)   Sasae Kenichiro, "Indo Taiheiyo no Atarashi Kokusai Chitsujo to Nichibeichu Kankei" [The New International Order of the Indo-Pacific and Japan-US-China Relations], *Gaiko* [Diplomacy], Vol. 53, 2019, p. 20.

4)   Ministry of Foreign Affairs, "Japan-US Joint Declaration on Security: Alliance for the 21st

Century," April 17, 1996.

5) Ministry of Foreign Affairs, "2. Former Japan's Official Development Assistance Charter" (Cabinet Decision of June 1992), June 30, 1992.

6) Ministry of Foreign Affairs, "TICAD I (First Tokyo International Conference on African Development) Tokyo Declaration on African Development 'Towards the 21st Century'," October 6, 1993.

7) Ministry of Foreign Affairs, "Minshuteki Hatten no tame no Patonashippu (PDD): Partnership for Democratic Development."

8) Ministry of Foreign Affairs, "Creating an Arc of Freedom and Prosperity," November 30, 2006.

9) Ministry of Foreign Affairs, "Free and Open Indo-Pacific."

10) Abe Shinzo, "Asia's Democratic Security Diamond," December 27, 2012.

11) Ministry of Foreign Affairs, "Japan-China Summit Meeting and Dinner," June 27, 2019.

12) Takei Tomohisa, "Kaiyo Shinjidai ni okeru Kaijo Jieitai: JMSDF in the New Maritime Era," *Hato* [Billows], Vol. 34, No. 4, November 2008, pp. 2-29.

13) Maritime Self-Defense Force, "International Maritime Exercise at Indian Ocean."

14) Ministry of Foreign Affairs, "Government Initiatives to Ensure the Security of Ships Related to Japan in the Middle East," December 27, 2019.

15) *Asahi Shimbun*, April 29, 2019.

16) *Sankei Shimbun*, April 28, 2019.

17) Ministry of Defense, "Jieikan no Kurusei ni tsuite (Tsutatsu)" [About the Crew System of MSDF Ships (Notification)], November 1, 2017.

18) Ministry of Defense, "Jieikan no Teinen Nenrei no Hikiage ni tsuite" [About the Raised Fixed Age of Retirement for SDF Personnel], December 21, 2018.

19) Ministry of Defense, "Dai 5 Kai Nichi ASEAN Boei Tanto Daijin Kaigo (Gaiyo)" [5th Japan-ASEAN Defense Ministers' Informal Meeting (Outline)], November 17, 2019.

20) *Sankei Shimbun*, September 23, 2019.

21) Ministry of Defense, "Dai 1 Kai 'Nichi ASEAN Boei Kyoryoku Kento Iinkai' no Kaisai ni tsuite" [About the Holding of the "1st Japan-ASEAN Defense Cooperation Committee"], December 22, 2018.

22) Prime Minister Abe's answers during the 193rd Session of the Diet House of Representatives plenary session on March 14, 2017.

23) Satake Tomohiko, "Osutoraria no Chiiki Boei Kanyo: Minami Taiheiyo to Tonan Ajia ni okeru 'Ashiato'" [Australia's Regional Defense Engagement: "Footprint" in the South Pacific and Southeast Asia], Sasakawa Peace Foundation, 2018, p. 6.

Authors

Hashimoto Yasuaki Former Director, Policy Studies Department Introduction

Ichimasa Sukeyuki Senior Fellow, Defense Policy Division, Policy Studies Department Chapter 1

Momma Rira Director, Regional Studies Department Chapter 2

Iwamoto Hiroshi Research Fellow, China Division, Regional Studies Department Chapter 2

Watanabe Takeshi Senior Fellow, Asia & Africa Division, Regional Studies Department Chapter 3

Koike Osamu Research Fellow, Government & Law Division, Security Studies Department Chapter 3

Matsuura Yoshihide Head, Government & Law Division, Security Studies Department Chapter 4

Tomikawa Hideo Senior Fellow, Security & Economy Division, Security Studies Department Chapter 4

Manabe Yuko Research Fellow, Asia & Africa Division, Regional Studies Department Chapter 4

Hyodo Shinji Director, Policy Studies Department Chapter 5

Hasegawa Takeyuki Research Fellow, America, Europe & Russia Division, Regional Studies Department Chapter 5

Sakaguchi Yoshiaki Senior Fellow, America, Europe & Russia Division, Regional Studies Department Chapter 5

Sawada Hiroto Research Fellow, Security & Economy Division, Security Studies Department Chapter 5

Arakaki Hiromu Senior Fellow, America, Europe & Russia Division, Regional Studies Department Chapter 6

Kiridori Ryo Research Fellow, America, Europe & Russia Division, Regional Studies Department Chapter 6

Satake Tomohiko Senior Fellow, Defense Policy Division, Policy Studies Department Chapter 7